Functional JavaScript

Michael Fogus

Beijing · Cambridge · Farnham · Köln · Sebastopol · Tokyo

Functional JavaScript

by Michael Fogus

Printed in the United States of America.

Published by O'Reilly Media, Inc., 1005 Gravenstein Highway North, Sebastopol, CA 95472.

O'Reilly books may be purchased for educational, business, or sales promotional use. Online editions are also available for most titles (*http://my.safaribooksonline.com*). For more information, contact our corporate/institutional sales department: 800-998-9938 or *corporate@oreilly.com*.

Editor: Mary Treseler	**Indexer:** Judith McConville
Production Editor: Melanie Yarbrough	**Cover Designer:** Karen Montgomery
Copyeditor: Jasmine Kwityn	**Interior Designer:** David Futato
Proofreader: Jilly Gagnon	**Illustrator:** Robert Romano

May 2013:   First Edition

Revision History for the First Edition:

2013-05-24:   First release

2013-08-02:   Second release

See *http://oreilly.com/catalog/errata.csp?isbn=9781449360726* for release details.

ISBN: 978-1-449-36072-6

[LSI]

For Yuki

Table of Contents

Foreword by Jeremy Ashkenas

This is a terribly exciting book.

Despite its ignominious origins as a "Java-lite" scripting language, intended to be embedded inline in HTML documents to allow a minimum modicum of interactivity, JavaScript has always been one of the most essentially flexible languages for general purpose programming.

You can sketch, smudge, and draft bits of code in JavaScript, while pushing and twisting the language in the direction that best suits your particular style. The reason that this is more natural in JavaScript than in other, more rigid languages is due to the small set of strong core ideas that lie at the heart of JavaScript: Everything is an object (everything is a value) to an even greater extent than in famously object-oriented languages like Ruby and Java. Functions are objects, are values. An object may serve as prototype (default values) for any other object. There is only *one* kind of function, and depending on how you employ it, it can either serve as a pure function, a mutating procedure, or as a method on an object.

JavaScript enables, but does not enforce, many different programming styles. In the early days, we tended to bring our traditional expectations and "best" practices with us when we started to learn to write JavaScript. Naturally this led to much JavaScript resembling Java without the omnipresent types or even with the types still there, just living inside of annotation comments above each method. Gradually, experiments were made: folks started generating functions at runtime, working with immutable data structures, creating different patterns for object-orientation, discovering the magic of chaining APIs, or extending built-in prototypes with custom functionality.

One of my favorite recent developments is the enthusiastic embrace of functional programming ideas as appropriate tools for building rich JavaScript applications. As we move beyond form validation and DOM animation towards full-featured apps, where the JavaScript in your codebase might be getting up to any manner of hijinks in any particular problem space, functional ideas are similarly moving beyond the basic callback, and towards more interesting arenas, such as:

- Building out a large API by partially applying a core set of functions with arguments in different configurations.
- Using recursive functions to smooth the gap between actions that need to occur for a period of time, and events coming in rapid-fire off the event loop.
- Structuring a piece of complex business logic as a pipeline of mutation-free changes that can later be plugged-into and pulled apart.

You're reading the ideal book with which to explore this territory. In the following nine chapters (and two appendixes), your friendly tour guide and resident mad scientist, Michael Fogus, breaks down functional programming into its basic atoms, and builds it back up again into edifices of terrifying cleverness that will leave you wondering. It's rare that a programming book can take you by surprise, but this one will.

Enjoy.

—Jeremy Ashkenas

Foreword by Steve Vinoski

I remember when I first read Douglas Crockford's wonderful book *JavaScript: The Good Parts*. Not only did I learn from it, but the fact that Crockford required only 172 pages to steer readers away from JavaScript's problematic parts makes his work that much more impressive. Brevity is often at odds with educative exposition, but when an author achieves both as Crockford did, the reader is more likely to fully digest the author's recommendations and benefit from them.

In the pages that follow, you'll find that Michael Fogus has given us a book as excellent as Crockford's, perhaps more so. He's built on the sound advice of Crockford and other predecessors to take us on a deep dive into the world of functional JavaScript programming. I've often heard and read (and even written myself) that JavaScript is a functional programming language, but such assertions (including my own) have always seemed light on the pragmatic details that practicing programmers need. Even Crockford devoted only a single chapter to functions, focusing instead, like many authors, on JavaScript's object support. Here, merely saying that Fogus fills in those missing details would be a serious understatement.

Functional programming has been a part of the computing field from its inception, yet traditionally it has not enjoyed significant interest or growth among practicing software professionals. But thanks to continuing advances in computing hardware speed and capacity, coupled with our industry's increasing interest in creating software systems of ever-escalating levels of concurrency, distribution and scale, functional programming is rapidly growing in popularity. This growth is due to the observation that functonal programming appears to help developers reason about, build and maintain such systems. Curiosity about languages that support functional programming, like Scala, Clojure, Erlang and Haskell, is at an all-time high and still increasing, with no abatement in sight.

As you read through Michael's insightful investigations of JavaScript's functional programming capabilities, you'll be impressed with the significant depth and breadth of the information he provides. He keeps things simple at first, explaining how functions and "data as abstraction" can avoid the desire to use JavaScript's powerful object prototype system to create yet another way of modeling classes. But as he explains and thoroughly reveals in subsequent chapters, the simple model of functional data transformation can yield sophisticated yet efficient building blocks and higher level abstractions. I predict you'll be amazed at just how far Fogus is able to take these innovative approaches as each chapter goes by.

Most software development efforts require pragmatism, though, and fortunately for us Fogus tackles this important requirement as well. Having beautiful, sophisticated and simple code is ultimately meaningless if it's not practical, and this is a large part of the reason functional programming stayed hidden in the shadows for so many years. Fogus addresses this issue by helping the reader explore and evaluate the computing costs associated with the functional programming approaches he champions here.

And of course books, just like software, are ultimately about communication. Like Crockford, Fogus writes in a manner that's both brief and informative, saying just enough to drive his ideas home without belaboring them. I can't overstate the importance of Michael's brevity and clarity, since without them we'd miss the incredible potential of the ideas and insights he's provided here. You'll find elegance not only in the approaches and code Fogus presents, but also in the way he presents them.

—Steve Vinoski

Preface

What Is Underscore?

Underscore.js (hereafter called Underscore) is a JavaScript library supporting functional programming. The Underscore website describes the library as such:

> Underscore is a utility-belt library for JavaScript that provides a lot of the functional programming support that you would expect in Prototype.js (or Ruby), but without extending any of the built-in JavaScript objects.

In case you didn't grow up watching the kitschy old Batman television show, the term "utility belt" means that it provides a set of useful tools that will help you solve many common problems.[1]

Getting Underscore

The Underscore website (*http://underscorejs.org*) has the latest version of the library. You can download the source from the website and import it into the applicable project directories.

Using Underscore

Underscore can be added to your own projects in the same way you would add any other JavaScript library. However, there are a few points to make about how you interact with Underscore. First, by default Underscore defines a global object named _ that contains all of its functions. To call an Underscore function, you simply call it as a method on _, as shown in the following code:

---

1. Batman actually had more than just useful tools—he had tools for every conceivable circumstance, including those that might require a Bat Alphabet Soup Container or Bat Shark Repellant. Underscore doesn't quite match that level of applicability.

```
_.times(4, function() { console.log("Major") });

// (console) Major
// (console) Major
// (console) Major
// (console) Major
```

Simple, no?

One thing that might not be so simple is if you already defined a global _ variable. In this case, Underscore provides a _.noConflict function that will rebind your old _ and return a reference to Underscore itself. Therefore, using _.noConflict works as follows:

```
var underscore = _.noConflict();

underscore.times(4, function() { console.log("Major") });

// (console) Major
// (console) Major
// (console) Major
// (console) Major


_;
//=> Whatever you originally bound _ to
```

You'll see many of the details of Underscore throughout this book, but bear in mind that while I use Underscore extensively (and endorse it), this is not a book about Underscore per se.

The Source Code for Functional JavaScript

Many years ago, I wanted to write a library for JavaScript based on functional programming techniques. Like many programmers, I had obtained a working understanding of JavaScript through a mixture of experimentation, use, and the writing of Douglas Crockford. Although I went on to complete my functional library (which I named Doris), I rarely used it for even my own purposes.

After completing Doris, I went on to other ventures, including extensive work with (and on) the functional programming languages Scala and Clojure. Additionally, I spent a lot of time helping to write ClojureScript, especially its compiler that targets JavaScript. Based on these experiences, I gained a very good understanding of functional programming techniques. As a result, I decided to resurrect Doris and try it again, this time using techniques learned in the intervening years. The product of this effort was called Lemonad, which was developed in conjunction with the content of this book.

While many of the functions in this book are created for the purpose of illustration, I've expanded on the lessons in this book in my Lemonad library (*http://www.github.com/fogus/lemonad*) and the official underscore-contrib library (*http://bit.ly/12xnnSp*).

Running the Code in This Book

The source code for *Functional JavaScript* is available on GitHub (*https://github.com/funjs*). Additionally, navigating to the book's website (*http://www.functionaljavascript.com*) will allow you to use your browser's JavaScript console to explore the functions defined herein.

Notational Conventions

Throughout the course of this book (and in general when writing JavaScript) I observe various rules when writing functions, including the following:

- Avoid assigning variables more than once.
- Do not use `eval`.[2]
- Do not modify core objects like `Array` and `Function`.
- Favor functions over methods.
- If a function is defined at the start of a project, then it should work in subsequent stages as well.

Additionally, I use various conventions in the text of this book, including the following:

- Functions of zero parameters are used to denote that the arguments don't matter.
- In some examples, ... is used to denote that the surrounding code segments are being ignored.
- Text like `inst#method` denotes a reference to an instance method.
- Text like `Object.method` denotes a reference to a type method.
- I tend to restrict `if`/`else` statements to a single line per branch, so I prefer to avoid using curly brackets to wrap the blocks. This saves precious vertical space.
- I like to use semicolons.

For the most part, the JavaScript code in this book is like the majority of JavaScript code that you'll see in the wild, except for the functional composition, which is the whole point of writing the book in the first place.

Whom Functional JavaScript Is Written For

This book started as an idea a few years ago, to write an introductory book on functional programming in the Scheme programming language. Although Scheme and JavaScript

---

2. Like all powerful tools, JavaScript's `eval` and `Function` constructors can be used for harm as well as for good. I have nothing against them per se, but I rarely need them.

have some common features, they are very different in many important ways. However, regardless of the language used, much of functional programming is transcendent. Therefore, I wrote this book to introduce functional programming in the context of what is and what is not possible with JavaScript.

I assume a base-level understanding of JavaScript. There are many amazing books on the topic and a bevy of online resources, so an introduction to the language is not provided herein. I also assume a working understanding of object-oriented programming, as commonly practiced in languages such as Java, Ruby, Python, and even JavaScript. While knowing object-oriented programming can help you to avoid my use of the occasional irrelevant phrase, an expert-level understanding of the subject is not required.

The ideal readers for *Functional JavaScript* are long-time JavaScript programmers hoping to learn about functional programming, or long-time functional programmers looking to learn JavaScript. For the latter case, it's advised that this book be supplemented with material focusing on JavaScript's...oddities. Of particular note is *JavaScript: The Good Parts* by Douglas Crockford (O'Reilly). Finally, this book is appropriate for anyone looking to learn more about functional programming, even those who have no intention of using JavaScript beyond the confines of these pages.

A Roadmap for Functional JavaScript

Here is an outline of the topics covered in *Functional JavaScript*:

Chapter 1, Introducing Functional JavaScript
> The book starts off by introducing some important topics, including functional programming and Underscore.js.

Chapter 2, First-Class Functions and Applicative Programming
> Chapter 2 defines first-class functions, shows how to use them, and describes some common applications. One particular technique using first-class functions—called applicative programming—is also described. The chapter concludes with a discussion of "data thinking," an important approach to software development central to functional programming.

Chapter 3, Variable Scope and Closures
> Chapter 3 is a transitional chapter that covers two topics of core importance to understanding functional programming in JavaScript. I start by covering variable scoping, including the flavors used within JavaScript: lexical scoping, dynamic scoping, and function scoping. The chapter concludes with a discussion of closures —how they operate, and how and why you might use them.

Chapter 4, Higher-Order Functions
Building on the lessons of Chapters 2 and 3, this chapter describes an important type of first-class function: higher-order functions. Although "higher-order functions" sound complicated, this chapter shows that they are instead straightfoward.

Chapter 5, Function-Building Functions
Moving on from the lessons of the previous chapters, Chapter 5 describes a way to "compose" functions from other functions. Composing functions is an important technique in functional programming, and this chapter will help guide you through the process.

Chapter 6, Recursion
Chapter 6 is another transitional chapter in which I'll discuss recursion, a term that describes a function that calls itself either directly or indirectly. Because recursion is limited in JavaScript, it's not often used; however, there are ways around these limitations, and this chapter will guide you through a few.

Chapter 7, Purity, Immutability, and Policies for Change
Chapter 7 deals with various ways to write functional code that doesn't change anything. Put simply, functional programming is facilitated when variables are not changed at all, and this chapter will guide you through just what that means.

Chapter 8, Flow-Based Programming
Chapter 8 deals with viewing tasks, and even whole systems, as virtual "assembly lines" of functions that transform and move data.

Chapter 9, Programming Without Class
The final chapter focuses on how functional programming allows you to structure applications in interesting ways that have nothing to do with class-based object-oriented programming.

Following these chapters, the book concludes with two appendixes of supplementary information: Appendix A, *Functional JavaScript in the Wild* and Appendix B, *Annotated Bibliography*.

Conventions Used in This Book

The following typographical conventions are used in this book:

Italic
Indicates new terms, URLs, email addresses, filenames, and file extensions.

`Constant width`
Used for program listings, as well as within paragraphs to refer to program elements such as variable or function names, databases, data types, environment variables, statements, and keywords.

Constant width bold

Shows commands or other text that should be typed literally by the user.

Constant width italic

Shows text that should be replaced with user-supplied values or by values determined by context.

Using Code Examples

This book is here to help you get your job done. In general, if this book includes code examples, you may use the code in your programs and documentation. You do not need to contact us for permission unless you're reproducing a significant portion of the code. For example, writing a program that uses several chunks of code from this book does not require permission. Selling or distributing a CD-ROM of examples from O'Reilly books does require permission. Answering a question by citing this book and quoting example code does not require permission. Incorporating a significant amount of example code from this book into your product's documentation does require permission.

We appreciate, but do not require, attribution. An attribution usually includes the title, author, publisher, and ISBN. For example: "*Functional JavaScript* by Michael Fogus (O'Reilly). Copyright 2013 Michael Fogus, 978-1-449-36072-6."

If you feel your use of code examples falls outside fair use or the permission given above, feel free to contact us at *permissions@oreilly.com*.

Safari® Books Online

 Safari Books Online (*www.safaribooksonline.com*) is an on-demand digital library that delivers expert content in both book and video form from the world's leading authors in technology and business.

Technology professionals, software developers, web designers, and business and creative professionals use Safari Books Online as their primary resource for research, problem solving, learning, and certification training.

Safari Books Online offers a range of product mixes and pricing programs for organizations, government agencies, and individuals. Subscribers have access to thousands of books, training videos, and prepublication manuscripts in one fully searchable database from publishers like O'Reilly Media, Prentice Hall Professional, Addison-Wesley Professional, Microsoft Press, Sams, Que, Peachpit Press, Focal Press, Cisco Press, John Wiley & Sons, Syngress, Morgan Kaufmann, IBM Redbooks, Packt, Adobe Press, FT Press, Apress, Manning, New Riders, McGraw-Hill, Jones & Bartlett, Course Technology, and dozens more. For more information about Safari Books Online, please visit us online.

How to Contact Us

Please address comments and questions concerning this book to the publisher:

O'Reilly Media, Inc.
1005 Gravenstein Highway North
Sebastopol, CA 95472
800-998-9938 (in the United States or Canada)
707-829-0515 (international or local)
707-829-0104 (fax)

We have a web page for this book, where we list errata, examples, and any additional information. You can access this page at *http://oreil.ly/functional_js*.

To comment or ask technical questions about this book, send email to *bookques tions@oreilly.com*.

For more information about our books, courses, conferences, and news, see our website at *http://www.oreilly.com*.

Find us on Facebook: *http://facebook.com/oreilly*

Follow us on Twitter: *http://twitter.com/oreillymedia*

Watch us on YouTube: *http://www.youtube.com/oreillymedia*

Acknowledgments

It takes a village to write a book, and this book is no different. First, I would like to thank my good friend Rob Friesel for taking the time to provide feedback throughout the course of writing this book. Additionally, I would like to thank Jeremy Ashkenas for putting me in touch with O'Reilly and really making this book possible from the start. Plus he wrote the Underscore.js library—no small matter.

The following people have provided great conversation, direct feedback, or even inspiration from afar over the years, and I thank them all just for being awesome: Chris Houser, David Nolen, Stuart Halloway, Tim Ewald, Russ Olsen, Alan Kay, Peter Seibel, Sam Aaron, Brenton Ashworth, Craig Andera, Lynn Grogan, Matthew Flatt, Brian McKenna, Bodil Stokke, Oleg Kiselyov, Dave Herman, Mashaaricda Barmajada ee Mahmud, Patrick Logan, Alan Dipert, Alex Redington, Justin Gehtland, Carin Meier, Phil Bagwell, Steve Vinoski, Reginald Braithwaite, Daniel Friedman, Jamie Kite, William Byrd, Larry Albright, Michael Nygard, Sacha Chua, Daniel Spiewak, Christophe Grand, Sam Aaron, Meikel Brandmeyer, Dean Wampler, Clinton Dreisbach, Matthew Podwysocki, Steve Yegge, David Liebke, and Rich Hickey.

I would also like to thank the O'Reilly staff who've helped me make this book better than I could have ever done alone: Mary Treseler, Melanie Yarbrough, Dan Fauxsmith, Meghan Connolly, and Jasmine Kwityn.

My soundtrack while writing *Functional JavaScript* was provided by Pantha du Prince, Black Ace, Brian Eno, Béla Bartók, Dieter Moebius, Sun Ra, Broadcast, Scientist, and John Coltrane.

Finally, nothing that I do would be possible without the support of the three loves of my life: Keita, Shota, and Yuki.

CHAPTER 1

Introducing Functional JavaScript

This chapter sets up the book in a number of important ways. In it, I will introduce Underscore and explain how you can start using it. Additionally, I will define the terms and goals of the rest of the book.

The Case for JavaScript

The question of why you might choose JavaScript is easily answered in a word: reach. In other words, aside from perhaps Java, there is no more popular programming language right now than JavaScript. Its ubiquity in the browser and its near-ubiquity in a vast sea of current and emerging technologies make it a nice—and sometimes the only—choice for portability.

With the reemergence of client-service and single-page application architectures, the use of JavaScript in discrete applications (i.e., single-page apps) attached to numerous network services is exploding. For example, Google Apps are all written in JavaScript, and are prime examples of the single-page application paradigm.

If you've come to JavaScript with a ready interest in functional programming, then the good news is that it supports functional techniques "right out of the box" (e.g., the function is a core element in JavaScript). For example, if you have any experience with JavaScript, then you might have seen code like the following:

```
[1, 2, 3].forEach(alert);
// alert box with "1" pops up
// alert box with "2" pops up
// alert box with "3" pops up
```

The `Array#forEach` method, added in the fifth edition of the ECMA-262 language standard, takes some function (in this case, `alert`) and passes each array element to the function one after the other. That is, JavaScript provides various methods and functions that take other functions as arguments for some inner purpose. I'll talk more about this style of programming as the book progresses.

JavaScript is also built on a solid foundation of language primitives, which is amazing, but a double-edged sword (as I'll discuss soon). From functions to closures to prototypes to a fairly nice dynamic core, JavaScript provides a well-stocked set of tools.[1] In addition, JavaScript provides a very open and flexible execution model. As a small example, all JavaScript functions have an `apply` method that allows you to call the function with an array as if the array elements were the arguments to the function itself. Using `apply`, I can create a neat little function named `splat` that just takes a function and returns another function that takes an array and calls the original with `apply`, so that its elements serve as its arguments:

```
function splat(fun) {
  return function(array) {
    return fun.apply(null, array);
  };
}

var addArrayElements = splat(function(x, y) { return x + y });

addArrayElements([1, 2]);
//=> 3
```

This is your first taste of functional programming—a function that returns another function—but I'll get to the meat of that later. The point is that `apply` is only one of many ways that JavaScript is a hugely flexible programming language.

Another way that JavaScript proves its flexibility is that any function may be called with any number of arguments of any type, at any time. We can create a function `unsplat` that works opposite from `splat`, taking a function and returning another function that takes any number of arguments and calls the original with an array of the values given:

```
function unsplat(fun) {
  return function() {
    return fun.call(null, _.toArray(arguments));
  };
}

var joinElements = unsplat(function(array) { return array.join(' ') });

joinElements(1, 2);
//=> "1 2"

joinElements('-', '$', '/', '!', ':');
//=> "- $ / ! :"
```

---

1. And, as with all tools, you can get cut and/or smash your thumb if you're not careful.

Every JavaScript function can access a local value named `arguments` that is an array-like structure holding the values that the function was called with. Having access to `arguments` is surprisingly powerful, and is used to amazing effect in JavaScript in the wild. Additionally, the `call` method is similar to `apply` except that the former takes the arguments one by one rather than as an array, as expected by `apply`. The trifecta of `apply`, `call`, and `arguments` is only a small sample of the extreme flexibility provided by JavaScript.

With the emergent growth of JavaScript for creating applications of all sizes, you might expect stagnation in the language itself or its runtime support. However, even a casual investigation of the `ECMAScript.next` initiative shows that it's clear that JavaScript is an evolving (albeit slowly) language.[2] Likewise, JavaScript engines like V8 are constantly evolving and improving JavaScript speed and efficiency using both time-tested and novel techniques.

Some Limitations of JavaScript

The case against JavaScript—in light of its evolution, ubiquity, and reach—is quite thin. You can say much about the language quirks and robustness failings, but the fact is that JavaScript is here to stay, now and indefinitely. Regardless, it's worth acknowledging that JavaScript is a flawed language.[3] In fact, the most popular book on JavaScript, Douglas Crockford's *JavaScript: The Good Parts* (O'Reilly), spends more pages discussing the terrible parts than the good. The language has true oddities, and by and large is not particularly succinct in expression. However, changing the problems with JavaScript would likely "break the Web," a circumstance that's unacceptable to most. It's because of these problems that the number of languages targeting JavaScript as a compilation platform is growing; indeed, this is a very fertile niche.[4]

As a language supporting—and at times preferring—imperative programming techniques and a reliance on global scoping, JavaScript is unsafe by default. That is, building programs with a key focus on mutability is potentially confusing as programs grow. Likewise, the very language itself provides the building blocks of many high-level features found by default in other languages. For example, JavaScript itself, prior to trunk versions of ECMAScript 6, provides no module system, but facilitates their creation using raw objects. That JavaScript provides a loose collection of basic parts ensures a bevy of custom module implementations, each incompatible with the next.

---

2. A draft specification for `ES.next` is found at *http://wiki.ecmascript.org/doku.php?id=harmony:specifica tion_drafts*.

3. The debate continues over just how deeply.

4. Some languages that target JavaScript include, but are not limited to, the following: ClojureScript, Coffee-Script, Roy, Elm, TypeScript, Dart, Flapjax, Java, and JavaScript itself!

Language oddities, unsafe features, and a sea of competing libraries: three legitimate reasons to think hard about the adoption of JavaScript. But there is a light at the end of the tunnel that's not just the light of an oncoming train. The light is that through discipline and an observance to certain conventions, JavaScript code can be not only safe, but also simple to understand and test, in addition to being proportionally scalable to the size of the code base. This book will lead you on the path to one such approach: functional programming.

Getting Started with Functional Programming

You may have heard of functional programming on your favorite news aggregation site, or maybe you've worked in a language supporting functional techniques. If you've written JavaScript (and in this book I assume that you have) then you indeed *have* used a language supporting functional programming. However, that being the case, you might not have used JavaScript in a functional way. This book outlines a functional style of programming that aims to simplify your own libraries and applications, and helps tame the wild beast of JavaScript complexity.

As a bare-bones introduction, functional programming can be described in a single sentence:

> Functional programming is the use of functions that transform values into units of abstraction, subsequently used to build software systems.

This is a simplification bordering on libel, but it's functional (ha!) for this early stage in the book. The library that I use as my medium of functional expression in JavaScript is Underscore, and for the most part, it adheres to this basic definition. However, this definition fails to explain the "why" of functional programming.

Why Functional Programming Matters

> The major evolution that is still going on for me is towards a more functional programming style, which involves unlearning a lot of old habits, and backing away from some OOP directions.
>
> —John Carmack

If you're familiar with object-oriented programming, then you may agree that its primary goal is to break a problem into parts, as shown in Figure 1-1 (Gamma 1995).

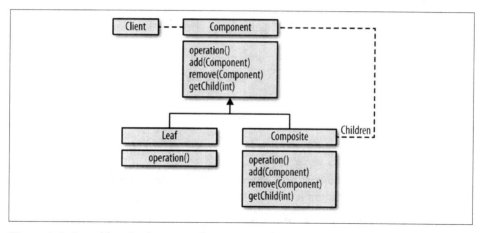

Figure 1-1. A problem broken into object-oriented parts

Likewise, these parts/objects can be aggregated and composed to form larger parts, as shown in Figure 1-2.

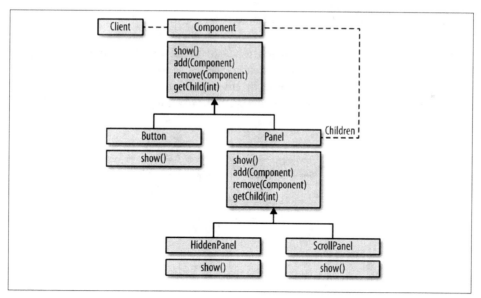

Figure 1-2. Objects are "composed" together to form bigger objects

Based on these parts and their aggregates, a system is then described in terms of the interactions and values of the parts, as shown in Figure 1-3.

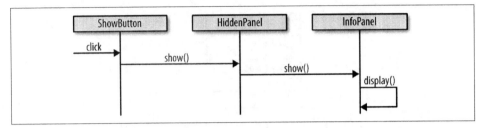

Figure 1-3. An object-oriented system and its interactions as a sequence diagram

This is a gross simplification of how object-oriented systems are formed, but I think that as a high-level description it works just fine.

By comparison, a strict functional programming approach to solving problems also breaks a problem into parts (namely, functions), as shown in Figure 1-4.

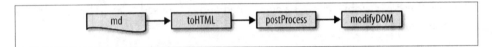

Figure 1-4. A problem broken into functional parts

Whereas the object-oriented approach tends to break problems into groupings of "nouns," or objects, a functional approach breaks the same problem into groupings of "verbs," or functions.[5] As with object-oriented programming, larger functions are formed by "gluing" or "composing" other functions together to build high-level behaviors, as shown in Figure 1-5.

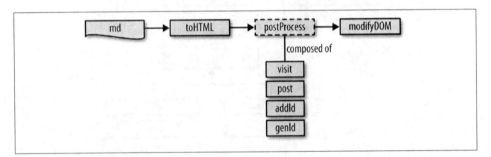

Figure 1-5. Functions are also composed together to form more behaviors

---

5. This is a simplistic way to view the composition of object-oriented versus functional systems, but bear with me as I develop a way to mix the two throughout the course of this book.

Finally, one way that the functional parts are formed into a system (as shown in Figure 1-6) is by taking a value and gradually "transforming" it—via one primitive or composed function—into another.

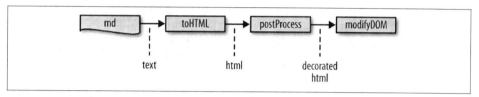

Figure 1-6. A functional system interacts via data transformation

In a system observing a strict object-oriented style, the interactions between objects cause internal change to each object, leading to an overall system state that is the amalgamation of many smaller, potentially subtle state changes. These interrelated state changes form a conceptual "web of change" that, at times, can be confusing to keep in your head. This confusion becomes a problem when the act of adding new objects and system features requires a working knowledge of the subtleties of potentially far-reaching state changes.

A functional system, on the other hand, strives to minimize observable state modification. Therefore, adding new features to a system built using functional principles is a matter of understanding how new functions can operate within the context of localized, nondestructive (i.e., original data is never changed) data transformations. However, I hesitate to create a false dichotomy and say that functional and object-oriented styles should stand in opposition. That JavaScript supports both models means that systems can and should be composed of both models. Finding the balance between functional and object-oriented styles is a tricky task that will be tackled much later in the book, when discussing mixins in Chapter 9. However, since this is a book about functional programming in JavaScript, the bulk of the discussion is focused on functional styles rather than object-oriented ones.

Having said that, a nice image of a system built along functional principles is an assembly-line device that takes raw materials in one end, and gradually builds a product that comes out the other end (Figure 1-7).

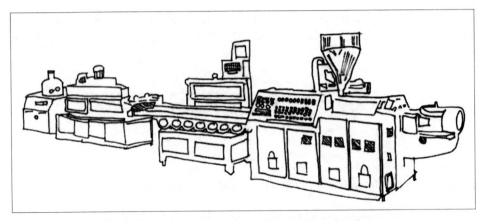

Figure 1-7. A functional program is a machine for transforming data

The assembly line analogy is, of course, not entirely perfect, because every machine I know consumes its raw materials to produce a product. By contrast, functional programming is what happens when you take a system built in an imperative way and shrink explicit state changes to the smallest possible footprint to make it more modular (Hughes 1984). Practical functional programming is not about eliminating state change, but instead about reducing the occurrences of mutation to the smallest area possible for any given system.

Functions as Units of Abstraction

One method of abstraction is that functions hide implementation details from view. In fact, functions are a beautiful unit of work allowing you to adhere to the long-practiced maxim in the UNIX community, set forth by Butler Lampson:

> Make it run, make it right, make it fast.

Likewise, functions-as-abstraction allow you to fulfill Kent Beck's similarly phrased mantra of test-driven development (TDD):

> Make it run, then make it right, then make it fast.

For example, in the case of reporting errors and warnings, you could write something like the following:

```
function parseAge(age) {
  if (!_.isString(age)) throw new Error("Expecting a string");
  var a;

  console.log("Attempting to parse an age");

  a = parseInt(age, 10);

  if (_.isNaN(a)) {
```

```
    console.log(["Could not parse age:", age].join(' '));
      a = 0;
    }

    return a;
}
```

This function, although not comprehensive for parsing age strings, is nicely illustrative. Use of `parseAge` is as follows:

```
parseAge("42");
// (console) Attempting to parse an age
//=> 42

parseAge(42);
// Error: Expecting a string

parseAge("frob");
// (console) Attempting to parse an age
// (console) Could not parse age: frob
//=> 0
```

The `parseAge` function works as written, but if you want to modify the way that errors, information, and warnings are presented, then changes need to be made to the appropriate lines therein, and anywhere else similar patterns are used. A better approach is to "abstract" the notion of errors, information, and warnings into functions:

```
function fail(thing) {
    throw new Error(thing);
}

function warn(thing) {
    console.log(["WARNING:", thing].join(' '));
}

function note(thing) {
    console.log(["NOTE:", thing].join(' '));
}
```

Using these functions, the `parseAge` function can be rewritten as follows:

```
function parseAge(age) {
    if (!_.isString(age)) fail("Expecting a string");
    var a;

    note("Attempting to parse an age");
    a = parseInt(age, 10);

    if (_.isNaN(a)) {
        warn(["Could not parse age:", age].join(' '));
        a = 0;
    }
```

```
    return a;
  }
```

Here's the new behavior:

```
parseAge("frob");
// (console) NOTE: Attempting to parse an age
// (console) WARNING: Could not parse age: frob
//=> 0
```

It's not very different from the old behavior, except that now the idea of reporting errors, information, and warnings has been abstracted away. The reporting of errors, information, and warnings can thus be modified entirely:

```
function note() {}
function warn(str) {
  alert("That doesn't look like a valid age");
}

parseAge("frob");
// (alert box) That doesn't look like a valid age
//=> 0
```

Therefore, because the behavior is contained within a single function, the function can be replaced by new functions providing similar behavior or outright different behaviors altogether (Abelson and Sussman 1996).

Encapsulation and Hiding

Over the years, we've been taught that a cornerstone of object-oriented programming is *encapsulation*. The term encapsulation in reference to object-oriented programming refers to a way of packaging certain pieces of data with the very operations that manipulate them, as seen in Figure 1-8.

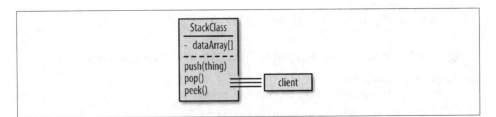

Figure 1-8. Most object-oriented languages use object boundaries to package data elements with the operations that work on them; a Stack class would therefore package an array of elements with the push, pop, and peek operations used to manipulate it

JavaScript provides an object system that does indeed allow you to encapsulate data with its manipulators. However, sometimes encapsulation is used to restrict the visibility of certain elements, and this act is known as *data hiding*. JavaScript's object system does not provide a way to hide data directly, so data is hidden using something called closures, as shown in Figure 1-9.

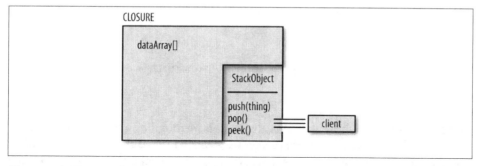

Figure 1-9. Using a closure to encapsulate data is a functional way to hide details from a client's view

Closures are not covered in any depth until Chapter 3, but for now you should keep in mind that closures are kinds of functions. By using functional techniques involving closures, you can achieve data hiding that is as effective as the same capability offered by most object-oriented languages, though I hesitate to say whether functional encapsulation or object-oriented encapsulation is better. Instead, while they are different in practice, they both provide similar ways of building certain kinds of abstraction. In fact, this book is not at all about encouraging you to throw away everything that you might have ever learned in favor of functional programming; instead, it's meant to explain functional programming on its own terms so that you can decide if it's right for your needs.

Functions as Units of Behavior

Hiding data and behavior (which has the side effect of providing a more agile change experience) is just one way that functions can be units of abstraction. Another is to provide an easy way to store and pass around discrete units of basic behavior. Take, for example, JavaScript's syntax to denote looking up a value in an array by index:

```
var letters = ['a', 'b', 'c'];

letters[1];
//=> 'b'
```

While array indexing is a core behavior of JavaScript, there is no way to grab hold of the behavior and use it as needed without placing it into a function. Therefore, a simple example of a function that abstracts array indexing behavior could be called nth. The naive implementation of nth is as follows:

```
function naiveNth(a, index) {
  return a[index];
}
```

As you might suspect, nth operates along the happy path perfectly fine:

```
naiveNth(letters, 1);
//=> "b"
```

However, the function will fail if given something unexpected:

```
naiveNth({}, 1);
//=> undefined
```

Therefore, if I were to think about the abstraction surrounding a function nth, I might devise the following statement: *nth returns the element located at a valid index within a data type allowing indexed access.* A key part of this statement is the idea of an indexed data type. To determine if something is an indexed data type, I can create a function isIndexed, implemented as follows:

```
function isIndexed(data) {
  return _.isArray(data) || _.isString(data);
}
```

The function isIndexed is also a function providing an abstraction over checking if a piece of data is a string or an array. Building abstraction on abstraction leads to the following complete implementation of nth:

```
function nth(a, index) {
  if (!_.isNumber(index)) fail("Expected a number as the index");
  if (!isIndexed(a)) fail("Not supported on non-indexed type");
  if ((index < 0) || (index > a.length - 1))
    fail("Index value is out of bounds");

  return a[index];
}
```

The completed implementation of nth operates as follows:

```
nth(letters, 1);
//=> 'b'

nth("abc", 0);
//=> "a"

nth({}, 2);
// Error: Not supported on non-indexed type

nth(letters, 4000);
// Error: Index value is out of bounds

nth(letters, 'aaaaa');
// Error: Expected a number as the index
```

In the same way that I built the nth abstraction out of an indexed abstraction, I can likewise build a second abstraction:

```
function second(a) {
  return nth(a, 1);
}
```

The second function allows me to appropriate the correct behavior of nth for a different but related use case:

```
second(['a','b']);
//=> "b"

second("fogus");
//=> "o"

second({});
// Error: Not supported on non-indexed type
```

Another unit of basic behavior in JavaScript is the idea of a *comparator*. A comparator is a function that takes two values and returns <0 if the first is less than the second, >0 if it is greater, and 0 if they are equal. In fact, JavaScript itself can appear to use the very nature of numbers themselves to provide a default sort method:

```
[2, 3, -6, 0, -108, 42].sort();
//=> [-108, -6, 0, 2, 3, 42]
```

But a problem arises when you have a different mix of numbers:

```
[0, -1, -2].sort();
//=> [-1, -2, 0]

[2, 3, -1, -6, 0, -108, 42, 10].sort();
//=> [-1, -108, -6, 0, 10, 2, 3, 42]
```

The problem is that when given no arguments, the Array#sort method does a string comparison. However, every JavaScript programmer knows that Array#sort expects a comparator, and instead writes:

```
[2, 3, -1, -6, 0, -108, 42, 10].sort(function(x,y) {
  if (x < y) return -1;
  if (y < x) return  1;
  return 0;
});

//=> [-108, -6, -1, 0, 2, 3, 10, 42]
```

That seems better, but there is a way to make it more generic. After all, you might need to sort like this again in another part of the code, so perhaps it's better to pull out the anonymous function and give it a name:

```
function compareLessThanOrEqual(x, y) {
  if (x < y) return -1;
```

```
  if (y < x) return  1;
  return 0;
}
```

```
[2, 3, -1, -6, 0, -108, 42, 10].sort(compareLessThanOrEqual);
//=> [-108, -6, -1, 0, 2, 3, 10, 42]
```

But the problem with the compareLessThanOrEqual function is that it is coupled to the idea of "comparatorness" and cannot easily stand on its own as a generic comparison operation:

```
if (compareLessThanOrEqual(1,1))
  console.log("less or equal");
```

```
// nothing prints
```

To achieve the desired effect, I would need to *know* about compareLessThanOrEqual's comparator nature:

```
if (_.contains([0, -1], compareLessThanOrEqual(1,1)))
  console.log("less or equal");
```

```
// less or equal
```

But this is less than satisfying, especially when there is a possibility for some developer to come along in the future and change the return value of compareLessThanOrEqual to -42 for negative comparisons. A better way to write compareLessThanOrEqual might be as follows:

```
function lessOrEqual(x, y) {
  return x <= y;
}
```

Functions that always return a Boolean value (i.e., true or false only), are called *predicates*. So, instead of an elaborate comparator construction, lessOrEqual is simply a "skin" over the built-in <= operator:

```
[2, 3, -1, -6, 0, -108, 42, 10].sort(lessOrEqual);
//=> [42, 10, 3, 2, 0, -1, -6, -108]
```

At this point, you might be inclined to change careers. However, upon further reflection, the result makes sense. If sort expects a comparator, and lessOrEqual only returns true or false, then you need to somehow get from the world of the latter to that of the former without duplicating a bunch of if/then/else boilerplate. The solution lies in creating a function, comparator, that takes a predicate and converts its result to the -1/0/1 result expected of comparator functions:

```
function comparator(pred) {
  return function(x, y) {
    if (truthy(pred(x, y)))
      return -1;
    else if (truthy(pred(y, x)))
```

```
      return 1;
    else
      return 0;
  };
};
```

Now, the `comparator` function can be used to return a new function that "maps" the results of the predicate `lessOrEqual` (i.e., `true` or `false`) onto the results expected of comparators (i.e., `-1`, `0`, or `1`), as shown in Figure 1-10.

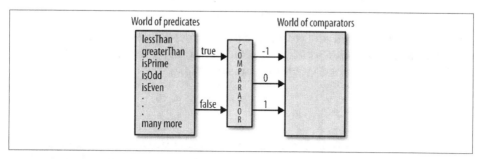

Figure 1-10. Bridging the gap between two "worlds" using the comparator function

In functional programming, you'll almost always see functions interacting in a way that allows one type of data to be brought into the world of another type of data. Observe `comparator` in action:

```
[2, 3, -1, -6, 0, -108, 42, 10].sort(comparator(lessOrEqual));
//=> [-108, -6, -1, 0, 2, 3, 10, 42]
```

The function `comparator` will work to map any function that returns "truthy" or "falsey" values onto the notion of "comparatorness." This topic is covered in much greater depth in Chapter 4, but it's worth noting now that `comparator` is a *higher-order function* (because it takes a function and returns a new function). Keep in mind that not every predicate makes sense for use with the `comparator` function, however. For example, what does it mean to use the `_.isEqual` function as the basis for a `comparator`? Try it out and see what happens.

Throughout this book, I will talk about the ways that functional techniques provide and facilitate the creation of abstractions, and as I'll discuss next, there is a beautiful synergy between functions-as-abstraction and data.

Data as Abstraction

JavaScript's object prototype model is a rich and foundational data scheme. On its own, the prototype model provides a level of flexibility not found in many other mainstream programming languages. However, many JavaScript programmers, as is their wont, immediately attempt to build a class-based object system using the prototype or closure features (or both).[6] Although a class system has its strong points, very often the data needs of a JavaScript application are much simpler than is served by classes.[7]

Instead, using JavaScript bare data primitives, objects, and arrays, much of the data modeling tasks that are currently served by classes are subsumed. Historically, functional programming has centered around building functions that work to achieve higher-level behaviors and work on very simple data constructs.[8] In the case of this book (and Underscore itself), the focus is indeed on processing arrays and objects. The flexibility in those two simple data types is astounding, and it's unfortunate that they are often overlooked in favor of yet another class-based system.

Imagine that you're tasked with writing a JavaScript application that deals with comma-separated value (CSV) files, which are a standard way to represent data tables. For example, suppose you have a CSV file that looks as follows:

```
name,    age, hair
Merble, 35,   red
Bob,     64,   blonde
```

It should be clear that this data represents a table with three columns (name, age, and hair) and three rows (the first being the header row, and the rest being the data rows). A small function to parse this very constrained CSV representation stored in a string is implemented as follows:

```
function lameCSV(str) {
  return _.reduce(str.split("\n"), function(table, row) {
    table.push(_.map(row.split(","), function(c) { return c.trim()}));
    return table;
  }, []);
};
```

You'll notice that the function lameCSV processes the rows one by one, splitting at \n and then stripping whitespace for each cell therein.[9] The whole data table is an array of sub-arrays, each containing strings. From the conceptual view shown in Table 1-1, nested arrays can be viewed as a table.

6. The ECMAScript.next initiative is discussing the possibility of language support for classes. However, for various reasons outside the scope of this book, the feature is highly controversial. As a result, it's unclear when and if classes will make it into JavaScript core.

7. One strong argument for a class-based object system is the historical use in implementing user interfaces.

8. Very often you will see a focus on list data structures in functional literature. In the case of JavaScript, the array is a nice substitute.

9. The function lameCSV is meant for illustrative purposes and is in no way meant as a fully featured CSV parser. Having said that, there are better ways to implement it but I wanted to highlight the use of _.reduce in this implementation.

Table 1-1. Simply nested arrays are one way to abstract a data table

name	age	hair
Merble	35	red
Bob	64	blonde

Using `lameCSV` to parse the data stored in a string works as follows:

```
var peopleTable = lameCSV("name,age,hair\nMerble,35,red\nBob,64,blonde");

peopleTable;
//=> [["name",   "age",  "hair"],
//    ["Merble", "35",   "red"],
//    ["Bob",    "64",   "blonde"]]
```

Using selective spacing highlights the table nature of the returned array. In functional programming, functions like `lameCSV` and the previously defined `comparator` are key in translating one data type into another. Figure 1-11 illustrates how data transformations in general can be viewed as getting from one "world" into another.

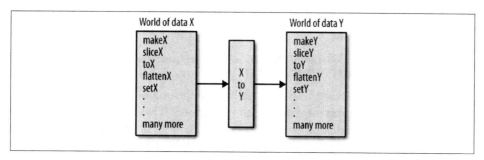

Figure 1-11. Functions can bridge the gap between two "worlds"

There are better ways to represent a table of such data, but this nested array serves us well for now. Indeed, there is little motivation to build a complex class hierarchy representing either the table itself, the rows, people, or whatever. Instead, keeping the data representation minimal allows me to use existing array fields and array processing functions and methods out of the box:

```
_.rest(peopleTable).sort();

//=> [["Bob",    "64",  "blonde"],
//    ["Merble", "35",  "red"]]
```

Likewise, since I know the form of the original data, I can create appropriately named selector functions to access the data in a more descriptive way:

```
function selectNames(table) {
  return _.rest(_.map(table, _.first));
}
```

```
function selectAges(table) {
  return _.rest(_.map(table, second));
}

function selectHairColor(table) {
  return _.rest(_.map(table, function(row) {
    return nth(row, 2);
  }));
}

var mergeResults = _.zip;
```

The select functions defined here use existing array processing functions to provide fluent access to simple data types:

```
selectNames(peopleTable);
//=> ["Merble", "Bob"]

selectAges(peopleTable);
//=> ["35", "64"]

selectHairColor(peopleTable);
//=> ["red", "blonde"]

mergeResults(selectNames(peopleTable), selectAges(peopleTable));
//=> [["Merble", "35"], ["Bob", "64"]]
```

The simplicity of implementation and use is a compelling argument for using Java-Script's core data structures for data modeling purposes. That's not to say that there is no place for an object-oriented or class-based approach. In my experience, I've found that a functional approach centered around generic collection processing functions is ideal for handling data about people and an object-oriented approach works best for simulating people.[10]

If you are so inclined, the data table could be changed to a custom class-based model, and as long as you use the selector abstractions, then the user would never know, nor care. However, throughout this book, I strive to keep the data needs as simple as possible and build abstract functions that operate on them. Constraining myself to functions operating on simple data, interestingly enough, increases my flexibility. You might be surprised how far these fundamental types will take you.

---

10. That the object-oriented paradigm sprung from the simulation community in the form of the Simula programming language is no coincidence. Having written my share of simulation systems, I feel very strongly that object orientation or actor-based modeling are compelling fits for simulation.

A Taste of Functional JavaScript

This is not a book about navigating around the quirks of JavaScript. There are many other books that will help you along that path. However, before I start any JavaScript project these days, I define two useful functions that I often find a need for: `existy` and `truthy`.

The function `existy` is meant to define the existence of something. JavaScript has two values—`null` and `undefined`—that signify nonexistence. Thus, `existy` checks that its argument is neither of these things, and is implemented as follows:

```
function existy(x) { return x != null };
```

Using the loose inequality operator (`!=`), it is possible to distinguish between `null`, `undefined`, and everything else. It's used as follows:

```
existy(null);
//=> false

existy(undefined);
//=> false

existy({}.notHere);
//=> false

existy((function(){})());
//=> false

existy(0);
//=> true

existy(false);
//=> true
```

The use of `existy` simplifies what it means for something to exist in JavaScript. Minimally, it collocates the existence check in an easy-to-use function. The second function mentioned, `truthy`, is defined as follows:[11]

```
function truthy(x) { return (x !== false) && existy(x) };
```

The `truthy` function is used to determine if something should be considered a synonym for `true`, and is used as shown here:[12]

---

11. You might come across the idea of JavaScript's truthiness referring to the true-ness and false-ness of the language's native types. Although it's important to know the details of what constitutes truth for JavaScript, I like to simplify matters by reducing the number of rules that I need to consider for my own applications.

12. That the number zero is considered "truthy" is by design. That it is often used as a synonym for `false` is a relic of a C heritage. If you wish to retain this behavior, then simply do not use `truthy` where you might expect 0.

```
truthy(false);
//=> false

truthy(undefined);
//=> false

truthy(0);
//=> true

truthy('');
//=> true
```

In JavaScript, it's sometimes useful to perform some action only if a condition is true and return something like undefined or null otherwise. The general pattern is as follows:

```
{
  if(condition)
    return _.isFunction(doSomething) ? doSomething() : doSomething;
  else
    return undefined;
}
```

Using truthy, I can encapsulate this logic in the following way:

```
function doWhen(cond, action) {
  if(truthy(cond))
    return action();
  else
    return undefined;
}
```

Now whenever that pattern rears its ugly head, you can do the following instead:[13]

```
function executeIfHasField(target, name) {
  return doWhen(existy(target[name]), function() {
    var result = _.result(target, name);
    console.log(['The result is', result].join(' '));
    return result;
  });
}
```

The execution of executeIfHasField for success and error cases is as follows:

```
executeIfHasField([1,2,3], 'reverse');
// (console) The result is 3, 2, 1
//=> [3, 2, 1]

executeIfHasField({foo: 42}, 'foo');
// (console) The result is 42
```

13. I use existy(target[name]) rather than Underscore's has(target, name) because the latter will only check self-keys.

```
//=> 42

executeIfHasField([1,2,3], 'notHere');
//=> undefined
```

Big deal, right? So I've defined two functions—this is hardly functional programming. The functional part comes from their use. You may be familiar with the `Array#map` method available in many JavaScript implementations. It's meant to take a function and call it for every element in an array, returning a new array with the new values. It's used as follows:

```
[null, undefined, 1, 2, false].map(existy);
//=> [false, false, true, true, true]

[null, undefined, 1, 2, false].map(truthy);
//=> [false, false, true, true, false]
```

This, ladies and gentlemen, is functional programming:

- The definition of an abstraction for "existence" in the guise of a function
- The definition of an abstraction for "truthiness" built from existing functions
- The use of said functions by other functions via parameter passing to achieve some behavior

This book is all about code like this, but to an exquisite level of detail.

On Speed

I know what you're thinking. This functional programming stuff has to be slow as a dog, right?

There's no way to deny that the use of the array index form `array[0]` will execute faster than either of `nth(array, 0)` or `_.first(array)`. Likewise, an imperative loop of the following form will be very fast:[14]

```
for (var i=0, len=array.length; i < len; i++) {
  doSomething(array[i]);
}
```

An analogous use of Underscore's `_.each` function will, all factors being equal, be slower:

```
_.each(array, function(elem) {
  doSomething(array[i]);
});
```

However, it's very likely that all factors will not be equal. Certainly, if you had a function that needed speed, then a reasonable manual transformation would be to convert the

---

14. A wonderful site that I use for JavaScript browser benchmarking is located at *http://www.jsperf.com*.

internal use of _.each into an analogous use of for or while. Happily, the days of the ponderously slow JavaScript are coming to an end, and in some cases are a thing of the past. For example, the release of Google's V8 engine ushered in an age of runtime optimizations that have worked to motivate performance gains across all JavaScript engine vendors (Bak 2012).[15] Even if other vendors were not following Google's lead, the prevalence of the V8 engine is growing, and in fact drives the very popular Chrome browser and Node.js itself. However, other vendors are following the V8 lead and introducing runtime speed enhancements such as native-code execution, just-in-time compilation, faster garbage collection, call-site caching, and in-lining into their own JavaScript engines.[16]

However, the need to support aging browsers like Internet Explorer 6 is a very real requirement for some JavaScript programmers. There are two factors to consider when confronted with legacy platforms: (1) the use of IE6 and its ilk is dying out, and (2) there are other ways to gain speed before the code ever hits the browser.[17] For example, the subject of in-lining is particularly interesting, because many in-lining optimizations can be performed *statically*, or before code is ever run. Code in-lining is the act of taking a piece of code contained in, say, a function, and "pasting" it in place of a call to that very function. Let's take a look at an example to make things clearer. Somewhere in the depths of Underscore's _.each implementation is a loop very similar to the for loop shown earlier (edited for clarity):

```
_.each = function(obj, iterator, context) {
  // bounds checking
  // check for native method
  // check for length property
    for (var i = 0, l = obj.length; i < l; i++) {
      // call the given function
    }
}
```

Imagine that you have a bit of code that looks as follows:

```
function performTask(array) {
  _.each(array, function(elem) {
    doSomething(elem);
  });
}
```

---

15. As with any story, there is always precedent. Prior to V8, the WebKit project worked on the SquirrelFish Extreme engine that compiled JavaScript to native code. Prior to SquirrelFish was the Tamarin VM, which was developed by Mozilla based on the ActionScript VM 2 by Adobe. Even more interesting is that most JavaScript optimization techniques were pioneered by the older programming languages Self and Smalltalk.

16. Don't worry if you're not familiar with these optimization techniques. They are not important for the purposes of this book, and will therefore not be on the test. I highly encourage studying up on them, however, as they are nonetheless a fascinating topic.

17. A fun site that tracks worldwide IE6 usage is found at *http://www.ie6countdown.com*.

```
// ... some time later

performTask([1,2,3,4,5]);
```

A static optimizer could transform the body of `performTask` into the following:

```
function performTask(array) {
  for (var i = 0, l = array.length; i < l; i++) {
    doSomething(array[i]);
  }
}
```

And a sophisticated optimization tool could optimize this further by eliminating the function call altogether:

```
// ... some time later

var array123 = [1,2,3,4,5];

for (var i = 0, l = array123.length; i < l; i++) {
  doSomething(array[i]);
}
```

Finally, a really amazing static analyzer could optimize it even further into five separate calls:

```
// ... some time later

doSomething(array[1]);
doSomething(array[2]);
doSomething(array[3]);
doSomething(array[4]);
doSomething(array[5]);
```

And to top off this amazing set of optimizing transformations, you can imagine that if these calls have no effects or are never called, then the optimal transformation is:

```
// ... some time later
```

That is, if a piece of code can be determined to be "dead" (i.e., not called), then it can safely be eliminated via a process known as *code elision*. There are already program optimizers available for JavaScript that perform these types of optimizations—the primary being Google's Closure compiler. The Closure compiler is an amazing piece of engineering that compiles JavaScript into highly optimized JavaScript.[18]

There are many different ways to speed up even highly functional code bases using a combination of best practices and optimization tools. However, very often we're too

---

18. There are caveats that go along with using the Google Closure compiler, primary among them being that it works to its optimal efficiency given a certain style of coding. However, when it works, it works wonders, as I learned during my work on the ClojureScript compiler.

quick to consider matters of raw computation speed before we've even written a stitch of correct code. Likewise, I sometimes find my mind drifting toward speed considerations even if raw speed is not needed for the types of systems that I create. Underscore is a very popular functional programming library for JavaScript, and a great many applications do just fine with it. The same can be said for the heavyweight champion of JavaScript libraries, jQuery, which fosters many functional idioms.

Certainly there are legitimate domains for raw speed (e.g., game programming and low-latency systems). However, even in the face of such systems' execution demands, functional techniques are not guaranteed to slow things down. You would not want to use a function like nth in the heart of a tight rendering loop, but functional structuring in the aggregate can still yield benefits.

The first rule of my personal programming style has always been the following: Write beautiful code. I've achieved this goal to varying degrees of success throughout my career, but it's always something that I strive for. Writing beautiful code allows me to optimize another aspect of computer time: the time that I spend sitting at a desk typing on a keyboard. I find a functional style of writing code to be exceptionally beautiful if done well, and I hope that you'll agree by the time you reach the end.

The Case for Underscore

Before moving on to the meat of the book, I'd like to explain why I chose Underscore as my mode of expression. First of all, Underscore is a very nice library that offers an API that is pragmatic and nicely functional in style. It would be fruitless for me to implement, from scratch, all of the functions useful for understanding functional programming. Why implement map when the idea of "mappiness" is more important? That's not to say that I will not implement core functional tools in this book, but I do so with Underscore as a foundation.[19]

Second, there is a greater than zero chance that running the preceding code snippets using Array#map did not work. The likely reason is that in whichever environment you chose to run it might not have had the map method on its array implementation. What I would like to avoid, at any cost, is getting bogged down in cross-browser incompatibility issues. This noise, while extremely important, is a distraction to the larger purpose of introducing functional programming. The use of Underscore eliminates that noise almost completely![20]

---

19. There are other functional libraries for JavaScript that could have served just as well as a foundation for this book, including Functional JavaScript, Bilby, and even JQuery. However, my go-to choice is Underscore. Your mileage may vary.

20. Cross-browser compatibility is an issue in the use of Underscore when it defers to the underlying methods; the speed of execution is likely to be much faster than the Underscore implementation.

Finally, JavaScript by its very nature enables programmers to reinvent the wheel quite often. JavaScript itself has the perfect mix of powerful low-level constructs coupled with the absence of mid- and high-level language features. It's this odd condition that almost dares people to create language features from the lower-level parts. Language evolution will obviate the need to reinvent some of the existing wheels (e.g., module systems), but we're unlikely to see a complete elimination of the desire or need to build language features.[21] However, I believe that when available, existing high-quality libraries should be reused.[22] It would be fun to re-implement Underscore's capabilities from scratch, but it would serve neither myself (or my employer) nor you to do so.

Summary

This chapter covered a few introductory topics, starting with the motivation for learning and using JavaScript. Among the current stable of popular programming languages, few seem more poised for growth than JavaScript. Likewise, the growth potential seems almost limitless. However, JavaScript is a flawed language that needs to call on powerful techniques, discipline, or a mixture of both to be used effectively. One technique for building JavaScript applications is called "functional programming," which in a nutshell, consists of the following techniques:

- Identifying an abstraction and building a function for it
- Using existing functions to build more complex abstractions
- Passing existing functions to other functions to build even more complex abstractions

However, functions are not enough. In fact, functional programming very often works best when implemented in concert with powerful data abstractions. There is a beautiful symmetry between functional programming and data, and the next chapter dives into this symmetry more deeply.

---

21. This a facet of the nature of programming in my opinion.

22. I'm particularly enamored with the microjs website (*http://microjs.com/*) for discovering JavaScript libraries.

CHAPTER 2

First-Class Functions and Applicative Programming

The basics of functional programming, which treats functions as first-class elements of a language, are covered in this chapter. I'll provide a basis in the three common functions: map, reduce, and filter. Since programmers will likely be familiar with these functions, using them as a starting point should provide a nice foundation for the rest of the book.

Functions as First-Class Things

Some programmers familiar with JavaScript, myself included, consider it to be a functional language. Of course, to say such a thing implies that others disagree with that assessment. The reason for this disagreement stems from the fact that functional programming often has a relative definition, differing in minor and major ways from one practitioner or theorist to another.[1]

This is a sad state of affairs, indeed. Thankfully, however, almost every single relative definition of functional programming seems to agree on one point: a functional programming language is one facilitating the use and creation of first-class functions.

Typically, you will see this point accompanied by other definitional qualifications including but not limited to static typing, pattern matching, immutability, purity, and so on. However, while these other points describe certain implementations of functional programming languages, they fail in broad applicability. If I boil down the definition to its essence, consisting of the terms "facilitating" and "first-class functions," then it covers a broad range of languages from Haskell to JavaScript—the latter being quite important

---

1. Aside from the fact that programmers rarely agree on even the most common terms.

to this book. Thankfully, this also allows first-class functions to be defined in a paragraph.[2]

The term "first-class" means that something is just a value. A first-class function is one that can go anywhere that any other value can go—there are few to no restrictions. A number in JavaScript is surely a first-class thing, and therefore a first-class function has a similar nature:

- A number can be stored in a variable and so can a function:

```
var fortytwo = function() { return 42 };
```

- A number can be stored in an array slot and so can a function:

```
var fortytwos = [42, function() { return 42 }];
```

- A number can be stored in an object field and so can a function:

```
var fortytwos = {number: 42, fun: function() { return 42 }};
```

- A number can be created as needed and so can a function:

```
42 + (function() { return 42 })();
//=> 84
```

- A number can be passed to a function and so can a function:

```
function weirdAdd(n, f) { return n + f() }

weirdAdd(42, function() { return 42 });
//=> 84
```

- A number can be returned from a function and so can a function:

```
return 42;

return function() { return 42 };
```

The last two points define by example what we would call a "higher-order" function; put directly, a higher-order function can do one or both of the following:

- Take a function as an argument
- Return a function as a result

---

2. Haskell programs dealing with matters of I/O are often highly imperative in nature, but you would be hard-pressed to find someone claiming that Haskell was not functional.

In Chapter 1, `comparator` was used as an example of a higher-order function, but here is yet another example:

```
_.each(['whiskey', 'tango', 'foxtrot'], function(word) {
  console.log(word.charAt(0).toUpperCase() + word.substr(1));
});

// (console) Whiskey
// (console) Tango
// (console) Foxtrot
```

Underscore's `_.each` function takes a collection (object or array) and loops over its elements, calling the function given as the second argument for *each* element.

I'll dive deeper into higher-order functions in Chapter 4. For now, I'll take a couple of pages to talk about JavaScript itself, because as you may already know, while it supports a functional style, it also supports a number of other programming paradigms.

JavaScript's Multiple Paradigms

Of course JavaScript is not strictly a functional programming language, but instead facilitates the use of other paradigms as well:

Imperative programming
> Programming based around describing actions in detail

Prototype-based object-oriented programming
> Programming based around prototypical objects and instances of them

Metaprogramming
> Programming manipulating the basis of JavaScript's execution model

Including only imperative, object-oriented, and metaprogramming restricts us to only those paradigms directly supported by the built-in language constructs. You could further support other paradigms, like class orientation and evented programming, using the language itself as an implementation medium, but this book does not deal with those topics in depth. Before I get into the definition and details of JavaScript's support for first-class functions, let me take a brief moment to elucidate how the other three models differ from functional programming. I'll dig deeper into each topic throughout this book, so for now a paragraph or two on each should suffice in transitioning you into the functional programming discussion.

Imperative programming

An imperative programming style is categorized by its exquisite (and often infuriating) attention to the details of algorithm implementation. Further, imperative programs are often built around the direct manipulation and inspection of program state. For example, imagine that you'd like to write a program to build a lyric sheet for the song "99

Bottles of Beer." The most direct way to describe the requirements of this program are as such:

- Start at 99
- Sing the following for each number down to 1:
  — X bottles of beer on the wall
  — X bottles of beer
  — Take one down, pass it around
  — X-1 bottles of beer on the wall
- Subtract one from the last number and start over with the new value
- When you finally get to the number 1, sing the following last line instead:
  — No more bottles of beer on the wall

As it turns out, this specification has a fairly straightforward imperative implementation in JavaScript, as shown here:

```
var lyrics = [];

for (var bottles = 99; bottles > 0; bottles--) {
  lyrics.push(bottles + " bottles of beer on the wall");
  lyrics.push(bottles + " bottles of beer");
  lyrics.push("Take one down, pass it around");

  if (bottles > 1) {
    lyrics.push((bottles - 1) + " bottles of beer on the wall.");
  }
  else {
    lyrics.push("No more bottles of beer on the wall!");
  }
}
```

This imperative version, while somewhat contrived, is emblematic of an imperative programming style. That is, the implementation describes a "99 Bottles of Beer" program and exactly a "99 Bottles of Beer" program. Because imperative code operates at such a precise level of detail, they are often one-shot implementations or at best, difficult to reuse. Further, imperative languages are often restricted to a level of detail that is good for their compilers rather than for their programmers (Sokolowski 1991).

By comparison, a more functional approach to this same problem might look as follows:

```
function lyricSegment(n) {
  return _.chain([])
    .push(n + " bottles of beer on the wall")
    .push(n + " bottles of beer")
    .push("Take one down, pass it around")
    .tap(function(lyrics) {
```

```
      if (n > 1)
        lyrics.push((n - 1) + " bottles of beer on the wall.");
      else
        lyrics.push("No more bottles of beer on the wall!");
    })
  .value();
}
```

The `lyricSegment` function does very little on its own—in fact, it only generates the lyrics for a single verse of the song for a given number:

```
lyricSegment(9);

//=> ["9 bottles of beer on the wall",
//     "9 bottles of beer",
//     "Take one down, pass it around",
//     "8 bottles of beer on the wall."]
```

Functional programming is about pulling programs apart and reassembling them from the same parts, abstracted behind function boundaries. Thinking in this way, you can imagine that the `lyricSegment` function is the part of the "99 Bottles" program that abstracts lyric generation. Therefore, the part of the program that abstracts the assembly of the verse segments into a song is as follows:

```
function song(start, end, lyricGen) {
  return _.reduce(_.range(start,end,-1),
    function(acc,n) {
      return acc.concat(lyricGen(n));
    }, []);
}
```

And using it is as simple as:

```
song(99, 0, lyricSegment);

//=> ["99 bottles of beer on the wall",
//     ...
//     "No more bottles of beer on the wall!"]
```

Abstracting in this way allows you to separate out domain logic (i.e., the generation of a lyrical verse) from the generic verse assembly machinery. If you were so inclined, you could pass different functions like `germanLyricSegment` or `agreementLyricSegment` into `song` to generate a different lyric sheet altogether. Throughout this book, I'll use this technique, and explain it in greater depth along the way.

Prototype-based object-oriented programming

JavaScript is very similar to Java or C# in that its constructor functions are classes (at least at the level of implementation details), but the method of use is at a lower level. Whereas every instance in a Java program is generated from a class serving as its template, JavaScript instances use existing objects to serve as prototypes for specialized instances.[3] Object specialization, together with a built-in dispatch logic that routes calls down what's called a *prototype chain,* is far more low-level than class-oriented programming, but is extremely elegant and powerful. I will talk about exploiting JavaScript's prototype chain later in Chapter 9.

For now, how this relates to functional programming is that functions can also exist as values of object fields, and Underscore itself is the perfect illustration:

```
_.each;

//=> function (array, n, guard) {
//    ...
//    }
```

This is great and beautiful, right? Well…not exactly. You see, because JavaScript is oriented around objects, it must have a semantics for self-references. As it turns out, its self-reference semantics conflict with the notion of functional programming. Observe the following:

```
var a = {name: "a", fun: function () { return this; }};

a.fun();
//=> {name: "a", fun: ...};
```

You'll notice that the self-reference this returned from the embedded fun function returns the object a itself. This is probably what you would expect. However, observe the following:

```
var bObj = {name: "b", fun: function(){ return this }};
bObj.fun();
//=> {name: "b", fun: function (){ return this }}

var bFunc = bObj.fun;
bFunc();
//=> some global object, probably Window
```

Well, this might be surprising. You see, when a function is called within the context of an object, its this reference points to the object itself. However, when I later bound bFunc to the field bObj.fun, its reference was changed to the global object when called. In most programming languages offering both functional and object-oriented styles, a trade-off is made in the way that self-reference is handled. JavaScript has its approach while Python has a different approach and Scala has a different approach still. Throughout this book, you'll notice a fundamental tension between an object-oriented style and a functional style, but Underscore provides some tools to relieve, if not eliminate, this tension. This will be covered in greater depth later, but for now keep in mind that when

---

3. There is an existential crisis lurking in the question, "who created the first object?"

I use the word "function" I mean a function that exists on its own and when I use "method" I mean a function created in the context of an object.

Metaprogramming

Related to prototype-based object-oriented programming are the facilities provided by JavaScript supporting metaprogramming. Many programming languages support metaprogramming, but rarely do they provide the level of power offered by JavaScript. A good definition of metaprogramming goes something like this: programming occurs when you write code to do something and metaprogramming occurs when you write code that changes the way that something is interpreted. Let's take a look at an example of metaprogramming so that you can better understand.

In the case of JavaScript, the dynamic nature of the `this` reference can be exploited to perform a bit of metaprogramming. For example, observe the following constructor function:

```
function Point2D(x, y) {
  this._x = x;
  this._y = y;
}
```

When used with `new`, the `Point2D` function gives a new object instance with the proper fields set as you might expect:

```
new Point2D(0, 1);

//=> {_x: 0, _y: 1}
```

However, the `Function.call` method can be used to metaprogram a derivation of the `Point2D` constructor's behavior for a new `Point3D` type:

```
function Point3D(x, y, z) {
  Point2D.call(this, x, y);
  this._z = z;
}
```

And creating a new instance works like a champ:

```
new Point3D(10, -1, 100);

//=> {_x: 10, _y: -1, _z: 100}
```

Nowhere did `Point3D` explicitly set the values for `this._x` and `this._y`, but by dynamically binding the `this` reference in a call to `Point2D` it became possible to change the target of its property creation code.

I will not go too deeply into JavaScript metaprogramming in this book because it's orthogonal to functional programming, but I'll take advantage of it occasionally throughout this book.[4]

Applicative Programming

So far in this book I've shown only one aspect of functional programming that deals with a narrow band of the capabilities of functions—namely, applicative programming. Applicative programming is defined as the calling by function B of a function A, supplied as an argument to function B originally. I will not use the term "applicative" very often in this book because variations of that word can appear in different contexts with different meanings, but it's good to know should you see it in the future. That said, the three canonical examples of applicative functions are map, reduce, and filter. Observe how they operate:

```
var nums = [1,2,3,4,5];

function doubleAll(array) {
  return _.map(array, function(n) { return n*2 });
}

doubleAll(nums);
//=> [2, 4, 6, 8, 10]

function average(array) {
  var sum = _.reduce(array, function(a, b) { return a+b });
  return sum / _.size(array);
}

average(nums);
//=> 3

/* grab only even numbers in nums */
function onlyEven(array) {
  return _.filter(array, function(n) {
    return (n%2) === 0;
  });
}

onlyEven(nums);
//=> [2, 4]
```

You can imagine that somewhere inside of map, reduce, and filter a call to the function that's passed in occurs, and indeed that is the case. In fact, the semantics of these functions can be defined in terms of that very relationship:

---

4. If you're interested in a great book about JavaScript metaprogramming, then petition O'Reilly to have me write it. ☺

- `_.map` calls a function on every value in a collection in turn, returning a collection of the results
- `_.reduce` collects a composite value from the incremental results of a function supplied with an accumulation value and each value in a collection
- `_.filter` calls a predicate function (one returning a true or false value) and grabs each value where said predicate returned `true`, returning them in a new collection

The functions `map`, `reduce`, and `filter` are as simple and as emblematic of applicative functional programming as you can get, but Underscore provides numerous others for your use. Before I get into those, let me take a moment to cover the idea of collection-centric programming, which is often coupled with functional programming itself.

Collection-Centric Programming

Functional programming is extremely useful for tasks requiring that some operation happen on many items in a collection. Certainly an array of numbers [1,2,3,4,5] is a collection of numbers, but we can also envision that an object {a: 1, b: 2} is a collection of key/value pairs. Take the simple case of `_.map` using the `_.identity` function (one that just returns its argument) as an example:

```
_.map({a: 1, b: 2}, _.identity);
//=> [1,2]
```

It would seem that `_.map` only deals with the value parts of the key/value pair, but this limitation is only a matter of use. If we want to deal with the key/value pairs, then we supply a function that expects them:

```
_.map({a: 1, b: 2}, function(v,k) {
  return [k,v];
});
//=> [['a', 1], ['b', 2]]
```

In the spirit of completeness, it's worth noting that the function given to `_.map` can also take a third argument, the collection itself:

```
_.map({a: 1, b: 2}, function(v,k,coll) {
  return [k, v, _.keys(coll)];
});
//=> [['a', 1, ['a', 'b']], ['b', 2, ['a', 'b']]]
```

The point of a collection-centric view, as advocated by Underscore and functional programming in general, is to establish a consistent processing idiom so that we can reuse a comprehensive set of functions. As the great luminary Alan Perlis once stated:

> It is better to have 100 functions operate on one data structure than 10 functions on 10 data structures.

Throughout this book, I emphasize the notion of empowering our data through the use of generic functions built on a collection-centric philosophy.

Other Examples of Applicative Programming

To close out my discussion of applicative programming, I offer examples illustrating it, with some dialog along the way.

reduceRight

You've already seen the _.reduce function, but I failed to mention its sibling _.reduce Right. The two functions operate in much the same way, except that _.reduce works from left to right, whereas _.reduceRight works from right to left. Observe the differences:

```
var nums = [100,2,25];

function div(x,y) { return x/y };

_.reduce(nums, div);
//=> 2

_.reduceRight(nums, div);
//=> 0.125
```

The work of _.reduce is similar to (100/2) / 25 while _.reduceRight is (25/2) / 100. If the function supplied to the reduce siblings is associative, then they wind up returning the same values, but otherwise the difference in ordering can prove useful. Many common functions can be created using _.reduceRight. Here are a couple more examples:

```
function allOf(/* funs */) {
  return _.reduceRight(arguments, function(truth, f) {
    return truth && f();
  }, true);
}

function anyOf(/* funs */) {
  return _.reduceRight(arguments, function(truth, f) {
    return truth || f();
  }, false);
}
```

Example usages of allOf and anyOf are as follows:

```
function T() { return true }
function F() { return false }

allOf();
//=> true
allOf(T, T);
//=> true
```

```
allOf(T, T, T , T , F);
//=> false

anyOf(T, T, F);
//=> true
anyOf(F, F, F, F);
//=> false
anyOf();
//=> false
```

The _.reduceRight function has further advantages in languages providing lazy evaluation, but since JavaScript is not such a language, evaluation *order* is the key factor
(Bird 1988).[5]

find

The find function is fairly straightforward; it takes a collection and a predicate and
returns the first element for which the predicate returns true. An example of find is as
follows:

```
_.find(['a', 'b', 3, 'd'], _.isNumber);
//=> 3
```

Notice the use of the built-in function _.isNumber as the predicate function. Underscore
comes with numerous predicates ready for use, including _.isEqual, _.isEmpty,
_.isElement, _.isArray, _.isObject, _.isArguments, _.isFunction, _.isString,
_.isNumber, _.isFinite, _.isBoolean, _.isDate, _.isRegExp, _.isNaN, _.isNull,
and _.isUndefined. I will use some or all of them over the course of this book.

reject

Underscore's _.reject is essentially the opposite of _.filter; it takes a predicate and
returns a collection of values that excludes values for which the predicate returned
true. For example:

```
_.reject(['a', 'b', 3, 'd'], _.isNumber);
//=> ['a', 'b', 'd']
```

This is the same as reversing the truthiness of the predicate to _.filter. In fact, a simple
function called complement would perform just such a task:[6]

```
function complement(pred) {
  return function() {
    return !pred.apply(null, _.toArray(arguments));
```

---

5. The allOf and anyOf functions could have just as easily been written using Underscore's reduce, but I chose
to use the former for the purpose of illustrating reduceRight.

6. Passing null as the first argument to apply is worth a mention. Recall that the first argument to apply is the
"target" object setting the this reference inside the called function. Since I can't know what the target object
should be, or even if it's needed at all, I use null to signal that this should just refer to the global object.

```
  };
}
```

The `complement` function takes a predicate and returns a function that reverses the sense of the result of said predicate. It can then be used with `_.filter` to achieve the same effect as `_.reject`:

```
_.filter(['a', 'b', 3, 'd'], complement(_.isNumber));
//=> ['a', 'b', 'd']
```

The `complement` function is an example of a higher-order function. Although I touched briefly on what that means earlier, I will defer a deeper discussion until Chapter 3.

all

The `_.all` function takes a collection and a predicate, and returns `true` if *all* of the elements within return `true` on the predicate check. For example:

```
_.all([1, 2, 3, 4], _.isNumber);
//=> true
```

Of course, if *any* of the elements fail the predicate test, then `_.all` returns `false`.

any

The `_.any` function takes a collection and a predicate, and returns `true` if *any* of the elements within return `true` on the predicate check. For example:

```
_.any([1, 2, 'c', 4], _.isString);
//=> true
```

Of course, if *all* of the elements fail the predicate test, then `_.any` returns `false`.

sortBy, groupBy, and countBy

The last three applicative functions that I'll discuss are related, in that they all perform some action based on the result of a given criteria function. The first of the three, `_.sortBy`, takes a collection and a function, and returns a sorted collection based on the criteria determined by the passed function. For example:

```
var people = [{name: "Rick", age: 30}, {name: "Jaka", age: 24}];

_.sortBy(people, function(p) { return p.age });

//=> [{name: "Jaka", age: 24}, {name: "Rick", age: 30}]
```

The `_.groupBy` function takes a collection and a criteria function, and returns an object where the keys are the criteria points returned by the function, and their associated values are the elements that matched. For example:

```
var albums = [{title: "Sabbath Bloody Sabbath", genre: "Metal"},
              {title: "Scientist", genre: "Dub"},
              {title: "Undertow", genre: "Metal"}];

_.groupBy(albums, function(a) { return a.genre });
```

```
//=> {Metal:[{title:"Sabbath Bloody Sabbath", genre:"Metal"},
//           {title:"Undertow", genre:"Metal"}],
//    Dub:  [{title:"Scientist", genre:"Dub"}]}
```

The _.groupBy function is extremely handy, and will show up numerous times throughout the course of this book.

The final applicative function I'll discuss is called _.countBy. This function works similarly to _.groupBy, except that it returns an object with keys of the match criteria
associated with its count, as shown in the following:

```
_.countBy(albums, function(a) { return a.genre });
```

```
//=> {Metal: 2, Dub: 1}
```

That wraps up this discussion of applicative functional programming. I started with the
most common case of a functional style that you're likely to encounter in JavaScript
code, so that you have some background knowledge before venturing deeper into the
wilderness. Up next, I'll cover one more common topic in JavaScript code: closures.

Defining a Few Applicative Functions

I've shown many of the applicative functions offered by Underscore, but what about
creating some of your own? The process is fairly straightforward: define a function that
takes a function and then calls it.

A simple function that takes some number of arguments and concatenates them is *not*
applicative:

```
function cat() {
  var head = _.first(arguments);
  if (existy(head))
    return head.concat.apply(head, _.rest(arguments));
  else
    return [];
}
```

```
cat([1,2,3], [4,5], [6,7,8]);
//=> [1, 2, 3, 4, 5, 6, 7, 8]
```

While considerably useful, cat doesn't expect to receive any functions as arguments.[7]
Likewise, a function construct that takes an element and an array and places the element in the front of the array may use cat:

```
function construct(head, tail) {
  return cat([head], _.toArray(tail));
}
```

---

7. The cat function might receive functions in the arrays that it takes, but that is tangential to the point.

```
construct(42, [1,2,3]);
//=> [42, 1, 2, 3]
```

While construct uses cat within its body, it does not receive it as an argument, so it fails the applicative test.

Instead, a function mapcat, defined as follows, is applicative:

```
function mapcat(fun, coll) {
    return cat.apply(null, _.map(coll, fun));
}
```

The function mapcat does indeed take a function, fun, that it uses in the same manner as _.map, calling it for every element in the given collection. This use of fun is the applicative nature of mapcat. Additionally, mapcat concatenates all of the elements of the result of _.map:

```
mapcat(function(e) {
    return construct(e, [","]);
}, [1,2,3]);
//=> [1, ",", 2, ",", 3, ","]
```

The operation of mapcat is such that when the mapped function returns an array, it can be flattened a level. We could then use mapcat and another function, butLast, to define a third function, interpose:

```
function butLast(coll) {
    return _.toArray(coll).slice(0, -1);
}

function interpose (inter, coll) {
    return butLast(mapcat(function(e) {
        return construct(e, [inter]);
    },
    coll));
}
```

Using interpose is straightforward:

```
interpose(",", [1,2,3]);

//=> [1, ",", 2, ",", 3]
```

This is a key facet of functional programming: the gradual definition and use of discrete functionality built from lower-level functions. Very often you will see (and in this book I will preach the case vociferously) a chain of functions called one after the other, each gradually transforming the result from the last to reach a final solution.

Data Thinking

Throughout this book, I'll take the approach of using minimal data types to represent abstractions, from sets to trees to tables. In JavaScript, however, although its object types are extremely powerful, the tools provided to work with them are not entirely functional. Instead, the larger usage pattern associated with JavaScript objects is to attach methods for the purposes of polymorphic dispatch. Thankfully, you can also view an unnamed (not built via a constructor function) JavaScript object as simply an associative data store.[8]

If the only operations that we can perform on a Book object or an instance of an Employee type are setTitle or getSSN, then we've locked our data up into per-piece-of-information micro-languages (Hickey 2011). A more flexible approach to modeling data is an associative data technique. JavaScript objects, even minus the prototype machinery, are ideal vehicles for associative data modeling, where named values can be structured to form higher-level data models, accessed in uniform ways.[9]

Although the tools for manipulating and accessing JavaScript objects as data maps are sparse within JavaScript itself, thankfully Underscore provides a bevy of useful operations. Among the simplest functions to grasp are _.keys, _.values, and _.pluck. Both _.keys and _.values are named according to their functionality, which is to take an object and return an array of its keys or values:

```
var zombie = {name: "Bub", film: "Day of the Dead"};

_.keys(zombie);
//=> ["name", "film"]

_.values(zombie);
//=> ["Bub", "Day of the Dead"]
```

The _.pluck function takes an array of objects and a string and returns all of the values at the given key for each object in the array:

```
_.pluck([{title: "Chthon", author: "Anthony"},
        {title: "Grendel", author: "Gardner"},
        {title: "After Dark"}],
        'author');

//=> ["Anthony", "Gardner", undefined]
```

---

8. There has been some discussion within the ECMAScript effort to provide simple map (and set) types, divorced from the prototype system. More information is found at *http://wiki.ecmascript.org/doku.php?id=harmo ny:simple_maps_and_sets*.

9. JavaScript's ability to provide uniform access across its associative data types is a boon in allowing you to write a powerful suite of functions for manipulating data generically. JavaScript's for...in loop and the indexed access operator form the basis for much of Underscore.

All three of these functions deconstruct the given objects into arrays, allowing you to perform sequential actions. Another way of viewing a JavaScript object is as an array of arrays, each holding a key and a value. Underscore provides a function named _.pairs that takes an object and turns it into this nested array:

```
_.pairs(zombie);

//=> [["name", "Bub"], ["film", "Day of the Dead"]]
```

This nested array view can be processed using sequential operations and reassembled into a new object using Underscore's _.object function:

```
_.object(_.map(_.pairs(zombie), function(pair) {
  return [pair[0].toUpperCase(), pair[1]];
}));

//=> {FILM: "Day of the Dead", NAME: "Bub"};
```

Aside from changing the key in some subtle way, another common function on maps is to flip the keys and values via the _.invert function:

```
_.invert(zombie);
//=> {"Bub": "name", "Day of the Dead": "film"}
```

It's worth mentioning that unlike in many other languages, JavaScript object keys can only ever be strings. This may occassionally cause confusion when using _.invert:

```
_.keys(_.invert({a: 138, b: 9}));
//=> ['9', '138']
```

Underscore also provides functions for filling in and removing values from objects according to the values that they take:

```
_.pluck(_.map([{title: "Chthon", author: "Anthony"},
               {title: "Grendel", author: "Gardner"},
               {title: "After Dark"}],
              function(obj) {
                return _.defaults(obj, {author: "Unknown"})
              }),
         'author');

//=> ["Anthony", "Gardner", "Unknown"]
```

In this example, each object is preprocessed with the _.defaults function to ensure that the author field contains a useful value (rather than undefined). While _.defaults augments incoming objects, two functions—_.pick and _.omit—(potentially) filter objects based on their arguments:

```
var person = {name: "Romy", token: "j3983ij", password: "tigress"};

var info = _.omit(person, 'token', 'password');
info;
//=> {name: "Romy"}
```

```
var creds = _.pick(person, 'token', 'password');
creds;

//=> {password: "tigress", token: "j3983ij"};
```

Using the same "dangerous" keys, token and password, shows that the _.omit function takes a blacklist to remove keys from an object, and _.pick takes a whitelist to take keys (both nondestructively).

Finally, Underscore provides selector functions useful in finding certain objects based on keyed criteria, _.findWhere and _.where. The _.findWhere function takes an array of objects and returns the first one that matches the criteria given in the object in the second argument:

```
var library = [{title: "SICP", isbn: "0262010771", ed: 1},
               {title: "SICP", isbn: "0262510871", ed: 2},
               {title: "Joy of Clojure", isbn: "1935182641", ed: 1}];

_.findWhere(library, {title: "SICP", ed: 2});

//=> {title: "SICP", isbn: "0262510871", ed: 2}
```

The _.where function operates similarly except that it operates over an array and returns *all* of the objects that match the criteria:

```
_.where(library, {title: "SICP"});

//=> [{title: "SICP", isbn: "0262010771", ed: 1},
//    {title: "SICP", isbn: "0262510871", ed: 2}]
```

This type of usage pattern points to a very important data abstraction: the table. In fact, using Underscore's object manipulation functions, you can derive an experience very similar to that of SQL, where logical data tables are filtered and processed according to a powerful declarative specification. However, as I'll show next, to achieve a more fluent table processing API, I'll need to step it up beyond what Underscore provides and take advantage of functional techniques. The functions created in this section implement a subset of the relational algebra on which all SQL engines are built (Date 2003). I will not dive deeply into the relational algebra, but will instead work at the level of a pseudo-SQL. I assume a base-level proficiency in SQL-like languages.

"Table-Like" Data

Table 2-1 presents one way to look at the data in the library array.

Table 2-1. A data table view of an array of JavaScript objects

title	isbn	ed
SICP	0262010771	1
SICP	0262510871	2
Joy of Clojure	1935182641	1

Here, each row is equivalent to a JavaScript object and each cell is a key/value pair in each object. The information in Table 2-2 corresponds to an SQL query of the form `SELECT title FROM library`.

Table 2-2. A table of the titles

title
SICP
SICP
Joy of Clojure

A way to achieve the same effect using the tools that I've explored so far is as follows:

```
_.pluck(library, 'title');

//=> ["SICP", "SICP", "Joy of Clojure"]
```

The problem is that the result from the `_.pluck` function is of a different abstraction than the table abstraction. While technically an array of strings *is* an array of objects, the abstraction is broken using `_.pluck`. Instead, you need a function that allows a similar capability to the SQL's SELECT statement, while preserving the table abstraction. The function `project` will serve as the stand-in for SELECT:[10]

```
function project(table, keys) {
  return _.map(table, function(obj) {
    return _.pick.apply(null, construct(obj, keys));
  });
};
```

The `project` function uses the `_.pick` function on each object in the array to pull out whitelisted keys into new objects, thus preserving the table abstraction:

```
var editionResults = project(library, ['title', 'isbn']);

editionResults;
//=> [{isbn: "0262010771", title: "SICP"},
//    {isbn: "0262510871", title: "SICP"},
//    {isbn: "1935182641", title: "Joy of Clojure"}];
```

---

10. It's an odd mistake of history that the traditional SQL SELECT is actually the PROJECT statement in relational algebra. I'll use `project` for now because Underscore already provides `select` as an alias for `filter`.

As shown, the `project` function itself returns a table-like data structure, which can be further processed using `project`:

```
var isbnResults = project(editionResults, ['isbn']);

isbnResults;
//=> [{isbn: "0262010771"},{isbn: "0262510871"},{isbn: "1935182641"}]
```

Finally, the abstraction can be intentionally broken by purposefully pulling out only the desired data:

```
_.pluck(isbnResults, 'isbn');
//=> ["0262010771", "0262510871", "1935182641"]
```

This intentional extraction is a deliberate act to "hand over" data from one module or function to the next. While `project` works on the table abstraction, another fictional function, `populateISBNSelectBox`, would probably work with arrays of strings that might then construct DOM elements of the form `<option value= "1935182641">1935182641</option>`. Functional programmers think deeply about their data, the transformations occurring on it, and the hand-over formats between the layers of their applications. Visually, you can picture the high-level data-centric thinking as in Figure 2-1 (Gruber 2004).

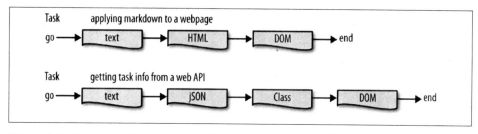

Figure 2-1. Data transformations can be used to abstract tasks

Let's explore this table abstraction just a little bit more before diving deeper into data transformation and hand overs. For example, most SQL engines provide an AS statement used to alias column names. In SQL, the AS looks like the following:

```
SELECT ed AS edition FROM library;
```

The preceding query would output the results shown in Table 2-3:

Table 2-3. A table of the aliased editions

edition
1
2
1

However, before I implement as to work against a table, it would behoove me to create a utility function, rename, that renames keys based on a given renaming criteria map:

```
function rename(obj, newNames) {
  return _.reduce(newNames, function(o, nu, old) {
    if (_.has(obj, old)) {
      o[nu] = obj[old];
      return o;
    }
    else
      return o;
  },
  _.omit.apply(null, construct(obj, _.keys(newNames))));
};
```

One important point about the implementation of rename is that it uses the _.reduce function to reconstruct an object using Underscore's alternative mode for traversing over the key/value pairings that preserves the "mappiness" of the accumulator. I take advantage of this fact by renaming keys via direct array manipulation, according to the renaming map. It will be more clear how this works with an example:

```
rename({a: 1, b: 2}, {'a': 'AAA'});

//=> {AAA: 1, b: 2}
```

I can implement an as function using rename to work against the table abstraction as follows:

```
function as(table, newNames) {
  return _.map(table, function(obj) {
    return rename(obj, newNames);
  });
};
```

As you'll notice, as works against the table abstraction by simply mapping the rename over each of the contained objects. Observe:

```
as(library, {ed: 'edition'});

//=> [{title: "SICP", isbn: "0262010771", edition: 1},
//    {title: "SICP", isbn: "0262510871", edition: 2},
//    {title: "Joy of Clojure", isbn: "1935182641", edition: 1}]
```

Because both as and project work against the same abstraction, I can chain the calls together to produce a new table like that given by the aforementioned SQL statement:

```
project(as(library, {ed: 'edition'}), ['edition']);

//=> [{edition: 1}, {edition: 2}, {edition: 1}];
```

Finally, I can square the circle of providing basic SQL capabilities against a table abstraction by implementing a function akin to SQL's WHERE clause, named restrict (Date 2011):

```
function restrict(table, pred) {
  return _.reduce(table, function(newTable, obj) {
    if (truthy(pred(obj)))
      return newTable;
    else
      return _.without(newTable, obj);
  }, table);
};
```

The restrict function takes a function that acts as a predicate against each object in the table. Whenever the predicate returns a falsey value, the object is disregarded in the final table. Here's how restrict can work to remove all first editions:

```
restrict(library, function(book) {
  return book.ed > 1;
});

//=> [{title: "SICP", isbn: "0262510871", ed: 2}]
```

And like the rest of the functions that work against the table abstraction, restrict can be chained:

```
restrict(
  project(
    as(library, {ed: 'edition'}),
    ['title', 'isbn', 'edition']),
  function(book) {
    return book.edition > 1;
});

//=> [{title: "SICP", isbn: "0262510871", edition: 2},]
```

An equivalent SQL statement could be written as follows:

```
SELECT title, isbn, edition FROM (
  SELECT ed AS edition FROM library
) EDS
WHERE edition > 1;
```

Although they're not as attractive as the equivalent SQL, the functions project, as, and restrict work against a common table abstraction—a simple array of objects. This is data thinking.

Summary

This chapter focused on first-class functions. First-class functions are functions that can be treated like any other piece of data:

- They can be stored in a variable.
- They can be stored in an array slot.

- They can be stored in an object field.

- They can be created as needed.

- They can be passed to other functions.

- They can be returned from functions.

That JavaScript supports first-class functions is a great boon to practicing functional programming. One particular form of functional programming—and one that most readers will be familiar with—is known as *applicative programming*. Examples of functions that allow applicative programming such as `_.map`, `_.reduce`, and `_.filter` were shown, and new applicative functions were created later.

What makes applicative programming particularly powerful is a focus in most JavaScript applications on dealing with collections of data, whether they're arrays, objects, arrays of objects, or objects of arrays. A focus on fundamental collection types allowed us to build a set of SQL-like relational operators working against a simple "table" abstraction built from arrays of objects.

The next chapter is a transition chapter to cover the fundamental topic of variable scope and closures.

CHAPTER 3

Variable Scope and Closures

This chapter introduces variable scope, an important foundational topic not only to functional programming, but to JavaScript in general. The term "binding" refers to the act of assigning a value to a name in JavaScript via var assignment, function arguments, this passing, and property assignment. This chapter first touches on dynamic scoping, as displayed in JavaScript's this reference, and proceeds onto function-level scoping and how it works. All of this builds up to a discussion of closures, or functions that capture nearby variable bindings when they are created. The mechanics of closures will be covered, along with their general use cases and some examples.

The term "scope" has various meanings in common use among JavaScript programmers:

- The value of the this binding
- The execution context defined by the value of the this binding
- The "lifetime" of a variable
- The variable value resolution scheme, or the lexical bindings

For the purposes of this book, I'll use *scope* to refer to the generic idea of the variable value resolution scheme. I'll dig deeper into various types of resolution schemes to cover the full spectrum of scope provided by JavaScript, starting with the most straightforward: global scope.

Global Scope

The *extent* of a scope refers to the lifetime of a variable (i.e., how long a variable holds a certain value). I'll start with variables with the longest lifespan—that of the "life" of the program itself—globals.

In JavaScript, the following variable would have global scope:

```
aGlobalVariable = 'livin la vida global';
```

Any variable declared in JavaScript without the var keyword is created in the global scope, or the scope accessible to every function and method in our program. Observe:

```
_.map(_.range(2), function() { return aGlobalVariable });
//=> ["livin la vida global", "livin la vida global"]
```

As shown, the variable aGlobalVariable is accessible from the anonymous function (one created without a name) supplied to the _.map call. Global scope is simple to understand and is used often in JavaScript programs (and sometimes with great effect). In fact, Underscore creates a global named _ that contains all of its functions. Although this may not provide the greatest name-spacing technique yet invented, it's what Java-Script uses, and Underscore at least provides an escape hatch with the _.noConflict function.

The funny thing about variables in JavaScript is that they are *mutable* by default (i.e., you can change their property values right in place):

```
aGlobalVariable = 'i drink your milkshake';

aGlobalVariable;
//=> "i drink your milkshake"
```

The problem with global variables, and the reason that they are so reviled, is that any piece of code can change them for any reason at any time. This anarchic condition can make for severe pain and missed holidays. In any case, the idea of global scope and its dangers should be known to you by now. However, being defined at the top of a file or lacking a var is not all that it takes for a variable to have global scope. Any object is wide open for change (unless it's frozen, which I'll talk about in Chapter 7):

```
function makeEmptyObject() {
  return new Object();
}
```

The makeEmptyObject function does exactly what it says: it makes an empty object. I can attach all manner of properties to the objects returned from this function, but so too can any other piece of code that gets a reference to them. Any mutable object that you pass around effectively allows change at a global scale on its properties. Heck, if I wanted, I could change every function in the Underscore object to return the string 'nerf herder'—no one can stop me. This presents somewhat of a challenge to functional programming in JavaScript. However, as I'll show throughout this book, there are ways to alleviate the problem of an implicit global scope.

Just because a global variable holds a certain value for the entire life of a program doesn't mean that when you refer to its name you'll get the global value. Scope becomes more interesting when we talk about something called *lexical scope*, described next.

Lexical Scope

Lexical scope refers to the visibility of a variable and its value analogous to its textual representation. For example, observe the following code:

```
aVariable = "Outer";

function afun() {
  var aVariable = "Middle";

  return _.map([1,2,3], function(e) {
    var aVariable = "In";

    return [aVariable, e].join(' ');
  });
}
```

What is the value of a call to `afun`?

```
afun();
//=> ["In 1", "In 2", "In 3"]
```

The innermost variable value, `In`, takes precedence when used within the function passed to `_.map`. Lexical scope dictates that since the assignment `aVariable` to `In` occurs textually close to its innermost use, then that is its value at the time of use. Figure 3-1 shows this condition graphically.

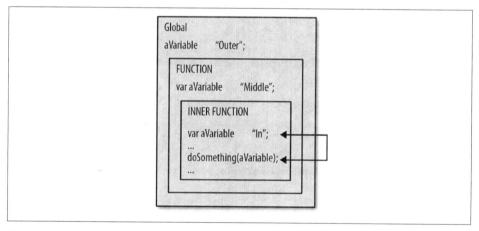

Figure 3-1. Variable lookup starts at the innermost scope and expands outward

In the simple case, variable lookup starts at the closest binding context and expands outward until it finds a binding.[1] Figure 3-1 describes *lexical scoping*, or the grouping of names with values according to the surrounding source code. I will cover the mechanics of different lookup schemes supported by JavaScript over the course of this chapter, starting with dynamic scope.

Dynamic Scope

One of the most underappreciated and over-abused concepts in programming is that of *dynamic scoping*. One reason for this is that very few languages use dynamic scope as their primary binding resolution scheme. Dynamic scoping, however, is a simplistic scheme used as the primary scoping mechanism in only a handful of modern programming languages, and has not seen widespread adoption outside of the earliest versions of Lisp.[2] Simulating a naive dynamic scoping mechanism requires very little code:

```
var globals = {};
```

First of all, dynamic scoping is built on the idea of a global table of named values.[3] At the heart of any JavaScript engine you will see—if not in implementation, then in spirit —one big honking lookup table:

```
function makeBindFun(resolver) {
  return function(k, v) {
    var stack = globals[k] || [];
    globals[k] = resolver(stack, v);
    return globals;
  };
}
```

With globals and makeBindFun in place, we can move onto the policies for adding bindings to the globals variable:

```
var stackBinder = makeBindFun(function(stack, v) {
  stack.push(v);
  return stack;
});

var stackUnbinder = makeBindFun(function(stack) {
  stack.pop();
```

1. There are other scoping modes that JavaScript provides that complicate lookup, including this resolution, function-level scope, and with blocks. I plan to cover all but the last of these.

2. To get a feel for what the early Lisps had to offer, read "Recursive Functions of Symbolic Expressions and Their Computation by Machine, Part I" by John McCarthy and the "LISP 1.5 Programmer's Manual" by McCarthy, Abrahams, Edwards, Hart, and Levin.

3. This is only one way to implement dynamic scoping, but it is likely the simplest.

```
    return stack;
  });
```

The function `stackBinder` performs a very simple task (i.e., it takes a key and a value and pushes the value onto the global `bindings` map at the slot associated with the key). Maintaining a global map of stacks associated with binding names is the core of dynamic scoping, as shown in Figure 3-2.

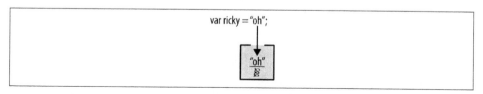

Figure 3-2. You can imagine that any time you declare a variable it comes with a little stack to hold its value; the current dynamic value is found at the top of the stack

The `stackUnbinder` function is the antithesis of `stackBinder` in that it pops the last value binding off of the stack associated with a name. Finally, we'll need a function to look up bound values:

```
var dynamicLookup = function(k) {
  var slot = globals[k] || [];
  return _.last(slot);
};
```

The `dynamicLookup` function provides a convenient way to look up the value at the top of a named value binding stack, and is used to simulate `this` reference resolution as you might visualize it in Figure 3-3.

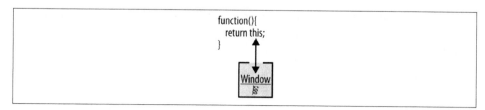

Figure 3-3. A lone function referencing "this" will deal with some global object (e.g., the window in the browser)

Now that our binding and lookup functions are defined, I can note the effects that various operations have on the simulated dynamic scope:

```
stackBinder('a', 1);
stackBinder('b', 100);

dynamicLookup('a');
//=> 1
```

```
globals;
//=> {'a': [1], 'b': [100]}
```

So far, everything looks as you might expect in the preceding code. Specifically, taking the keyed arrays in globals as stacks, you might see that since a and b have been bound only once each, the stacks would have only a single value inside. While dynamicLook up cannot easily simulate the this resolution in an object method, you can think of it as yet another push onto the stack, as shown in Figure 3-4.

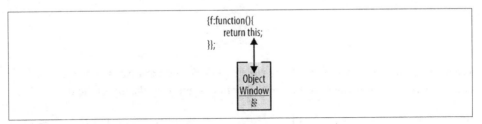

Figure 3-4. An object method referencing "this" will deal with the object itself

In a dynamic scoping scheme, the value at the top of a stack in a binding is the current value. Let's investigate what would happen if we bind again:

```
stackBinder('a', '*');

dynamicLookup('a');
//=> '*'

globals;
//=> {'a': [1, '*'], 'b': [100]}
```

As you'll notice, the new stack bound at a contains the stack [1, '*'], so any lookup occurring with that condition will result in *. To retrieve the previous binding is as simple as unbinding by popping the stack:

```
stackUnbinder('a');

dynamicLookup('a');
//=> 1
```

You may already imagine (or know) how a scheme like this (i.e., the manipulation of global named stacks) may cause trouble, but if not observe the following:

```
function f() { return dynamicLookup('a'); };
function g() { stackBinder('a', 'g'); return f(); };

f();

//=> 1
```

```
g();
//=> 'g'

globals;
// {a: [1, "g"], b: [100]}
```

Here we see that though f never manipulated the binding of a, the value that it saw was subject to the whim of its caller g! This is the poison of dynamic scoping: the value of any given binding cannot be known until the caller of any given function is known—which may be too late.

A point of note in the preceding code is that I had to explicitly "unbind" a dynamic binding, whereas in programming languages supporting dynamic binding this task is done automatically at the close of the dynamic binding's context.

JavaScript's Dynamic Scope

This section has not been an exercise in theory, but instead has set up the discussion for the one area where dynamic scoping rules apply to JavaScript, the this reference. In Chapter 2, I mentioned that the this reference can point to different values depending on the context in which it was first created, but it's actually much worse than that. Instead, the value of the this reference, like our binding of a, is also determined by the caller, as shown in the following:

```
function globalThis() { return this; }

globalThis();
//=> some global object, probably Window

globalThis.call('barnabas');
//=> 'barnabas'

globalThis.apply('orsulak', [])
//=> 'orsulak'
```

Yep, the value of the this reference is directly manipulable through the use of apply or call, as shown in Figure 3-5. That is, whatever object is passed into them as the first argument becomes the referenced object. Libraries like jQuery use this as a way to pass context objects and event targets into first-class functions, and as long as you keep your wits about you, it can prove to be a powerful technique. However, dynamic scope can confuse this.

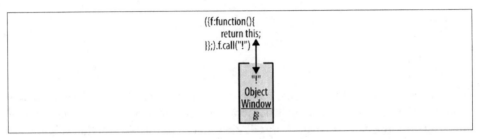

Figure 3-5. Using the Function#call method allows you to set the "this" reference to a known value

Thankfully, this problem does not arise if a `this` reference is never passed to `call` or `apply`, or if it is bound to `null`. Additionally, Underscore provides the function `_.bind` that allows you to lock the `this` reference from changing, like the following:

```
var nopeThis   = _.bind(globalThis, 'nope');

nopeThis.call('wat');
//=> 'nope';
```

Because the `this` reference is dynamically scoped, you may often find, especially in the case of event handling functions, that the `this` you get on something like a button click is not useful and may break your app. To tackle a problem like this, you can use the `_.bindAll` function to lock the `this` reference to a stable value for all of the named methods, as shown here:

```
var target = {name: 'the right value',
              aux: function() { return this.name; },
              act: function() { return this.aux(); }};

target.act.call('wat');
// TypeError: Object [object String] has no method 'aux'

_.bindAll(target, 'aux', 'act');

target.act.call('wat');
//=> 'the right value'
```

And thus, Underscore saves us from the perils of dynamic scoping. Now that I've covered dynamic scope in detail, it's high time to cover function scope.

Function Scope

In order to illustrate the difference between dynamic and function scoping, I'll need to modify the logic for binding and lookup. Instead of accessing bindings in a global hash map, the new model will instead require that all bindings be constrained to the smallest area possible (namely, the function). This follows the scoping model adhered to by JavaScript.[4]

To simulate a function scoping scheme requires a bit of imagination. As you know, each JavaScript function can refer to a this reference. In the previous section, I talked about the dangers of the dynamic nature of this, but for the sake of illustration, I'll use it to prove a different point. First, observe how JavaScript acts by default:

```
function strangeIdentity(n) {
  // intentionally strange
  for(var i=0; i<n; i++);
  return i;
}

strangeIdentity(138);
//=> 138
```

In a language like Java, an attempt to access a variable like i, defined locally to a for block, would provoke an access error. However, in JavaScript, all var declarations in a function body are implicitly moved to the top of the function in which they occur. The action of JavaScript to rearrange variable declarations is called *hoisting*. In other words, the previously defined function would become something like:[5]

```
function strangeIdentity(n) {
  var i;
  for(i=0; i<n; i++);
  return i;
}
```

The implications of this are that any piece of code in the function can see all of the variables defined inside. Needless to say, this can cause problems at times, especially if you are not careful about how the variables are captured via closures (discussed in the following section).

In the meantime, I can show how function scope can be simulated quite easily by using the this reference:

```
function strangerIdentity(n) {
  // intentionally stranger still
  for(this['i'] = 0; this['i']<n; this['i']++);
  return this['i'];
```

---

4. The ECMAScript.next activity has defined numerous ways to define "lexical" variable scoping (*http:// wiki.ecmascript.org/doku.php?id=harmony:specification_drafts*). Lexical scoping works similarly to function scoping except that it's "tighter." That is, it binds variables within JavaScript blocks and does not raise the declaration to the top of function bodies. I will not go into detail about lexical scoping here, but it's a topic well worth studying yourself.

5. The ECMAScript.next initiative is working through the specification of block-scope that would provide another level of scoping finer-grained than function scope. It's unclear when this feature will make it into JavaScript core. Its eventual inclusion should help justify the next edition of this book (crossing fingers).

```
    }

    strangerIdentity(108);
    //=> 108
```

Of course, this is not a true simulation because in this circumstance I've actually modified the global object:

```
    i;
    //=> 108
```

Whoops! Instead, it would be more precise to supply a scratch space for the function to operate on, and thanks to the magic of the this reference, I can supply it on the call:

```
    strangerIdentity.call({}, 10000);
    //=> 10000

    i;
    //=> 108
```

Although our original global i persists, at least I've stopped modifying the global environment. I've again not provided a true simulator, because now I can only access locals inside of functions. However, there is no reason that I need to pass in an empty object as context. In fact, in this faked-out JavaScript, it would be more appropriate to pass in the global context, but not directly, or else I'd be back in the soup. Instead, a clone should do:

```
    function f () {
      this['a'] = 200;
      return this['a'] + this['b'];
    }

    var globals = {'b': 2};

    f.call(_.clone(globals));
    //=> 202
```

And checking the global context proves clean:

```
    globals;
    //=> {'b': 2}
```

This model is a reasonable facsimile of how function scoping operates. For all intents and purposes, this is precisely what JavaScript does, except variable access is done implicitly within the function body instead of requiring an explicit lookup in this. Regardless of your thoughts about function-level scoping, at least JavaScript takes care of the underlying machinery for us—small victories and all that.

Closures

JavaScript closures are one of life's great mysteries. A recent survey on total Internet size places blog posts about JavaScript closures at around 23%.[6]

I kid. Closures, for whatever reason, remain a mystery to a substantial number of programmers for numerous reasons. In this section, I will take some time to go into detail on closures in JavaScript, but thankfully for you, they're quite simple. In fact, throughout this section, I'll build a small library that simulates scoping rules and closures. I'll then use this library to explore the details of this chapter, which include global scope, function scope, free variables, and closures.

To start, it's worth mentioning that closures go hand in hand with first-class functions. Languages without first-class functions can support closures, but they're often greatly stunted. Thankfully, JavaScript supports first-class functions, so its closures are a powerful way to pass around ad hoc encapsulated states.

 For the remainder of this chapter and the next, I will capitalize all of the variables that are captured by a closure. This is in no way standard practice in the JavaScript you're likely to see in the wild, nor an endorsement of such activity, but only meant to teach. After these two chapters I will no longer use this convention.

Having said all of that, a closure is a function that "captures" values near where it was born. Figure 3-6 is a graphical representation of a closure.

---

6. If you factor in the commentary on Hacker News, it's closer to 36%. I have no citation for this because I just made it up for fun.

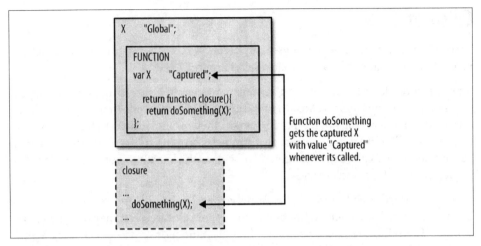

Figure 3-6. A closure is a function that "captures" values near where it was born

In the next few sections, I'll cover closures in depth, starting with a closure simulator.

Simulating Closures

It took only 30 years, but closures are finally becoming a key feature of mainstream programming languages. What is a closure? In a sentence, a closure is a function that captures the external bindings (i.e., not its own arguments) contained in the scope in which it was defined for later use (even after that scope has completed).

Before we go any further with how to simulate closures, let's take a look at how they behave by default. The simplest example of a closure is a first-class function that captures a local variable for later use:

```
function whatWasTheLocal() {
  var CAPTURED = "Oh hai";

  return function() {
    return "The local was: " + CAPTURED;
  };
}
```

Using the whatWasTheLocal function is as follows:

```
var reportLocal = whatWasTheLocal();
```

I've already talked about how function-local variables live only for the lifetime of a function's body, but when a closure captures a variable, it's able to live for an indeterminate extent:[7]

```
reportLocal();
//=> "The local was: Oh hai"
```

So it seems that the local variable CAPTURED was able to travel with the closure returned by whatWasTheLocal—indeed, this is effectively what happened. But local variables are not the only things that can be captured. As shown here, function arguments can be captured as well:

```
function createScaleFunction(FACTOR) {
  return function(v) {
    return _.map(v, function(n) {
      return (n * FACTOR);
    });
  };
}

var scale10 = createScaleFunction(10);

scale10([1,2,3]);
//=> [10, 20, 30]
```

The function createScaleFunction takes a scaling factor and returns a function that, given a collection of numbers, returns a list of its elements multiplied by the original scaling factor. As you may have noticed, the returned function refers to a variable FACTOR that seemingly falls out of scope once the createScaleFunction function exits. This observation is only partially true because in fact, the variable FACTOR is retained within the body of the return scaling function and is accessible anytime that function is called. This variable retention is precisely the definition of a closure.

So how would we simulate a closure using our function-scoped this scratchpad from the previous section? First of all, I'll need to devise a way for capturing closed variables while simultaneously maintaining access to non-closed variables normally. The most straightforward way to do that is to grab the variables defined in the outer function individually and bind them to the this of the returned function, as in the following:

```
function createWeirdScaleFunction(FACTOR) {
  return function(v) {
    this['FACTOR'] = FACTOR;
    var captures = this;

    return _.map(v, _.bind(function(n) {
```

---

7. Closures are the programming language equivalent of vampires—they capture minions and give them everlasting life until they themselves are destroyed. The only difference is that closures don't sparkle when exposed to sunlight.

```
      return (n * this['FACTOR']);
    }, captures));
  };
}

var scale10 = createWeirdScaleFunction(10);

scale10.call({}, [5,6,7]);
//=> [50, 60, 70];
```

Wow, keeping track of which variables are needed within the body of inner functions seems like a real pain. If you needed to keep track manually, like in this example, then JavaScript would be exceedingly difficult to write.[8] Thankfully for us, the machinery driving variable capture is automatic and straightforward to use.

Free variables

Free variables are related to closures in that it is the free variables that will be closed over in the creation of said closure. The basic principle behind closures is that if a function contains inner functions, then they can all see the variables declared therein; these variables are called "free" variables.[9] However, these variables can be grabbed and carried along for later use in inner functions that "escape" from a higher-level function via return.[10] The only caveat is that the capturing function *must be defined* within the outer function for the capture to occur. Variables used in the body of any function without prior local declaration (neither passed into, nor defined locally) within a function are then captured variables. Observe:

```
function makeAdder(CAPTURED) {
  return function(free) {
    return free + CAPTURED;
  };
}

var add10 = makeAdder(10);

add10(32);
//=> 42
```

The variable CAPTURED in the outer function is indeed captured in the returned function performing the addition because the inner never declares CAPTURED, but refers to it anyway. Thereafter, the function returned from makeAdder retains the variable CAPTURED that was captured when it was created and uses it in its calculation. Creating another

---

8. I could just refer directly to captures instead of dynamically passing it to the inner function passed to map via Underscore's bind, but then I would be using a closure to simulate a closure! That's cheating.

9. Not free as in beer, and not free as in freedom, but instead free as in theft.

10. Another name for this could be higher-order since the function returns another function. I go more in depth in Chapter 3.

adder will capture the same named variable CAPTURED but with a different value, because it will be created during a later invocation of makeAdder:

```
var add1024 = makeAdder(1024);
add1024(11);
//=> 1035

add10(98);
//=> 108
```

And finally, as shown in the preceding code, each new adder function retains its own unique instance of CAPTURED—the one captured when each was created. The value captured can be of any type, including another function. The following function, averageDamp, captures a function and returns a function that calculates the average of some value and the result of passing it to the captured function:[11]

```
function averageDamp(FUN) {
  return function(n) {
    return average([n, FUN(n)]);
  }
}

var averageSq = averageDamp(function(n) { return n * n });
averageSq(10);
//=> 55
```

Higher-order functions that capture other functions are a very powerful technique for building abstractions. I will perform this kind of act throughout the course of this book to great effect.

What happens if you create a function with a variable named the same as a variable in a higher scope? I'll talk briefly about this presently.

Shadowing

Variable shadowing happens in JavaScript when a variable of name x is declared within a certain scope and then another variable of the same name is declared later in a lower scope. Observe a simple example to illustrate how shadowing variables work:

```
var name = "Fogus";
var name = "Renamed";

name;
//=> "Renamed"
```

That two consecutive declarations of variables with the same name assign the value of the second should be no surprise. However, shadowing via function parameters is where the complexity level rises:

---

11. I defined average in Chapter 2.

```
var shadowed = 0;

function argShadow(shadowed) {
  return ["Value is", shadowed].join(' ');
}
```

What do you think is the value of the function call `argShadow(108)`? Observe:

```
argShadow(108)
//=> "Value is 108"

argShadow();
//=> "Value is "
```

The argument named `shadowed` in the function `argShadow` overrides the value assigned to the same named variable at the global scope. Even when no arguments are passed, the binding for `shadowed` is still set. In any case, the "closest" variable binding takes precedence. You can also see this in action via the use of `var`:

```
var shadowed = 0;

function varShadow(shadowed) {
  var shadowed = 4320000;
  return ["Value is", shadowed].join(' ');
}
```

If you guessed the value returned value of `varShadow(108)` is now `"Value is 4320000"` then you're absolutely correct. Shadowed variables are also carried along with closures, as shown in the following:

```
function captureShadow(SHADOWED) {
  return function(SHADOWED) {
    return SHADOWED + 1;
  };
}

var closureShadow = captureShadow(108);

closureShadow(2);
//=> 3 (it would stink if I were expecting 109 here)
```

I tend to avoid shadowed variables when writing JavaScript code, but I do so only via careful attention to naming. If you're not careful, then shadowing can cause confusion if you've not accounted for it. I'll now move on to some quick closure usage examples before wrapping up this chapter.

Using Closures

In this section, I'll touch briefly on the cases for using closures. Since the remainder of the book will use closures extensively, there's no need for me to belabor the point, but it's useful to show a few in action.

If you recall from "Other Examples of Applicative Programming" on page 36, the function `complement` took a predicate function and returned a new function that returned its opposite truthiness. While I glossed over the fact at the time, `complement` used a closure to great effect. Rewriting to illustrate the closure:

```
function complement(PRED) {
  return function() {
    return !PRED.apply(null, _.toArray(arguments));
  };
}
```

The `PRED` predicate is captured by the returned function. Take the case of a predicate that checks for evenness:

```
function isEven(n) { return (n%2) === 0 }
```

We can use `complement` to now define `isOdd`:

```
var isOdd = complement(isEven);

isOdd(2);
//=> false

isOdd(413);
//=> true
```

But what happens if the definition of `isEven` changes at some later time?

```
function isEven(n) { return false }

isEven(10);
//=> false
```

Will this change the behavior of `isOdd`? Observe:

```
isOdd(13);
//=> true;

isOdd(12);
//=> false
```

As you can see, the capture of a variable in a closure grabs the reference of the captured thing (in this case, the predicate PRED) at the time that the closure is created. Since I created a new reference for `isEven` by creating a fresh variable, the change was transparent to the closure `isOdd`. Let's run this to ground:

```
function showObject(OBJ) {
  return function() {
    return OBJ;
  };
}

var o = {a: 42};
var show0 = showObject(o);
```

```
showO();
//=> {a: 42};
```

Everything is fine and good, no? Well, not exactly:

```
o.newField = 108;
showO();
//=> {a: 42, newField: 108};
```

Since the reference to o exists inside and outside of the closure, its changes can be communicated across seemingly private boundaries. This is potentially a recipe for confusion, so the typical use case minimizes the exposure of captured variables. A pattern you will see very often in JavaScript is to use captured variables as private data:

```
var pingpong = (function() {
  var PRIVATE = 0;

  return {
    inc: function(n) {
      return PRIVATE += n;
    },
    dec: function(n) {
      return PRIVATE -= n;
    }
  };
})();
```

The object pingpong is constructed within the anonymous function serving as a scope block, and contains two closures inc and dec. The interesting part is that the captured variable PRIVATE is private to the two closures and cannot be accessed through any means but by calling one of the two functions:

```
pingpong.inc(10);
//=> 10

pingpong.dec(7);
//=> 3
```

Even adding another function is safe:

```
pingpong.div = function(n) { return PRIVATE / n };

pingpong.div(3);
// ReferenceError: PRIVATE is not defined
```

The access protection provided by this closure pattern is a powerful technique available to JavaScript programmers for keeping sanity in the face of software complexity.

Closures as an Abstraction

While closures provide for private access in JavaScript, they are a wonderful way to offer abstraction (i.e., closures often allow you to create functions based solely on some "configuration" captured at creation time). The implementations of makeAdder and complement are good examples of this technique. Another example is a function named plucker that takes a key into an associative structure—such as an array or an object—and returns a function that, given a structure, returns the value at the key. The implementation is as follows:

```
function plucker(FIELD) {
  return function(obj) {
    return (obj && obj[FIELD]);
  };
}
```

Testing the implementation reveals its behavior:

```
var best = {title: "Infinite Jest", author: "DFW"};

var getTitle = plucker('title');

getTitle(best);
//=> "Infinite Jest"
```

As I mentioned, plucker also works with arrays:

```
var books = [{title: "Chthon"}, {stars: 5}, {title: "Botchan"}];

var third = plucker(2);

third(books);
//=> {title: "Botchan"}
```

plucker comes in handy in conjunction with _.filter, which is used to grab objects in an array with a certain field:

```
_.filter(books, getTitle);
//=> [{title: "Chthon"}, {title: "Botchan"}]
```

As this book proceeds, I will explore other uses and advantages of closures, but for now I think the groundwork for understanding them has been laid.

Summary

This chapter focused on two foundational topics not only in JavaScript, but also for functional programming in general: variable scope and closures.

The focus on variable scope started with global scope, the largest available to JavaScript, and worked its way inward through lexical scope and function scope. Additionally, I covered dynamic scoping, especially as it manifests in the use and behavior of the this reference, based on the use of the `call` and `apply` methods. While potentially confusing, the dynamic `this` could be fixed to a certain value using Underscore's `_.bind` and `_.bindAll` functions.

My coverage of closures focused on how you could simulate them in a language with all of JavaScript's features, including the dynamic `this`. After simulating closures, I showed how to not only use closures in your own functions, but also how they can be viewed as a way to "tweak" existing functions to derive new functional abstractions.

In the next chapter, I will expand on first-class functions and delve into higher-order functions, defined in terms of these points:

- Functions can be passed to other functions
- Functions can be returned from functions

If you're unclear about the content of this chapter, then you might want to go back and reread before proceeding on to the next chapter. Much of the power of higher-order functions is realized in concert with variable scoping, and especially closures.

CHAPTER 4

Higher-Order Functions

This chapter builds on Chapter 3 by extending the idea that functions are first-class elements. That is, this chapter will explain that functions can not only reside in data structures and pass as data; they can return from functions, too. Discussion of these first "higher-order" functions will comprise the bulk of this chapter.

A higher-order function adheres to a very specific definition:

- It's first-class (refer back to Chapter 2 if you need a refresher on this topic)
- Takes a function as an argument
- Returns a function as a result

I've already shown many functions that take other functions as arguments, but it's worth exploring this realm more deeply, especially since its dominance is palpable in functional programming style.

Functions That Take Other Functions

You've already seen a gaggle of functions that take other functions, the more prominent being `_.map`, `_.reduce`, and `_.filter`. All of these functions adhere to the definition of higher-order. However, simply showing a few uses of each is insufficient for getting a feel for the importance of function-taking functions in functional programming. Therefore, I'll spend some time talking more about functions that take functions, and tie the practice together with a discussion of closures. Once again, whenever showing code utilizing a closure, I will capitalize the variable name of the captured value. It bears repeating that the capitalization of captured variables is not a recommended practice, but it serves well for book writing.

Thinking About Passing Functions: max, finder, and best

To start this discussion of function-taking functions, it's worth working through a few examples. Many programming languages with even modest core libraries include a function called something like max, which is used to find the largest value (usually a number) in a list or array. In fact, Underscore itself has such a function that performs this very task:

```
_.max([1, 2, 3, 4, 5]);
//=> 5

_.max([1, 2, 3, 4.75, 4.5])
//=> 4.75
```

There's nothing surprising in either result, but there is a limitation in this particular use case. That is, what if we want to find the maximum value in an array of objects rather than numbers? Thankfully, _.max is a higher-order function that takes an optional second argument. This second argument is, as you might have guessed, a function that is used to generate a numeric value from the object supplied to it.[1] For example:

```
var people = [{name: "Fred", age: 65}, {name: "Lucy", age: 36}];

_.max(people, function(p) { return p.age });

//=> {name: "Fred", age: 65}
```

This is a very useful approach to building functions because rather than baking in the comparison of numeric values, _.max provides a way to compare arbitrary objects. However, this function is still somewhat limited and not truly functional. To explain, in the case of _.max, the comparison is always via the greater-than operator (>).

However, we can make a new function, finder, that takes two functions: one to build a comparable value, and another to compare two values and return the "best" value of the two. The implementation of finder is as follows:

```
function finder(valueFun, bestFun, coll) {
  return _.reduce(coll, function(best, current) {
    var bestValue = valueFun(best);
    var currentValue = valueFun(current);

    return (bestValue === bestFun(bestValue, currentValue)) ? best : current;
  });
}
```

Now, using the finder function, the operation of Underscore's _.max can be simulated via the following:

---

1. Underscore's min function works similarly.

```
finder(_.identity, Math.max, [1,2,3,4,5]);

//=> 5
```

You'll notice the use of the handy-dandy _.identity function that just takes a value and returns it. Seems kinda useless, right? Perhaps, but in the realm of functional programming one needs to think in terms of functions, even when the best value is a value itself.

In any case, we can now use finder to find different types of "best-fit" functions:

```
finder(plucker('age'), Math.max, people);

//=> {name: "Fred", age: 65}

finder(plucker('name'),
       function(x,y) { return (x.charAt(0) === "L") ? x : y },
       people);

//=> {name: "Lucy", age: 36}
```

This function of course prefers names that start with the letter L.

Tightening it up a bit

The implementation of finder is fairly small and works as we expect, but it duplicates some logic for the sake of maximum flexibility. Notice a similarity in the implementation of finder and the comparison logic for the best-value first-class function:

```
// in finder
return (bestValue === bestFun(bestValue, currentValue)) ? best : current);

// in the best-value function
return (x.charAt(0) === "L") ? x : y;
```

You'll notice that the logic is exactly the same in both instances. That is, both algorithms are returning some value or other based on the fitness of the first. The implementation of finder can be tightened by making two assumption:

- That the best-value function returns true if the first argument is "better" than the second argument
- That the best-value function knows how to "unwrap" its arguments

Keeping these assumptions in mind leads to the following implementation of a cleaner best function (Graham 1993):

```
function best(fun, coll) {
  return _.reduce(coll, function(x, y) {
    return fun(x, y) ? x : y
  });
}
```

```
best(function(x,y) { return x > y }, [1,2,3,4,5]);
//=> 5
```

With the duplication of logic removed, we now have a tighter, more elegant solution. In fact, the preceding example shows once again that the pattern best(function(x,y) { return x > y }, ...) provides the same functionality as Underscore's _.max or even Math.max.apply(null, [1,2,3,4,5]). Chapter 5 discusses how functional programmers capture patterns like this to create a suite of useful functions, so for now I'll defer that topic and instead hammer home the point about higher-order functions.

More Thinking About Passing Functions: repeat, repeatedly, and iterateUntil

In the previous section, I created a function, finder, that took two functions. As it turned out, the need to take two functions (one to unwrap a value and another to perform a comparison), was overkill for that purpose—leading to the simplification to best. In fact, you'll find that in JavaScript it's often overkill to create functions that take more than one function in their arguments. However, there are cases where such a creation is wholly justified, as I'll discuss in this section.

The elimination of the extra function argument to finder was made because the same functionality requiring two functions (i.e., unwrapping and comparison) was eliminated, due to the adoption of an assumption on the function given to best. However, there are circumstances where placing assumptions on an algorithm is inappropriate.

I'll walk through three related functions one by one and will discuss how they can be made more generic (and the trade-offs of doing so) along the way.

First, let me start with a very simple function, repeat, which takes a number and a value and builds an array containing some number of the value, duplicated:

```
function repeat(times, VALUE) {
  return _.map(_.range(times), function() { return VALUE; });
}

repeat(4, "Major");
//=> ["Major", "Major", "Major", "Major"]
```

The implementation of repeat uses the _.map function to loop over an array of the numbers 0 to times - 1, plopping VALUE into an array 4 times. You'll notice that the anonymous function closes over the VALUE variable, but that's not very important (nor terribly interesting, in this case) at the moment. There are many alternatives to _.map for implementing repeat, but I used it to highlight an important point, summarized as "use functions, not values."

Use functions, not values

The implementation of `repeat` in isolation is not a bad thing. However, as a generic implementation of "repeatness," it leaves something to be desired. That is, while a function that repeats a value some number of times is good, a function that repeats a computation some number of times is better. I can modify `repeat` slightly to perform just such a task:

```
function repeatedly(times, fun) {
  return _.map(_.range(times), fun);
}

repeatedly(3, function() {
  return Math.floor((Math.random()*10)+1);
});
//=> [1, 3, 8]
```

The function `repeatedly` is a nice illustration of the power of functional thinking. By taking a function instead of a value, I've opened up "repeatness" to a world of possibility. Instead of bottoming out immediately on a fixed value at the call-site, as `repeat` does, we can fill an array with anything. If we truly want to plug in constant values using `repeatedly`, then we need only do the following:

```
repeatedly(3, function() { return "Odelay!"; });

//=> ["Odelay!", "Odelay!", "Odelay!"]
```

In fact, the pattern illustrated by the use of a function returning a constant, no matter what its arguments will pop up various times in this book, as well as in functional libraries in the wild, but I'll talk about that more in the next section and also in Chapter 5.

You'll notice that I failed to list any parameters on the functions supplied to `repeated ly`. This was a matter of expediency, since I chose not to use the incoming arguments. In fact, because `repeatedly` is implemented as a call to `_.map` over the results of a call to `_.range`, a number representing the current repeat count is supplied to the function and could be used as you see fit. I've found this technique useful in generating some known number of DOM nodes, each with an `id` containing the repeat count value, like so:

```
repeatedly(3, function(n) {
  var id = 'id' + n;
  $('body').append($("<p>Odelay!</p>").attr('id', id));
  return id;
});

// Page now has three Odelays
//=> ["id0", "id1", "id2"]
```

In this case, I've used the jQuery library to append some nodes for me. This is a perfectly legitimate use of `repeatedly`, but it makes changes to the "world" outside of the function. In Chapter 7 I will talk about why this is potentially problematic, but for now I'd like to make `repeatedly` even more generic.

I said, "Use functions, not values"

I've moved away from the use of the static value in `repeat`, to a function that takes one function instead in `repeatedly`. While this has indeed made `repeatedly` more open-ended, it's still not as generic as it could be. I'm still relying on a constant to determine how many times to call the given function. Often you'll know precisely how many times a function should be called, but there will be other times when knowing when to quit is not about "times" but about conditions. In other words, you may want to instead call a given function until its return value crosses some threshold, changes sign, becomes uppercase, and so on, and a simple value will not be sufficient. Instead, I can define another function that is the logical progression beyond `repeat` and `repeatedly` named `iterateUntil`; it's defined as follows:

```
function iterateUntil(fun, check, init) {
  var ret = [];
  var result = fun(init);

  while (check(result)) {
    ret.push(result);
    result = fun(result);
  }

  return ret;
};
```

The function `iterateUntil` takes two functions: a function that performs some action and another that checks a result, returning `false` if the result is a "stop" value. This is truly `repeatedly` taken to the next level in that now even the repeat count is open-ended and subject to the result of a function call. So how could you use `iterateUntil`? A simple use would be to collect all of the results of some repeated computation until the value crosses some threshold. For example, suppose you want to find all of the doubles starting at 2 up to, at most, 1024:

```
iterateUntil(function(n) { return n+n },
             function(n) { return n <= 1024 },
             1);

//=> [2, 4, 8, 16, 32, 64, 128, 256, 512, 1024]
```

To accomplish the same task with `repeatedly` requires that you know, before calling, the number of times you need to call your function to generate the correct array:

```
repeatedly(10, function(exp) { return Math.pow(2,exp+1) });

//=> [2, 4, 8, 16, 32, 64, 128, 256, 512, 1024]
```

Sometimes you know how many times you need to run some calculation, and sometimes you know only how to calculate when to stop. An added advantage that iterateUntil provides is that the repeating loop is a feed-forward function. In other words, the result of some call to the passed function is fed into the next call of the function as its argument. I will show how this is a powerful technique later in "Pipelining" on page 176, but for now I think that we can proceed to the next section and talk about functions that return other functions.

Functions That Return Other Functions

You've already seen a few functions that return a function as a result—namely, makeAdder, complement, and plucker. As you might have guessed, all of these functions are higher-order functions. In this section, I will talk more in depth about higher-order functions that return (and sometimes also take) functions and closures. To start, recall my use of repeatedly, which used a function that ignored its arguments and instead returned a constant:

```
repeatedly(3, function() { return "Odelay!"; });

//=> ["Odelay!", "Odelay!", "Odelay!"]
```

This use of a function returning a constant is so useful that it's almost a design pattern for functional programming and is often simply called k. However, for the sake of clarity, I'll call it always; it's implemented in the following way:

```
function always(VALUE) {
  return function() {
    return VALUE;
  };
};
```

The operation of always is useful for illustrating some points about closures. First, a closure will capture a single value (or reference) and repeatedly return the same value:

```
var f = always(function(){});

f() === f();
//=> true
```

Because the function always produces a unique value, you can see that from one invocation of always to another, the captured function bound to VALUE is always the same (Braithwaite 2013).

Any function created with function will return a unique instance, regardless of the contents of its body. Using (function(){}) is a quick way to ensure that unique values are generated. Keeping that in mind, a second important note about closures is that each new closure captures a different value than every other:

```
var g = always(function(){});

f() === g();
//=> false
```

Keeping these two rules in mind when using closures will help avoid confusion.

Moving on, plugging in `always` as a replacement for my anonymous function is a bit more succinct:

```
repeatedly(3, always("Odelay!"));

//=> ["Odelay!", "Odelay!", "Odelay!"]
```

The `always` function is what's known as a *combinator*. This book will not focus heavily on combinators, but it's worth covering the topic somewhat, as you will see them used in code bases built in a functional style. However, I will defer that discussion until Chapter 5; for now, I'd rather run through more examples of function-returning functions, especially focusing on how closures empower this approach.

However, before moving on, I'll show the implementation of another function-returning-function, `invoker`, that takes a method and returns a function that will invoke that method on any object given. Observe:

```
function invoker (NAME, METHOD) {
  return function(target /* args ... */) {
    if (!existy(target)) fail("Must provide a target");

    var targetMethod = target[NAME];
    var args = _.rest(arguments);

    return doWhen((existy(targetMethod) && METHOD === targetMethod), function() {
      return targetMethod.apply(target, args);
    });
  };
};
```

The form of `invoker` is very similar to `always`; that is, it's a function returning a function that uses an original argument, `METHOD`, during a later invocation. The returned function in this case is a closure. However, rather than returning a constant, `invoker` performs some specialized action based on the value of the original call. Using `invoker` is as follows:

```
var rev = invoker('reverse', Array.prototype.reverse);

_.map([[1,2,3]], rev);
//=> [[3,2,1]]
```

While it's perfectly legitimate to directly invoke a particular method on an instance, a functional style prefers functions taking the invocation target as an argument. Taking advantage of the fact that `invoker` returns `undefined` when an object does not have a given method allows you to use JavaScript's natural polymorphism to build polymorphic functions. However, I'll discuss that in Chapter 5.

Capturing Arguments to Higher-Order Functions

A useful way to think about why you might create functions that return another function is that the arguments to the higher-order function serve to "configure" the behavior of the returned function. In the case of the makeAdder higher-order function, its argument serves to configure its returned function to always add that value to whatever number it takes. Observe:

```
var add100 = makeAdder(100);
add100(38);
//=> 138
```

Specifically, by binding the function returned by makeAdder to the name add100, I've specifically highlighted just how the return function is "configured." That is, it's configured to always add 100 to whatever you pass into it. This is a useful technique, but somewhat limited in its ability. Instead, you'll often see a function returning a function that captures a variable, and this is what I'll talk about presently.

Capturing Variables for Great Good

Imagine that you have a need for a function that generates unique strings. One such naive implementation might look like the following:[2]

```
function uniqueString(len) {
  return Math.random().toString(36).substr(2, len);
};

uniqueString(10);
//=> "3rm6ww5w0x"
```

However, what if the function needed to generate unique strings with a certain prefix? You could modify the uniqueString in the following way:

```
function uniqueString(prefix) {
  return [prefix, new Date().getTime()].join('');
};

uniqueString("argento");
//=> "argento1356107740868"
```

The new uniqueString seems to do the job. However, what if the requirements for this function change once again and it needs to return a prefixed string with an increasing

---

2. The primary naïveté being that there is no uniqueness guarantee on the strings generated, but I hope the intent is clear.

suffix starting at some known value? In that case, you'd like the function to behave as follows:

```
uniqueString("ghosts");
//=> "ghosts0"

uniqueString("turkey");
//=> "turkey1"
```

The new implementation can include a closure to capture some increasing value, used as the suffix:

```
function makeUniqueStringFunction(start) {
  var COUNTER = start;

  return function(prefix) {
    return [prefix, COUNTER++].join('');
  }
};

var uniqueString = makeUniqueStringFunction(0);

uniqueString("dari");
//=> "dari0"

uniqueString("dari");
//=> "dari1"
```

In the case of makeUniqueStringFunction, the free variable COUNTER is captured by the returned function and manipulated whenever it's called. This seems to work just fine, but couldn't you get the same functionality with an object? For example:

```
var generator = {
  count: 0,
  uniqueString: function(prefix) {
    return [prefix, this.count++].join('');
  }
};

generator.uniqueString("bohr");
//=> bohr0

generator.uniqueString("bohr");
//=> bohr1
```

But there is a downside to this (aside from the fact that it's not functional) in that it's a bit unsafe:

```
// reassign the count
generator.count = "gotcha";
generator.uniqueString("bohr");
//=> "bohrNaN"
```

```
// dynamically bind this
generator.uniqueString.call({count: 1337}, "bohr");
//=> "bohr1337"
```

By this time, your system is in a perilous state indeed. The approach used in makeUni
queStringFunction hides the instance of COUNTER from prying eyes. That is, the
COUNTER variable is "private" to the closures returned. Now I'm not a stickler for private
variables and object properties, but there are times when hiding a critical implementation detail from access is important. In fact, we could hide the counter in generator
using the JavaScript secret sauce:

```
var omgenerator = (function(init) {
  var COUNTER = init;

  return {
    uniqueString: function(prefix) {
      return [prefix, COUNTER++].join('');
    }
  };
})(0);

omgenerator.uniqueString("lichking-");
//=> "lichking-0"
```

But what's the point? Creating a monstrosity like this is sometimes necessary, especially
when building module/namespace-like qualifications, but it's not something that I'd like
to use often.[3] The closure solution is clean, simple, and quite elegant, but it is also fraught
with dread.

Take care when mutating values

I plan to talk more about the dangers of mutating (i.e., changing) variables in Chapter 7, but I can take a moment to touch on it. The implementation of makeUniqueS
tringFunction uses a little piece of state named COUNTER to keep track of the current
value. While this piece of data is safe from outside manipulation, that it exists at all
causes a bit of complexity. When a function is reliant on only its arguments for the value
that it will return, it is known to exhibit something called *referential transparency*.

This seems like a fancy term, but it simply means that you should be able to replace any
call to a function with its expected value without breaking your programs. When you
use a closure that mutates a bit of internal code, you cannot necessarily do that because
the value that it returns is wholly dependent on the number of times that it was previously called. That is, calling uniqueString ten times will return a different value than
if it were called 10,000 times. The only way that you can replace uniqueString with its

---

3. The ECMAScript.next initiative is working through the specification of a module system that would handle
visibility matters (among other things) based on simple declarations. More information is found at *http://
wiki.ecmascript.org/doku.php?id=harmony:modules*.

value is if you knew *exactly* how many times it was called at any given point, but that's not possible.

Again, I will talk more about this in Chapter 7, but it's worth noting that I will avoid functions like `makeUniqueStringFunctions` unless they're absolutely necessary. Instead, I think you'll be surprised how seldom mutating a little bit of state is required in functional programming. It takes some time to change your mind-set when faced with designing functional programs for the first time, but I hope that after you finish reading this book you'll have a better idea of why a mutable state is potentially harmful, and that you will have a desire to avoid it.

A Function to Guard Against Nonexistence: fnull

Before I move into Chapter 5, I'd like to build a couple higher-order functions for illustrative purposes. The first that I'll discuss is named `fnull`. To describe the purpose of `fnull`, I'd like to show a few error conditions that it's meant to solve. Imagine that we have an array of numbers that we'd like to multiply:

```
var nums = [1,2,3,null,5];

_.reduce(nums, function(total, n) { return total * n });
//=> 0
```

Well, clearly multiplying a number by `null` is not going to give us a helpful answer. Another problem scenario is a function that takes a configuration object as input to perform some action:

```
doSomething({whoCares: 42, critical: null});
// explodes
```

In both cases, a function like `fnull` would be useful. The use for `fnull` is in a function that takes a function as an argument and a number of additional arguments, and returns a function that just calls the original function given. The magic of `fnull` is that if any of the arguments to the function that it returns are `null` or `undefined`, then the original "default" argument is used instead. The implementation of `fnull` is the most complicated higher-order function that I'll show to this point, but it's still fairly reasonable. Observe:

```
function fnull(fun /*, defaults */) {
  var defaults = _.rest(arguments);

  return function(/* args */) {
    var args = _.map(arguments, function(e, i) {
      return existy(e) ? e : defaults[i];
    });

    return fun.apply(null, args);
  };
};
```

How fnull works is that it circumvents the execution of some function, checks its incomming arguments for null or undefined, fills in the original defaults if either is found, and then calls the original with the patched args. One particularly interesting aspect of fnull is that the cost of mapping over the arguments to check for default values is incured *only* if the guarded function is called. That is, assigning default values is done in a *lazy* fashion—only when needed.

You can use fnull in the following ways:

```
var safeMult = fnull(function(total, n) { return total * n }, 1, 1);

_.reduce(nums, safeMult);
//=> 30
```

Using fnull to create the safeMult function protects a product from receiving a null or undefined. This also gives the added advantage of providing a multiplication function that has an identity value when given no arguments at all.

To fix our configuration object problem, fnull can be used in the following way:

```
function defaults(d) {
  return function(o, k) {
    var val = fnull(_.identity, d[k]);
    return o && val(o[k]);
  };
}

function doSomething(config) {
  var lookup = defaults({critical: 108});

  return lookup(config, 'critical');
}

doSomething({critical: 9});
//=> 9

doSomething({});
//=> 108
```

This use of fnull ensures that for any given configuration object, the critical values are set to sensible defaults. This helps to avoid long sequences of guards at the beginning of functions and the need for the o[k] || someDefault pattern. Using fnull in the body of the defaults function is illustrative of the propensity in functional style to build higher-level parts from lower-level functions. Likewise, that defaults returns a function is useful for providing an extra layer of checks onto the raw array access.[4] Therefore,

---

4. The ECMAScript.next effort is working through a specification for default function parameters and the assignment of their values (often called optional arguments). It's unclear when this will make it into JavaScript core, but from my perspective it's a welcome feature. More information is found at *http://wiki.ecmascript.org/doku.php?id=harmony:parameter_default_values.*

using this functional style allows you to encapsulate the defaults and check logic in isolated functions, separate from the body of the doSomething function. Sticking with this theme, I'm going to wrap up this chapter with a function for building object-field validating functions.

Putting It All Together: Object Validators

To end this chapter, I'll work through a solution to a common need in JavaScript: the need to validate the veracity of an object based on arbitrary criteria. For example, imagine that you're creating an application that receives external commands via JSON objects. The basic form of these commands is as follows:

```
{message: "Hi!",
 type: "display"
 from: "http://localhost:8080/node/frob"}
```

It would be nice if there were a simple way to validate this message, besides simply taking it and iterating over the entries. What I would like to see is something more fluent and easily composed from parts, that reports all of the errors found with any given command object. In functional programming, the flexibility provided by functions that take and return other functions cannot be understated. In fact, the solution to the problem of command validation is a general one, with a little twist to provide nice error reporting.

Here I present a function named checker that takes a number of predicates (functions returning true or false) and returns a validation function. The returned validation function executes each predicate on a given object, and it adds a special error string to an array for each predicate that returns false. If all of the predicates return true, then the final return result is an empty array; otherwise, the result is a populated array of error messages. The implementation of checker is as follows:

```
function checker(/* validators */) {
  var validators = _.toArray(arguments);

  return function(obj) {
    return _.reduce(validators, function(errs, check) {
      if (check(obj))
        return errs
      else
        return _.chain(errs).push(check.message).value();
    }, []);
  };
}
```

The use of _.reduce is appropriate in this case because, as each predicate is checked, the errs array is either extended or left alone. Incidentally, I like to use Underscore's _.chain function to avoid the dreaded pattern:

```
{
  errs.push(check.message);
```

```
    return errs;
  }
```

The use of _.chain definitely requires more characters, but it hides the array mutation nicely. (I'll talk more about hiding mutation in Chapter 7.) Notice that the checker function looks for a message field on the predicate itself. For purposes like this, I like to use special-purpose validating functions that contain their own error messages attached as pseudo-metadata. This is not a general-purpose solution, but for code under my control it's a valid use case.

A basic test for validating a command object is as follows:

```
var alwaysPasses = checker(always(true), always(true));
alwaysPasses({});
//=> []

var fails = always(false);
fails.message = "a failure in life";
var alwaysFails = checker(fails);

alwaysFails({});
//=> ["a failure in life"]
```

It's a bit of a pain to remember to set a message property on a validator every time you create one. Likewise, it would be nice to avoid putting properties on validators that you don't own. It's conceivable that message is a common enough property name that setting it could wipe a legitimate value. I could obfuscate the property key to something like _message, but that doesn't help the problem of remembrance. Instead, I would prefer a specific API for creating validators—one that is recognizable at a glance. My solution is a validator higher-order function defined as follows:

```
function validator(message, fun) {
  var f = function(/* args */) {
    return fun.apply(fun, arguments);
  };

  f['message'] = message;
  return f;
}
```

A quick check of the validator function bears out this strategy:

```
var gonnaFail = checker(validator("ZOMG!", always(false)));

gonnaFail(100);
//=> ["ZOMG!"]
```

I prefer to isolate the definition of individual "checkers" rather than defining them in place. This allows me to give them descriptive names, like so:

```
function aMap(obj) {
  return _.isObject(obj);
}
```

The aMap function can then be used as an argument to checker to provide a virtual sentence:

```
var checkCommand = checker(validator("must be a map", aMap));
```

And, of course, the use is as you might expect:

```
checkCommand({});
//=> true

checkCommand(42);
//=> ["must be a map"]
```

Adding straightforward checkers is just as easy. However, maintaining a high level of fluency might require a few interesting tricks. If you recall from earlier in this chapter, I mentioned that arguments to a function-returning function can serve as behavior configuration for the returned closure. Keeping this in mind will allow you to return tweaked closures anywhere that a function is expected.

Take, for example, the need to validate that the command object has values associated with certain keys. What would be the best possible way to describe this checker? I would say that a simple list of the required keys would be beautifully fluent—for example, something like hasKeys('msg', 'type'). To implement hasKeys to conform to this calling convention, return a closure and adhere to the contract of returning an error array as follows:

```
function hasKeys() {
  var KEYS = _.toArray(arguments);

  var fun = function(obj) {
    return _.every(KEYS, function(k) {
      return _.has(obj, k);
    });
  };

  fun.message = cat(["Must have values for keys:"], KEYS).join(" ");
  return fun;
}
```

You'll notice that the closure (capturing KEYS) does the real work of checking the validity of a given object.[5] The purpose of the function hasKeys is to provide an execution configuration to fun. Additionally, by returning a function outright, I've provided a

---

5. Underscore's has function in hasKeys checks an object for the existence of a keyed binding. I was tempted to use existy(obj[k]), but that fails when the keyed value is null or undefined, both of which are conceivably legal values.

nicely fluent interface for describing required keys. This technique of returning a function from another function—taking advantage of captured arguments along the way—is known as "currying" (I will talk more about currying in Chapter 5). Finally, before returning the closure bound to `fun`, I attach a useful `message` field with a list of all the required keys. This could be made more informative with some additional work, but it's good enough as an illustration.

Using the `hasKeys` function is as follows:

```
var checkCommand = checker(validator("must be a map", aMap),
                           hasKeys('msg', 'type'));
```

The composition of the `checkCommand` function is quite interesting. You can think of its operation as a staged validation module on an assembly line, where an argument is passed through various checkpoints and examined for validity. In fact, as you proceed through this book, you'll notice that functional programming can indeed be viewed as a way to build virtual assembly lines, where data is fed in one end of a functional "machine," transformed and (optionally) validated along the way, and finally returned at the end as *something else*.

In any case, using the new `checkCommand` checker to build a "sentence of conformity," works as you might have guessed:

```
checkCommand({msg: "blah", type: "display"});
//=> []

checkCommand(32);
//=> ["must be a map", "Must have values for keys: msg type"]

checkCommand({});
//=> ["Must have values for keys: msg type"]
```

And that nicely highlights the use of all that you've seen in this chapter. I will dig further into these topics and `checker` will make appearances again throughout this book.

Summary

In this chapter, I discussed higher-order functions that are first-class functions that also do one or both of the following:

- Take a function as an argument
- Return a function as a result

To illustrate passing a function to another, numerous examples were given, including `max`, `finder`, `best`, `repeatedly`, and `iterateUntil`. Very often, passing values to functions to achieve some behavior is valuable, but sometimes such a task can be made more generic by instead passing a function.

The coverage of functions that return other functions started with the ever-valuable `always`. An interesting feature of `always` is that it returned a closure, a technique that you'll see time and time again in JavaScript. Additionally, functions returning functions allow for building powerful functions, such as `fnull` guards against unexpected `nulls`, and let us define argument defaults. Likewise, higher-order functions were used to build a powerful constraint-checking system, `checker`, using very little code.

In the next chapter, I will take everything that you've learned so far and put it in the context of "composing" new functions entirely from other functions.

CHAPTER 5

Function-Building Functions

This chapter builds on the idea of first-class functions by explaining how and why one builds functions on the fly. It explores various ways to facilitate function "composition" —snapping together functions like Lego blocks to build richer functionality from parts.

The Essence of Functional Composition

Recall that the function invoker from Chapter 4 built a function taking an object as its first argument and attempted to call a method on it. If you'll recall, invoker returned undefined if the method was not available on the target object. This can be used as a way to compose multiple invokers together to form polymorphic functions, or functions that exhibit different behaviors based on their argument(s). To do this, I'll need a way to take one or more functions and keep trying to invoke each in turn, until a non-undefined value is returned. This function, dispatch, is defined imperatively as follows:

```
function dispatch(/* funs */) {
  var funs = _.toArray(arguments);
  var size = funs.length;

  return function(target /*, args */) {
    var ret = undefined;
    var args = _.rest(arguments);

    for (var funIndex = 0; funIndex < size; funIndex++) {
      var fun = funs[funIndex];
      ret = fun.apply(fun, construct(target, args));

      if (existy(ret)) return ret;
    }

    return ret;
  };
}
```

This is a lot of code to perform a simple task.[1]

To be clear, what you want to do is return a function that loops through an array of functions, calls each with an object, and returns the first actual value it finds (i.e., "existy"). However, despite its seeming complexity, dispatch fulfills the definition of polymorphic JavaScript functions. It does so in a way that simplifies the task of delegating to concrete method behaviors. For example, in the implementation of Underscore, you'll very often see the following pattern repeated in many different functions:

1. Make sure the target exists.
2. Check if there is a native version and use it if so.
3. If not, then do some specific tasks implementing the behavior:

   - Do type-specific tasks, if applicable.
   - Do argument-specific tasks, if applicable.
   - Do argument count–specific tasks, if applicable.

In code-speak, this same pattern is expressed in the implementation of Underscore's _.map function:

```
_.map = _.collect = function(obj, iterator, context) {
  var results = [];
  if (obj == null) return results;
  if (nativeMap && obj.map === nativeMap) return obj.map(iterator, context);
  each(obj, function(value, index, list) {
    results[results.length] = iterator.call(context, value, index, list);
  });
  return results;
};
```

The use of dispatch can work to simplify some of this code and allow easier extensibility. Imagine you're tasked with writing a function to generate the string representation for both array and string types. Using dispatch leads to an elegant implementation:

```
var str = dispatch(invoker('toString', Array.prototype.toString),
                   invoker('toString', String.prototype.toString));


str("a");
//=> "a"

str(_.range(10));
//=> "0,1,2,3,4,5,6,7,8,9"
```

---

1. Recall that the construct function was defined all the way back in Chapter 2.

That is, by coupling `invoker` with `dispatch`, I can delegate down to concrete implementations like `Array.prototype.toString` rather than using a single function that groups type and existence checks via `if-then-else`.[2]

Of course, the operation of `dispatch` is not dependent on the use of `invoker`, but instead adheres to a certain contract. That is, it will keep trying to execute functions until it runs out or one returns an existy value. I can tap into this contract by supplying a function that adheres to the contract at hand, as in `stringReverse`:

```
function stringReverse(s) {
  if (!_.isString(s)) return undefined;
  return s.split('').reverse().join("");
}

stringReverse("abc");
//=> "cba"

stringReverse(1);
//=> undefined
```

Now `stringReverse` can be composed with the `Array#reverse` method to define a new, polymorphic function, `rev`:

```
var rev = dispatch(invoker('reverse', Array.prototype.reverse), stringReverse);

rev([1,2,3]);
//=> [3, 2, 1]

rev("abc");
//=> "cba"
```

In addition, we can exploit the contract of `dispatch` to compose a terminating function that provides some default behavior by always returning an existy value or one that always throws an exception. As a nice bonus, a function created by `dispatch` can *also* be an argument to `dispatch` for maximum flexibility:

```
var sillyReverse = dispatch(rev, always(42));

sillyReverse([1,2,3]);
//=> [3, 2, 1]

sillyReverse("abc");
//=> "cba"

sillyReverse(100000);
//=> 42
```

2. Using `Array.prototype.toString` directly.

A more interesting pattern that `dispatch` eliminates is the switch statement manual dispatch, which looks like the following:

```
function performCommandHardcoded(command) {
  var result;

  switch (command.type)
  {
  case 'notify':
    result = notify(command.message);
    break;
  case 'join':
    result = changeView(command.target);
    break;
  default:
    alert(command.type);
  }

  return result;
}
```

The `switch` statement in the `performCommandHardcoded` function looks at a field on a command object and dispatches to relevant code depending on the command string:

```
performCommandHardcoded({type: 'notify', message: 'hi!'});
// does the nofity action

performCommandHardcoded({type: 'join', target: 'waiting-room'});
// does the changeView action

performCommandHardcoded({type: 'wat'});
// pops up an alert box
```

I can eliminate this pattern nicely using dispatch in the following way:

```
function isa(type, action) {
  return function(obj) {
    if (type === obj.type)
      return action(obj);
  }
}

var performCommand = dispatch(
  isa('notify', function(obj) { return notify(obj.message) }),
  isa('join',   function(obj) { return changeView(obj.target) }),
  function(obj) { alert(obj.type) });
```

The preceding code starts with an `isa` function that takes a `type` string and an `action` function and returns a new function. The returned function will call the `action` function only if the `type` string and the `obj.type` field match; otherwise, it returns `undefined`.

It's the return of undefined that signals to dispatch to try the next dispatch sub-function.[3]

To extend the performCommandHardcoded function, you would need to go in and changed the actual switch statement itself. However, you can extend the performCom mand function with new behavior by simply wrapping it in another dispatch function:

```
var performAdminCommand = dispatch(
  isa('kill', function(obj) { return shutdown(obj.hostname) }),
  performCommand);
```

The newly created performAdminCommand states that it first tries to dispatch on the kill command, and if that fails then it tries the commands handled by performCommand:

```
performAdminCommand({type: 'kill', hostname: 'localhost'});
// does the shutdown action

performAdminCommand({type: 'flail'});
// alert box pops up

performAdminCommand({type: 'join', target: 'foo'});
// does the changeView action
```

You can also restrict the behavior by overriding commands earlier in the dispatch chain:

```
var performTrialUserCommand = dispatch(
  isa('join', function(obj) { alert("Cannot join until approved") }),
  performCommand);
```

Running through a couple of examples shows the new behavior:

```
performTrialUserCommand({type: 'join', target: 'foo'});
// alert box denial pops up

performTrialUserCommand({type: 'notify', message: 'Hi new user'});
// does the notify action
```

This is the essence of functional composition: using existing parts in well-known ways to build up new behaviors that can later serve as behaviors themselves. In the remainder of this chapter, I will discuss other ways to compose functions to create new behavior, starting with the notion of currying.

Mutation Is a Low-Level Operation

You've already been exposed to examples of functions implemented in an imperative fashion, and you will continue to see more as the book progresses. While often it's ideal to write code in a functional way, there are times when the primitives of a library, for

---

3. Some languages provide this kind of dispatch automatically as multimethods, i.e., function behavior determined by the result of a list of predicates or an arbitrary function.

the sake of speed or expediency, should be implemented using imperative techniques. Functions are quanta of abstraction, and the most important part of any given function is that it adheres to its contract and fulfills a requirement. No one cares if a variable was mutated deep within the confines of a function and never escaped. Mutation is sometimes necessary, but I view it as a low-level operation—one that should be kept out of sight and out of mind.

This book is not about spewing dogma regarding the virtues of functional programming. I think there are many functional techniques that offer ways to rein in the complexities of software development, but I realize that at times, there are better ways to implement any given individual part (Figure 5-1).

| Uses a stick to catch ants | Lives "close to the metal" | OOP (s) | λλλ | Thinks logically | Uses the right tool |

Figure 5-1. An "evolved" programmer knows when to use the right tool

Whenever you're building an application, it's always wise to explore the parameters of your personal execution needs to determine if a given implementation technique is appropriate. This book, while about functional programming, advocates above all else a full understanding of your problem and solution spaces to come to an understanding of your best-possible solution. I will discuss this theme throughout Chapter 7, but for now I present a recipe for delicious curry![4]

Currying

You've already seen an example of a curried function (namely, `invoker`). A curried function is one that returns a new function for every logical argument that it takes. In

---

4. The term "currying" has nothing at all to do with the delicious foodstuff. Instead, it's named after the mathematician Haskell Curry, who rediscovered a technique devised by another mathematician named Moses Schönfinkel. While Haskell Curry certainly contributed heaps to computer science, I think we've missed a fun opportunity to have a useful programming technique called schönfinkeling.

the case of `invoker`, you can imagine it operating in a slightly different (and more naive) way, as shown here:

```
function rightAwayInvoker() {
  var args = _.toArray(arguments);
  var method = args.shift();
  var target = args.shift();

  return method.apply(target, args);
}

rightAwayInvoker(Array.prototype.reverse, [1,2,3])
//=> [3, 2, 1]
```

That is, the function `rightAwayInvoker` does not return a function that then awaits a target object, but instead calls the method on the target taken as its second argument. The `invoker` function, on the other hand, is curried, meaning that the invocation of the method on a given target is deferred until its logical number of arguments (i.e., two) is exhausted. You can see this in action via the following:

```
invoker('reverse', Array.prototype.reverse)([1,2,3]);
//=> [3, 2, 1]
```

The double parentheses give away what's happening here (i.e., the function returned from `invoker` bound to the execution of `reverse` is immediately called with the array [1,2,3]).

Recall the idea that it's useful to return functions (closures) that are "configured" with certain behaviors based on the context in which they were created. This same idea can be extended to curried functions as well. That is, for every logical parameter, a curried function will keep returning a gradually more configured function until all parameters have been filled (Figure 5-2).

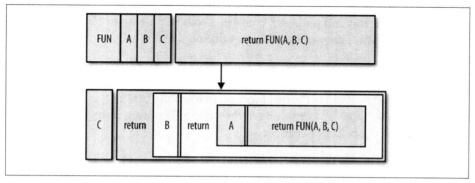

Figure 5-2. An illustration of currying

The idea of currying is simple, but there is one consideration that must be addressed. That is, if a curried function returns one function per parameter, then which parameter does the "uncurrying" start with, and with which does it end?

To Curry Right, or To Curry Left

The direction that you curry doesn't really matter, but the choice will have some implications on your API. For the purposes of this book (and my preference in general), I will curry starting at the rightmost argument and move left. In a language like JavaScript that allows you to pass any number of arguments, right-to-left currying allows you to fix the optional arguments to certain values.

To illustrate what I mean by the difference in argument direction, observe the following two functions:

```
function leftCurryDiv(n) {
  return function(d) {
    return n/d;
  };
}

function rightCurryDiv(d) {
  return function(n) {
    return n/d;
  };
}
```

The use of a division operation to illustrate currying works nicely because the result changes if the arguments are switched (i.e., it's not associative). Using the `leftCurry Div` function, observe how the curried parameters produce a result:

```
var divide10By = leftCurryDiv(10);
```

The function produced on the initial call, with `10` named `divide10By`, produces a function that, for all intents and purposes, contains a body pertaining to `10 / ?`, where ? is the curried rightmost parameter awaiting a value on the next call:

```
divide10By(2);
//=> 5
```

The second invocation of the curried function (named `divide10By`) now executes the fully populated body `10 / 2`, resulting in the value 5. However, if the `rightCurryDiv` function is used, the behavior changes:

```
var divideBy10 = rightCurryDiv(10);
```

Now the body of the curried function named `divideBy10` is instead `? / 10`, awaiting the leftmost argument before executing:

```
divideBy10(2);
//=> 0.2
```

As I mentioned, I will begin currying from the rightmost argument, so my calculations will operate as shown in Figure 5-2.

Another reason for currying from the right is that partial application handles working from the left (partial application will be discussed in greater depth in the next section). Between partial application and currying, I have both directions covered, allowing the full range of parameter specialization. Having said all of that, I'll presently implement a few functions both manually curried (as in leftCurryDiv and rightCurryDiv) and with an auto-currying function or two that I'll also implement.

Automatically Currying Parameters

The functions divide10By and divideBy10 were both curried by hand. That is, I explicitly wrote the functions to return the right number of functions corresponding to the number of function parameters. Likewise, for the purposes of illustration, my function rightCurryDiv returned a function corresponding to a division function taking two logical arguments. However, there is value in a simple higher-order function that takes a function and returns a function "pinned" to receive only one argument; I'll call this function curry and implement it as follows:

```
function curry(fun) {
  return function(arg) {
    return fun(arg);
  };
}
```

The operation of curry can be summarized as follows:

- Takes a function
- Returns a function expecting one parameter

This seems like a fairly useless function, no? Why not simply use the function directly instead? In many functional programming languages, there are few compelling reasons to provide an unadorned delegation like curry provides, but in JavaScript the story is slightly different. Very often in JavaScript, functions will take some number of expected arguments and an additional number of "specialization" arguments. For example, the JavaScript function parseInt takes a string and returns its equivalent integer:

```
parseInt('11');
//=> 11
```

Additionally, parseInt will accept a second argument that defines the radix to use when parsing (i.e., the number base):

```
parseInt('11', 2);
//=> 3
```

The preceding call, given a radix value of 2, means that the number is parsed as a binary (base-2) number. Complications arise using `parseInt` in a first-class way because of that optional second argument, as shown here:

```
['11','11','11','11'].map(parseInt)
//=> [11, NaN, 3, 4]
```

The problem here is that in some versions of JavaScript, the function given to Array#map will be invoked with each element of the array, the index of the element, plus the array itself.[5] So as you might have guessed, the radix argument for `parseInt` starts with 0 and then becomes 1, 2, and then 3. Ouch! Thankfully, using `curry`, you can force `parseInt` to receive only one argument on each call:

```
['11','11','11','11'].map(curry(parseInt));
//=> [11, 11, 11, 11]
```

I could have just as easily written a function that takes an arbitrary number of arguments and figures out how to curry the remaining arguments, but I like to be explicit when currying. The reason is that the use of a function like `curry` allows me to explicitly control the behavior of the function being called by fixing (or ignoring) the optional right-leaning arguments used for specialization.

Take, for example, the act of currying two function parameters using a `curry2` function, defined as such:

```
function curry2(fun) {
  return function(secondArg) {
    return function(firstArg) {
      return fun(firstArg, secondArg);
    };
  };
}
```

The `curry2` function takes a function and curries it up to two parameters deep. Using it to implement a version of the previously defined `divideBy10` function is shown here:

```
function div(n, d) { return n / d }

var div10 = curry2(div)(10);

div10(50);
//=> 5
```

Just like `rightCurryDiv`, the `div10` function awaits its first argument with a logical body corresponding to `? / 10`. And just for the sake of completion, `curry2` can also be used to fix the behavior of `parseInt` so that it handles only binary numbers when parsing:

5. The Underscore `map` function is subject to this problem as well.

```
var parseBinaryString = curry2(parseInt)(2);

parseBinaryString("111");
//=> 7

parseBinaryString("10");
//=> 2
```

Currying is a useful technique for specifying the specialized behavior of JavaScript functions and for "composing" new functions from existing functions, as I'll show next.

Building new functions using currying

I showed a way to use `curry2` to build a simple `div10` function that expects a numerator in a division operator, but that's not the full extent of its usefulness. In fact, in exactly the same way that closures are used to customize function behavior based on captured variables, currying can do the same via fulfilled function parameters. For example, Underscore provides a `_.countBy` function that, given an array, returns an object keying the count of its items tagged with some piece of data. Observe the operation of `_.count By`:

```
var plays = [{artist: "Burial", track: "Archangel"},
             {artist: "Ben Frost", track: "Stomp"},
             {artist: "Ben Frost", track: "Stomp"},
             {artist: "Burial", track: "Archangel"},
             {artist: "Emeralds", track: "Snores"},
             {artist: "Burial", track: "Archangel"}];

_.countBy(plays, function(song) {
  return [song.artist, song.track].join(" - ");
});

//=> {"Ben Frost - Stomp": 2,
//     "Burial - Archangel": 3,
//     "Emeralds - Snores": 1}
```

The fact that `_.countBy` takes an arbitrary function as its second argument should provide a hint about how you might use `curry2` to build customized functionality. That is, you can curry a useful function with `_.countBy` to implement custom counting functions. In the case of my artist counting activity, I might create a function named song Count as follows:

```
function songToString(song) {
  return [song.artist, song.track].join(" - ");
}

var songCount = curry2(_.countBy)(songToString);

songCount(plays);
//=> {"Ben Frost - Stomp": 2,
```

```
//    "Burial - Archangel": 3,
//    "Emeralds - Snores": 1}
```

The use of currying in this way forms a virtual sentence, effectively stating "to implement songCount, countBy songToString." You often see currying in the wild used to build fluent functional interfaces. In this book you'll see the same.

Currying three parameters to implement HTML hex color builders

Using the same pattern of implementation as curry2, I can also define a function that curries up to three parameters:

```
function curry3(fun) {
  return function(last) {
    return function(middle) {
      return function(first) {
        return fun(first, middle, last);
      };
    };
  };
};
```

I can use curry3 in various interesting ways, including using Underscore's _.uniq function to build an array of all of the unique songs played:

```
var songsPlayed = curry3(_.uniq)(false)(songToString);

songsPlayed(plays);

//=> [{artist: "Burial", track: "Archangel"},
//    {artist: "Ben Frost", track: "Stomp"},
//    {artist: "Emeralds", track: "Snores"}]
```

By spacing out the call to curry3 and aligning it with the direct call of _.uniq, you might see the relationship between the two more clearly: [6]

```
        _.uniq(plays, false,  songToString);

    curry3(_.uniq)     (false) (songToString);
```

In my own adventures, I've used curry3 as a way to generate HTML hexadecimal values with specific hues. I start with a function rgbToHexString, defined as follows:

```
function toHex(n) {
  var hex = n.toString(16);
  return (hex.length < 2) ? [0, hex].join(''): hex;
}

function rgbToHexString(r, g, b) {
```

6. Underscore's _.uniq function will take the boolean flag *or* the iterator as the second argument. Therefore, the currying above works correctly, but because of implementation details. The main reason for using it this way is to illustrate the correspondence between the arguments to curry3 and the direct call to _.uniq.

```
        return ["#", toHex(r), toHex(g), toHex(b)].join('');
}

rgbToHexString(255, 255, 255);
//=> "#ffffff"
```

This function can then be curried to varying depths to achieve specific colors or hues:

```
var blueGreenish = curry3(rgbToHexString)(255)(200);

blueGreenish(0);
//=> "#00c8ff"
```

And that is that.

Currying for Fluent APIs

A tangential benefit of currying is that it very oftens lead to fluent functional APIs. In the Haskell programming language, functions are curried by default, so libraries naturally take advantage of that fact. In JavaScript, however, functional APIs must be designed to take advantage of currying and must be documented to show how. However, a general-purpose rule when determining if currying is an appropriate tool for any given circumstance is this: does the API utilize higher-order functions? If the answer is yes, then curried functions, at least to one parameter, are appropriate. Take, for example, the checker function built in Chapter 4. It indeed accepts a function as an argument used to check the validity of a value. Using curried functions to build a fluent checker call is as simple as this:

```
var greaterThan = curry2(function (lhs, rhs) { return lhs > rhs });
var lessThan    = curry2(function (lhs, rhs) { return lhs < rhs });
```

By currying two functions that calculate greater-than and less-than, the curried version can be used directly where validator expects a predicate:

```
var withinRange = checker(
  validator("arg must be greater than 10", greaterThan(10)),
  validator("arg must be less than 20", lessThan(20)));
```

This use of curried functions is much easier on the eyes than directly using the anonymous versions of the greater-than and less-than calculations. Of course, the within Range checker works as you might expect:

```
withinRange(15);
//=> []

withinRange(1);
//=> ["arg must be greater than 10"]

withinRange(100);
//=> ["arg must be less than 20"]
```

So as you might agree, the use of curried functions can provide tangible benefits in creating fluent interfaces. The closer your code gets to looking like a description of the activity that it's performing, the better. I will strive to achieve this condition throughout the course of this book.

The Disadvantages of Currying in JavaScript

While it's nice to provide both `curry2` and `curry3`, perhaps it would be better to provide a function named `curryAll` that curries at an arbitrary depth. In fact, creating such a function is possible, but in my experience it's not very practical. In a programming language like Haskell or Shen, where functions are curried automatically, APIs are built to take advantage of arbitrarily curried functions. That JavaScript allows a variable number of arguments to functions actively works against currying in general and is often confusing. In fact, the Underscore library offers a plethora of different function behaviors based on the type and count of the arguments provided to many of its functions, so currying, while not impossible, must be applied with careful attention.

The use of `curry2` and `curry3` is occasionally useful, and in the presence of an API designed for currying, they can be an elegant approach to functional composition. However, I find it much more common to partially apply functions at arbitrary depths than to curry them, which is what I will discuss next.

Partial Application

You'll recall that I stated, in effect, that a curried function is one that returns a progressively more specific function for each of its given arguments until it runs out of parameters. A partially applied function, on the other hand, is a function that is "partially" executed and is ready for immediate execution given the remainder of its expected arguments, as shown in Figure 5-3.[7]

---

7. More recent versions of JavaScript provide a method `Function.bind` that performs partial application (Herman 2012).

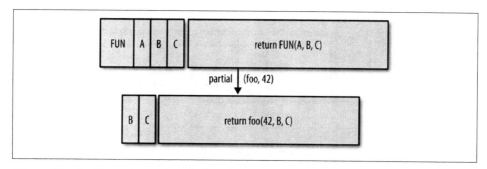

Figure 5-3. An illustration of partial application

Textual descriptions and pictures are nice, but the best way to understand partial application is to see it in action. Imagine a different implementation of `divide10By`, as shown here:

```
function divPart(n) {
  return function(d) {
    return n / d;
  };
}

var over10Part = divPart(10);
over10Part(2);
//=> 5
```

The implementation of `over10Part` looks almost exactly like the implementation of `leftCurryDiv`, and that fact highlights the relationship between currying and partial application. At the moment that a curried function will accept only one more argument before executing, it is effectively the same as a partially applied function expecting one more argument. However, partial application doesn't necessarily deal with one argument at a time, but instead deals with some number of partially applied arguments stored for later execution, given the remaining arguments.

The relationship between currying and partial application is shown in Figure 5-4.

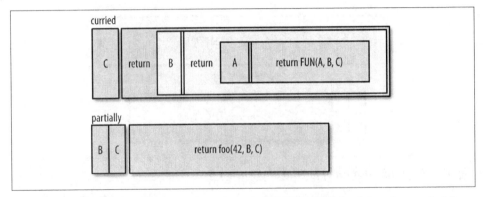

Figure 5-4. The relationship between currying and partial application; the curried function needs three cascading calls (e.g. curried(3)(2)(1)) before FUN runs, whereas the partially applied function is ready to rock, needing only one call of two args (e.g., partially(2, 3))

While currying and partial application are related, they are used quite differently. Never mind that my curry2 and curry3 functions work from right to left in the parameter list, although that fact alone would be enough to motivate different API shapes and usage patterns. The main difference with partial application is that it's less confusing in the face of the varargs function. JavaScript functions utilizing varargs usually directly bind the first few arguments and reserve the final arguments as optional or behavior specializing. In other words, JavaScript APIs, while allowing any functionality, usually concretely specify a known set of parameters, leading to concrete and default behavior. The use of partial application can take advantage of this, as I'll show next.

Partially Applying One and Two Known Arguments

Like currying, a discussion of partial application is best started simply. A function that partially applies its first argument is written as follows:[8]

```
function partial1(fun, arg1) {
  return function(/* args */) {
    var args = construct(arg1, arguments);
    return fun.apply(fun, args);
  };
}
```

Observe that the function returned from partial1 captures the argument arg1 from the original call and puts it at the front of the arglist of the executing call. You can see this operation in action in the following:

---

8. You can also use the native bind method (if it's available) to implement partial1 by replacing its body with return fun.bind(undefined, arg1);.

```
var over10Part1 = partial1(div, 10);

over10Part1(5);
//=> 2
```

So again, I've re-created the operation of the `divide10By` function by composing a function from another function and a "configuration" argument.[9] A function to partially apply up to two arguments is implemented similarly:

```
function partial2(fun, arg1, arg2) {
  return function(/* args */) {
    var args = cat([arg1, arg2], arguments);
    return fun.apply(fun, args);
  };
}

var div10By2 = partial2(div, 10, 2)

div10By2()
//=> 5
```

Partially applying one or two arguments is typically what you'll see in practice, but it would be useful to instead capture an arbitrary number of arguments for later execution, as I'll explain presently.

Partially Applying an Arbitrary Number of Arguments

Unlike currying, which is complicated by `varargs` in JavaScript, partial application of an arbitrary number of arguments is a legitimate composition strategy. Thankfully, the implementation of a function `partial` is not significantly more complex than either `partial1` nor `partial2`. In fact, the same basic implementation premise applies:

```
function partial(fun /*, pargs */) {
  var pargs = _.rest(arguments);

  return function(/* arguments */) {
    var args = cat(pargs, _.toArray(arguments));
    return fun.apply(fun, args);
  };
}
```

---

9. Likewise, `divide10By` can be implemented via native `bind`, when available, as `var divide10By = div.bind(undefined, 10)`; you can also use the native `bind` method, if it's available, to implement `partial2` by replacing its body with `return fun.bind(undefined, arg1, arg2)`.

As you might have noticed, the principle is the same: `partial` captures some number of arguments and returns a function that uses them as the prefix arguments for its final call.[10] In action, `partial` works exactly as you might expect:

```
var over10Partial = partial(div, 10);
over10Partial(2);
//=> 5
```

While the presence of varargs in JavaScript does not completely defeat the usefulness of partial application, it can still complicate matters, as shown below:[11]

```
var div10By2By4By5000Partial = partial(div, 10, 2, 4, 5000);
div10By2By4By5000Partial();
//=> 5
```

While you might be aware that a number that you're attempting to partially apply expects a fixed number of arguments, the fact that it will accept any number can at times cause confusion. In fact, the partially applied `div` function is just called one time with the arguments 10 and 2, and the remaining arguments are simply ignored. Adding partial application as a level of misdirection only exacerbates the confusion. The good news is that I've rarely run into this problem in practice.

Partial Application in Action: Preconditions

Recall the `validator` function from Chapter 4:

```
validator("arg must be a map", aMap)(42);
//=> false
```

The `validator` higher-order function takes a validation predicate and returns an array of the errors encountered along the way. If the error array is empty, then there were no reported errors. `validator` can also be used for more general purposes, such as the manual validation of arguments to functions:

```
var zero = validator("cannot be zero", function(n) { return 0 === n });
var number = validator("arg must be a number", _.isNumber);

function sqr(n) {
  if (!number(n)) throw new Error(number.message);
  if (zero(n))    throw new Error(zero.message);
```

10. JavaScript's native bind, when available, allows you to partially apply a function up to any number of arguments. To achieve the same effect as the body of `partial`, you can perform the following: `fun.bind.apply(fun, construct(undefined, args))`.

11. Underscore also has a `partial` function that works just like the one in this chapter. However, Underscore's very nature is that the default argument ordering is not amenable to its use. Where `partial` really shines is in creating new functions from existing functions. Having the collection first, as is the prevailing case in Underscore, eliminates the power potential to specialize higher-order functions by partially applying a modifier function in the first argument position.

```
  return n * n;
}
```

Calls to the sqr function are checked as such:

```
sqr(10);
//=> 100

sqr(0);
// Error: cannot be zero

sqr('');
// Error: arg must be a number
```

This is fairly nice to my eyes, but it can be even better using partial application. While there is certainly a class of errors that fall within the purview of essential data-check failures, there is another set of errors that do not. That is, there is a class of errors that pertains to the guarantees of a computation. In the latter case, you would say that there are two types of guarantees:

Preconditions
> Guarantees on the caller of a function

Postconditions
> Guarantees on the result of a function call, assuming the preconditions were met

In English, the relationship between pre- and postconditions is described as follows: given that you've provided a function data that it can handle, it will ensure that the return meets a specific criteria.

I showed one function—sqr—that had two preconditions pertaining to the "number-ness" and "zeroness" of its lone argument. We could check these conditions every single time, and that might be fine, but really they refer to a guarantee of sqr relative to the context of a running application. Therefore, I can use a new function, condition1, and partial application to attach the preconditions separately from essential calculations:

```
function condition1(/* validators */) {
  var validators = _.toArray(arguments);

  return function(fun, arg) {
    var errors = mapcat(function(isValid) {
      return isValid(arg) ? [] : [isValid.message];
    }, validators);

    if (!_.isEmpty(errors))
      throw new Error(errors.join(", "));

    return fun(arg);
  };
}
```

You'll notice that the function returned from `condition1` is meant to take only a single argument. This is done primarily for illustrative purposes, as the `vararg` version is a bit more complicated and obfuscates the point I'm trying to make.[12] The point is that the function returned by `condition1` takes a function and a set of functions, each created with `validator`, and either builds an `Error` or returns the value of the execution of `fun`. This is a very simple but powerful pattern, used as shown here:

```
var sqrPre = condition1(
    validator("arg must not be zero", complement(zero)),
    validator("arg must be a number", _.isNumber));
```

This is a very fluent validation API, as far as JavaScript goes. Very often you'll find that, through function composition, your code becomes more declarative (i.e., it says what it's supposed to do rather than how). A run-through of the operation of `sqrPre` bears out the operation of `condition1`:

```
sqrPre(_.identity, 10);
//=> 10

sqrPre(_.identity, '');
// Error: arg must be a number

sqrPre(_.identity, 0);
// Error: arg must not be zero
```

Recalling the definition of `sqr`, with its built-in error handling, you might have guessed how we can use `sqrPre` to check its arguments. If not, then imagine an "unsafe" version of `sqr` defined as follows:

```
function uncheckedSqr(n) { return n * n };

uncheckedSqr('');
//=> 0
```

Clearly, the square of the empty string shouldn't be 0, even if it can be explained by JavaScript's foibles. Thankfully, I've been building a set of tools, realized in the creation of `validator`, `partial1`, `condition1`, and `sqrPre`, to solve this particular problem, shown here:[13]

```
var checkedSqr = partial1(sqrPre, uncheckedSqr);
```

The creation of the new function `checkedSqr` was fully formed through the creation of functions, function-creating functions, and their interplay to build functions anew:

```
checkedSqr(10);
//=> 100
```

12. I leave this as an exercise for the reader.

13. I could have used `partial` instead of `partial1` in this example, but sometimes I like more explicitness in my code.

```
checkedSqr('');
// Error: arg must be a number

checkedSqr(0);
// Error: arg must not be zero
```

As shown in the preceding code, the new checkedSqr works exactly like sqr, except that by separating the validity checks from the main calculation, I've achieved an ideal level of flexibility. That is, I can now turn off condition checking altogether by not applying conditions to functions at all, or even mix in additional checks at a later time:

```
var sillySquare = partial1(
  condition1(validator("should be even", isEven)),
  checkedSqr);
```

Because the result of condition1 is a function expecting another function to delegate to, the use of partial1 combines the two:

```
sillySquare(10);
//=> 100

sillySquare(11);
// Error: should be even

sillySquare('');
// Error: arg must be a number

sillySquare(0);
// Error: arg must not be zero
```

Now obviously you wouldn't want to constrain the squaring of numbers to such a silly degree, but I hope the point is clear. The functions that compose other functions should themselves compose. Before moving on to the next section, it's worth taking a step back and seeing how to re-implement the command object (from Chapter 4) creation logic with validation:

```
var validateCommand = condition1(
  validator("arg must be a map", _.isObject),
  validator("arg must have the correct keys", hasKeys('msg', 'type')));

var createCommand = partial(validateCommand, _.identity);
```

Why use the _.identity function as the logic part of the createCommand function? In JavaScript, much of the safety that we achieve is built via discipline and careful thinking. In the case of createCommand, the intention is to provide a common gateway function used for creating and validating command objects, as shown below:

```
createCommand({});
// Error: arg must have right keys

createCommand(21);
```

```
// Error: arg must be a map, arg must have right keys

createCommand({msg: "", type: ""});
//=> {msg: "", type: ""}
```

However, using functional composition allows you to later build on top of the existing creation abstraction in order to customize the actual building logic or the validation itself. If you wanted to build a derived command type that required the existence of another key, then you would further compose with the following:

```
var createLaunchCommand = partial1(
  condition1(
    validator("arg must have the count down", hasKeys('countDown'))),
  createCommand);
```

And as you might expect, `createLaunchCommand` works as follows:

```
createCommand({msg: "", type: ""});
// Error: arg must have the count down

createCommand({msg: "", type: "", countDown: 10});
//=> {msg: "", type: "", countDown: 10}
```

Whether you use currying or partial application to build functions, there is a common limitation on both: they only compose based on the specialization of one or more of their arguments. However, it's conceivable that you might want to compose functions based on the relationships between their arguments and their return values. In the next section, I will talk about a `compose` function that allows the end-to-end stitching of functions.

Stitching Functions End-to-End with Compose

An idealized (i.e., not one that you're likely to see in production) functional program is a pipeline of functions fed a piece of data in one end and emitting a whole new piece of data at the other. In fact, JavaScript programmers do this all the time. Observe:

```
!_.isString(name)
```

The pipeline in play here is built from the function `_.isString` and the `!` operator, where:

- `_.isString` expects an object and returns a Boolean value
- `!` expects a Boolean value (in principle) and returns a Boolean

Functional composition takes advantage of this type of data chain by building new functions from multiple functions and their data transformations along the way:

```
function isntString(str) {
  return !_.isString(str);
}
```

```
isntString(1);
//=> true
```

But this same function can be built from function composition, using the Underscore function _.compose as follows:

```
var isntString = _.compose(function(x) { return !x }, _.isString);

isntString([]);
//=> true
```

The _.compose function works from right to left in the way that the resulting function executes. That is, the result of the rightmost functions are fed into the functions to their left, one by one. Using selective spacing, you can see how this maps to the original:

```
        !         _.isString("a");

_.compose(function(str) { return !str }, _.isString)("a");
```

In fact, the ! operator is useful enough to encapsulate it into its own function:

```
function not(x) { return !x }
```

The not function then composes as you'd expect:

```
var isntString = _.compose(not, _.isString);
```

Using composition this way effectively turns a string into a Boolean value without explicitly changing either one—a worthy result indeed. This model for composition can form the basis for entire function suites where primitive data transformers are plugged together like Lego blocks to build other functionality.

A function that I've already defined, mapcat, can be defined using _.compose in the following way:[14]

```
var composedMapcat = _.compose(splat(cat), _.map);

composedMapcat([[1,2],[3,4],[5]], _.identity);
//=> [1, 2, 3, 4, 5]
```

There are infinite ways to compose functions to form further functionality, one of which I'll show presently.

Pre- and Postconditions Using Composition

If you recall from the previous section, I mentioned that preconditions define the constraints under which a function's operation will produce a value adhering to a different set of constraints. These production constraints are called postconditions. Using con

---

14. I defined splat way back in Chapter 1.

dition1 and `partial`, I was able to build a function (`checkedSqr`) that checked the input arguments to `uncheckedSqr` for conformance to its preconditions. However, if I want to define the postconditions of the act of squaring, then I need to define them using `condition1` as such:

```
var sqrPost = condition1(
  validator("result should be a number", _.isNumber),
  validator("result should not be zero", complement(zero)),
  validator("result should be positive", greaterThan(0)));
```

I can run through each error case manually using the following:

```
sqrPost(_.identity, 0);
// Error: result should not be zero, result should be positive

sqrPost(_.identity, -1);
// Error: result should be positive

sqrPost(_.identity, '');
// Error: result should be a number, result should be positive

sqrPost(_.identity, 100);
//=> 100
```

But the question arises: how can I glue the postcondition check function onto the existing `uncheckedSqr` and `sqrPre`? The answer, of course, is to use `_.compose` for the glue: [15]

```
var megaCheckedSqr = _.compose(partial(sqrPost, _.identity), checkedSqr);
```

And its use is exactly the same as `checkedSqr`:

```
megaCheckedSqr(10);
//=> 100

megaCheckedSqr(0);
// Error: arg must not be zero
```

Except:

```
megaCheckedSqr(NaN);
// Error: result should be positive
```

Of course, if the function ever throws a postcondition error, then that means that either my preconditions are under-specified, my postconditions are over-specified, or my internal logic is busted. As the provider of a function, a post-condition failure is *always* my fault.

---

15. Another option is to rewrite `condition1` to work with an intermediate object type named `Either` that holds *either* the resulting value or an error string.

Summary

In this chapter, I worked through the idea that new functions can be built from existing functions, be they generic or special-purpose. The first phase of composition is done manually by just calling one function after another, then wrapping the calls in another function. However, using specialized composition functions was often easier to read and reason about.

The first composition function covered was _.curry, which took a function and some number of arguments and returned a function with the rightmost arguments fixed to those given. Because of the nature of JavaScript, which allows a variable number of arguments, a few static currying functions—curry and curry2—were used to create functions of known parameter sizes to a known number of curried arguments. In addition to introducing currying, I implemented a few interesting functions using the technique.

The second composition function covered was partial, which took a function and some number of arguments and returned a function that fixed the leftmost arguments to those given. Partial application via partial, partial1, and partial2 proved a much more broadly applicable technique than currying.

The final composition function covered was _.compose, which took some number of functions and strung them end to end from the rightmost to the leftmost. The _.compose higher-order function was used to build on the lessons learned from Chapter 4's implementation of checker to provide a pre- and postcondition function "decorator," using a surprisingly small amount of code.

The next chapter is again a transition chapter covering a topic not very prevalent in JavaScript, though more so in functional programming in general: recursion.

CHAPTER 6

Recursion

This chapter is a transitional chapter meant to smooth the way from thinking about functions to thinking about a deeper understanding of a functional style, including when to break from it and why doing so is sometimes a good idea. Specifically, this chapter covers recursion, or functions calling themselves directly or through other functions.

Self-Absorbed Functions (Functions That Call Themselves)

Historically, recursion and functional programming were viewed as related, or at least they were often taught together. Throughout this chapter, I'll explain how they're related, but for now, I can say that an understanding of recursion is important to functional programming for three reasons:

- Recursive solutions involve the use of a single abstraction applied to subsets of a common problem.
- Recursion can hide mutable state.
- Recursion is one way to implement laziness and infinitely large structures.

If you think about the essential nature of a function, myLength, that takes an array and returns its length (i.e., number of elements), then you might land on the following description:[1]

1. Start with a size of zero.
2. Loop through the array, adding one to the size for each entry.

---

[1] You might actually think, "why not just use the length field on the array?" While this kind of pragmatic thinking is extremely important for building great systems, it's not helpful for learning recursion.

3. If you get to the end, then the size is the length.

This is a correct description of myLength, but it doesn't involve recursive thinking. Instead, a recursive description would be as follows:

1. An array's length is zero if it's empty.

2. Add one to the result of myLength with the remainder of the array.

I can directly encode these two rules in the implementation of myLength, as shown here:

```
function myLength(ary) {
  if (_.isEmpty(ary))
    return 0;
  else
    return 1 + myLength(_.rest(ary));
}
```

Recursive functions are very good at building values. The trick in implementing a recursive solution is to recognize that certain values are built from subproblems of a larger problem. In the case of myLength, the total solution can really be seen as adding the lengths of some number of single-element arrays with the length of an empty array. Since myLength calls itself with the result of _.rest, each recursive call gets an array that is one element shorter, until the last call gets an empty array (see Figure 6-1).

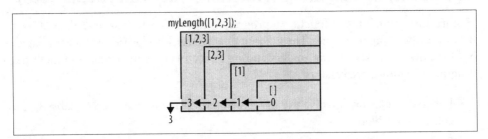

Figure 6-1. A recursive myLength that "consumes" an array

Observe the operation of myLength below:

```
myLength(_.range(10));
//=> 10

myLength([]);
//=> 0

myLength(_.range(1000));
//=> 1000
```

It's important to know that for minimal confusion, recursive functions should not change the arguments given them:

```
var a = _.range(10);

myLength(a);
//=> 10

a;
//=> [0, 1, 2, 3, 4, 5, 6, 7, 8, 9]
```

While a recursive function may *logically* consume its input arguments, it should never actually do so. While myLength built up an integer return value based on its input, a recursive function can build any type of legal value, including arrays and objects. Consider, for example, a function called cycle that takes a number and an array and builds a new array filled with the elements of the input array, repeated the specified number of times:

```
function cycle(times, ary) {
  if (times <= 0)
    return [];
  else
    return cat(ary, cycle(times - 1, ary));
}
```

The form of the cycle function looks similar to the myLength function. That is, while myLength "consumed" the input array, cycle "consumes" the repeat count. Likewise, the value built up on each step is the new cycled array. This consume/build action is shown in Figure 6-2.

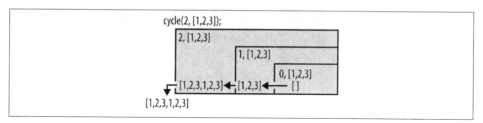

Figure 6-2. A recursive cycle that builds an array

Here's cycle in action:

```
cycle(2, [1,2,3]);
//=> [1, 2, 3, 1, 2, 3]

_.take(cycle(20, [1,2,3]), 11);
//=> [1, 2, 3, 1, 2, 3, 1, 2, 3, 1, 2]
```

Another self-recursive function that I'll create is called unzip, which is the inverse of Underscore's _.zip function, constrained to pairs, shown here:

```
_.zip(['a', 'b', 'c'], [1, 2, 3]);

//=> [['a', 1], ['b', 2], ['c', 3]]
```

Underscore's `_.zip` takes two arrays and pairs each element in the first array with each corresponding element in the second array. To implement a function that "unzips" arrays like those generated by `_.zip` requires that I think about the "pairness" of the array needing unzipping. In other words, if I think about the basic case, one array needing unzipping, then I can begin to deconstruct how to solve the problem as a whole:

```
var zipped1 = [['a', 1]];
```

Even more basic than `zipped1` would be the empty array `[]`, but an unzipped empty array is the resulting array `[[],[]]` (that seems like a good candidate for a terminating case, so put that in the back of your mind for now). The array `zipped1` is the simplest interesting case and results in the unzipped array `[['a'], [1]]`. So given the terminating case `[[],[]]` and the base case `zipped`, how can I get to `[['a'], [1]]`?

The answer is as simple as a function that makes an array of the first element in `zipped1` and puts it into the first array in the terminating case and the second element in `zipped1`, and puts that into the second array of the terminating case. I can abstract this operation in a function called `constructPair`:

```
function constructPair(pair, rests) {
  return [construct(_.first(pair), _.first(rests)),
          construct(second(pair),  second(rests))];
}
```

While the operation of `constructPair` is not enough to give me general "unzippability," I can achieve an unzipped version of `zipped1` manually by using it and the empty case:

```
constructPair(['a', 1], [[],[]]);
//=> [['a'], [1]]

_.zip(['a'], [1]);
//=> [['a', 1]]

_.zip.apply(null, constructPair(['a', 1], [[],[]]));
//=> [['a', 1]]
```

Likewise, I can gradually build up an unzipped version of a larger zipped array using `constructPair`, as shown here:

```
constructPair(['a', 1],
  constructPair(['b', 2],
    constructPair(['c', 3], [[],[]])));

//=> [['a','b','c'],[1,2,3]]
```

Graphically, these manual steps are shown in Figure 6-3.

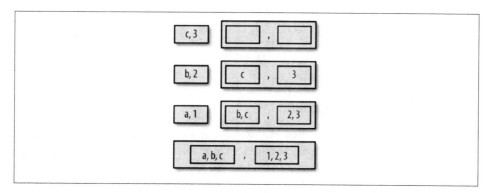

Figure 6-3. Illustrating the operation of constructPair graphically

So using the knowledge of how `constructPair` works, I can now build a self-recursive function `unzip`:

```
function unzip(pairs) {
  if (_.isEmpty(pairs)) return [[],[]];

  return constructPair(_.first(pairs), unzip(_.rest(pairs)));
}
```

The recursive call in `unzip` walks the given array of zipped pairs until it gets to an empty array. It then walks back down the subarrays, using `constructPair` along the way to build an unzipped representation of the array. Having implemented `unzip`, I should be able to "undo" the result of a call to `_.zip` that has built an array of pairs:

```
unzip(_.zip([1,2,3],[4,5,6]));
//=> [[1,2,3],[4,5,6]]
```

All instances of `myLength`, `cycle`, and `unzip` were examples of *self-recursion* (or, in other words, functions that call themselves). The rules of thumb when writing self-recursive functions are as follows(Touretzky 1990):

- Know when to stop
- Decide how to take one step
- Break the problem into that step and a smaller problem

Table 6-1 presents a tabular way of observing how these rules operate.

Table 6-1. The rules of self-recursion

Function	Stop When	Take One Step	Smaller Problem
myLength	_.isEmpty	1 + ...	_.rest
cycle	times <= 0	cat(ary ...	times - 1
unzip	_.isEmpty	constructPair(_.first ...	_.rest

Observing these three rules will provide a template for writing your own recursive functions. To illustrate that self-recursive functions of any complexity fall into this pattern, I'll run through a more complex example and explain the similarities along the way.

Graph Walking with Recursion

Another suitable problem solved by recursion in an elegant way is the task of walking the nodes in a graph-like data structure. If I wanted to create a library for navigating a graph-like structure, then I would be hard pressed to find a solution more elegant than a recursive one. A graph that I find particularly interesting is a (partial) graph of the programming languages that have influenced JavaScript either directly or indirectly.

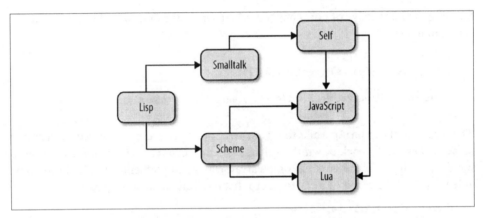

Figure 6-4. A partial graph of programming language influences

I could use a class-based or object-based representation, where each language and connection is represented by objects of type Node and Arc, but I think I'd prefer to start with something simple, like an array of arrays of strings:

```
var influences = [
  ['Lisp', 'Smalltalk'],
  ['Lisp', 'Scheme'],
  ['Smalltalk', 'Self'],
  ['Scheme', 'JavaScript'],
  ['Scheme', 'Lua'],
  ['Self', 'Lua'],
  ['Self', 'JavaScript']];
```

Each nested array in influences represents a connection of "influencer" to "influenced" (e.g., Lisp influenced Smalltalk) and encodes the graph shown in Figure 6-4. A recursive function, nexts, is defined recursively as follows(Paulson 1996):

```
function nexts(graph, node) {
  if (_.isEmpty(graph)) return [];
```

```
    var pair = _.first(graph);
    var from = _.first(pair);
    var to   = second(pair);
    var more = _.rest(graph);

    if (_.isEqual(node, from))
      return construct(to, nexts(more, node));
    else
      return nexts(more, node);
}
```

The function `nexts` walks the graph recursively and builds an array of programming languages influenced by the given node, as shown here:

```
nexts(influences, 'Lisp');
//=> ["Smalltalk", "Scheme"]
```

The recursive call within `nexts` is quite different than what you've seen so far; there's a recursive call in both branches of the `if` statement. The "then" branch of `nexts` deals directly with the target node in question, while the `else` branch ignores unimportant nodes.

Table 6-2. The rules of self-recursion according to nexts

Function	Stop When	Take One Step	Smaller Problem
nexts	_.isEmpty	construct(...)	_.rest

It would take very little work to make `nexts` take and traverse multiple nodes, but I leave that as an exercise to the reader. Instead, I'll now cover a specific type of graph-traversal recursive algorithm called depth-first search.

Depth-First Self-Recursive Search with Memory

In this section I'll talk briefly about graph searching and provide an implementation of a depth-first search function. In functional programming, you'll often need to search a data structure for a piece of data. In the case of hierarchical graph-like data (like `influ ences`), the search solution is naturally a recursive one. However, to find any given node in a graph, you'll need to (potentially) visit every node in the graph to see if it's the one you're looking for. One node traversal strategy called depth-first visits every leftmost node in a graph before visiting every rightmost node (as shown in Figure 6-5).

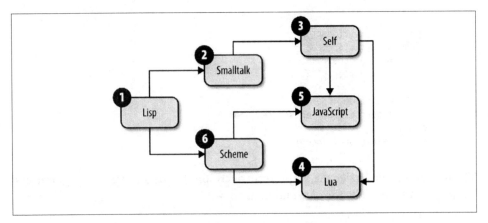

Figure 6-5. Traversing the influences graph depth-first

Unlike the previous recursive implementations, a new function `depthSearch` should maintain a memory of nodes that it's already seen. The reason, of course, is that another graph might have cycles in it, so without memory, a "forgetful" search will loop until JavaScript blows up. However, because a self-recursive call can only interact from one invocation to another via arguments, the memory needs to be sent from one call to the next via an "accumulator." An accumulator argument is a common technique in recursion for communicating information from one recursive call to the next. Using an accumulator, the implementation of `depthSearch` is as follows:

```
function depthSearch(graph, nodes, seen) {
  if (_.isEmpty(nodes)) return rev(seen);

  var node = _.first(nodes);
  var more = _.rest(nodes);

  if (_.contains(seen, node))
    return depthSearch(graph, more, seen);
  else
    return depthSearch(graph,
                       cat(nexts(graph, node), more),
                       construct(node, seen));
}
```

As you'll notice, the third parameter, `seen`, is used to hold the accumulation of seen nodes to avoid revisiting old nodes and their children. A usage example of `depth Search` is as follows:

```
depthSearch(influences, ['Lisp'], []);
//=> ["Lisp", "Smalltalk", "Self", "Lua", "JavaScript", "Scheme"]

depthSearch(influences, ['Smalltalk', 'Self'], []);
//=> ["Smalltalk", "Self", "Lua", "JavaScript"]
```

```
depthSearch(construct(['Lua','Io'], influences), ['Lisp'], []);
//=> ["Lisp", "Smalltalk", "Self", "Lua", "Io", "JavaScript", "Scheme"]
```

You may have noticed that the depthSearch function doesn't actually do anything. Instead, it just builds an array of the nodes that it would do something to (if it did anything) in depth-first order. That's OK because later I'll re-implement a depth-first strategy using functional composition and mutual recursion. First, let me take a moment to talk about "tail calls."

Tail (self-)recursion

While the general form of depthSearch looks very similar to the functions that came before, there is one difference that is key. To highlight what I mean, consider Table 6-3.

Table 6-3. The rules of self-recursion according to depthSearch

Function	Stop When	Take One Step	Smaller Problem
nexts	_.isEmpty	construct(...	_.rest
depthSearch	_.isEmpty	depthSearch(more...	depthSearch(cat...

The clear difference is that the "take one step" and "smaller problem" elements of depth Search are recursive calls. When either or both of these elements are recursive calls, then the function is known as tail-recursive. In other words, the last action that happens in the function (besides returning a termination element) is a recursive call. Since the last call in depthSearch is a recursive call, there is no way that the function body will ever be used again. A language like Scheme takes advantage of this fact to deallocate the resources used in a tail-recursive function body.

A reimplementation of myLength using a tail-recursive call is as follows:

```
function tcLength(ary, n) {
  var l = n ? n : 0;

  if (_.isEmpty(ary))
    return l;
  else
    return tcLength(_.rest(ary), l + 1);
}

tcLength(_.range(10));
//=> 10
```

By contrast, the recursive call in myLength (i.e., 1 + ...) revisits the function body to perform that final addition. Perhaps one day JavaScript engines will optimize tail-recursive functions to preserve memory. Until that time, we're cursed to blow the call stack on deeply recursive calls.[2] However, as you'll see later in this chapter, the tail position of a function is still interesting.

Recursion and Composing Functions: Conjoin and Disjoin

Throughout this book, I've implemented some common function composition functions—curry1, partial, and compose—but I didn't describe how to create your own. Fortunately, the need to create composition functions is rare, as much of the composition capabilities needed are provided by Underscore or are implemented herein. However, in this section, I'll describe the creation of two new combinators, orify and andify, implemented using recursion.

Recall that I created a checker function way back in Chapter 4 that took some number of predicates and returned a function that determined if they all returned truthiness for *every* argument supplied. I can implement the spirit of checker as a recursive function called andify:[3]

```
function andify(/* preds */) {
  var preds = _.toArray(arguments);

  return function(/* args */) {
    var args = _.toArray(arguments);

    var everything = function(ps, truth) {
      if (_.isEmpty(ps))
        return truth;
      else
        return _.every(args, _.first(ps))
               && everything(_.rest(ps), truth);
    };

    return everything(preds, true);
  };
}
```

Take note of the recursive call in the function returned by andify, as it's particularly interesting. Because the logical and operator, &&, is "lazy," the recursive call will never happen should the _.every test fail. This type of laziness is called "short-circuiting," and it is useful for avoiding uneccessary computations. Note that I use a local function, everything, to consume the predicates given in the original call to andify. Using a nested function is a common way to hide accumulators in recursive calls.

---

2. The ECMAScript 6 proposal currently has a section for tail-call optimization, so cross your fingers... I'll cross mine. See *http://wiki.ecmascript.org/doku.php?id=harmony:proper_tail_calls*.

3. A short-circuiting andify function can also be implemented via Underscore's every function. Can you see how?

Observe the action of andify here:

```
var evenNums = andify(_.isNumber, isEven);

evenNums(1,2);
//=> false

evenNums(2,4,6,8);
//=> true

evenNums(2,4,6,8,9);
//=> false
```

The implementation of orify is almost exactly like the form of andify, except for some logic reversals:[4]

```
function orify(/* preds */) {
  var preds = _.toArray(arguments);

  return function(/* args */) {
    var args = _.toArray(arguments);

    var something = function(ps, truth) {
      if (_.isEmpty(ps))
        return truth;
      else
        return _.some(args, _.first(ps))
                 || something(_.rest(ps), truth);
    };

    return something(preds, false);
  };
}
```

Like andify, should the _.some function ever succeed, the function returned by ori fy short-circuits (i.e., any of the arguments match any of the predicates). Observe:

```
var zeroOrOdd = orify(isOdd, zero);

zeroOrOdd();
//=> false

zeroOrOdd(0,2,4,6);
//=> true

zeroOrOdd(2,4,6);
//=> false
```

---

4. The orify function can also be implemented via Underscore's some function. Can you see how?

This ends my discussion of self-recursive functions, but I'm not done with recursion quite yet. There is another way to achieve recursion and it has a catchy name: mutual recursion.

Codependent Functions (Functions Calling Other Functions That Call Back)

Two or more functions that call each other are known as mutually recursive. Two very simple mutually recursive functions are the predicates to check for even and odd numbers, shown here:

```
function evenSteven(n) {
  if (n === 0)
    return true;
  else
    return oddJohn(Math.abs(n) - 1);
}

function oddJohn(n) {
  if (n === 0)
    return false;
  else
    return evenSteven(Math.abs(n) - 1);
}
```

The mutually recursive calls bounce back and forth between each other, decrementing some absolute value until one or the other reaches zero. This is a fairly elegant solution that works as you expect:

```
evenSteven(4);
//=> true

oddJohn(11);
//=> true
```

If you adhere to the strict use of higher-order functions, then you're likely to encounter mutually exclusive functions more often. Take, for example, the _.map function. A function that calls _.map with itself is a mind-bendingly indirect way to perform mutual recursion. A function to flatten an array to one level serves as an example:[5]

```
function flat(array) {
  if (_.isArray(array))
    return cat.apply(cat, _.map(array, flat));
  else
    return [array];
}
```

---

5. A better solution is to use Underscore's flatten function.

The operation of `flat` is a bit subtle, but the point is that in order to flatten a nested array, it builds an array of each of its nested elements and recursively concatenates each on the way back. Observe:

```
flat([[1,2],[3,4]]);
//=> [1, 2, 3, 4]

flat([[1,2],[3,4,[5,6,[[[7]]],8]]]);
//=> [1, 2, 3, 4, 5, 6, 7, 8]
```

Again, this is a fairly obscure use of mutual recursion, but one that fits well with the use of higher-order functions.

Deep Cloning with Recursion

Another example where recursion seems like a good fit is to implement a function to "deep" clone an object. Underscore has a `_.clone` function, but it's "shallow" (i.e., it only copies the objects at the first level):

```
var x = [{a: [1, 2, 3], b: 42}, {c: {d: []}}];

var y = _.clone(x);

y;
//=> [{a: [1, 2, 3], b: 42}, {c: {d: []}}];

x[1]['c']['d'] = 1000000;

y;
//=> [{a: [1, 2, 3], b: 42}, {c: {d: 1000000}}];
```

While in many cases, `_.clone` will be useful, there are times when you'll really want to clone an object and all of its subobjects.[6] Recursion is a perfect task for this because it allows us to walk every object in a nested fashion, copying along the way. A recursive implementation of `deepClone`, while not robust enough for production use, is shown here:

```
function deepClone(obj) {
  if (!existy(obj) || !_.isObject(obj))
    return obj;

  var temp = new obj.constructor();
  for (var key in obj)
    if (obj.hasOwnProperty(key))
      temp[key] = deepClone(obj[key]);
```

---

6. I'm using the term "clone" in the way often seen in JavaScript circles. In other prototypal languages (e.g., Self or Io) a clone operation delegates to the original, cloned object until a change is made, whereby a copy occurs.

```
    return temp;
  }
```

When deepClone encounters a primitive like a number, it simply returns it. However, when it encounters an object, it treats it like an associative structure (hooray for generic data representations) and recursively copies all of its key/value mappings. I chose to use the obj.hasOwnProperty(key) to ensure that I do not copy fields from the prototype. I tend to use objects as associative data structures (i.e., maps) and avoid putting data onto the prototype unless I must. The use of deepClone is as follows:

```
var x = [{a: [1, 2, 3], b: 42}, {c: {d: []}}];

var y = deepClone(x);

_.isEqual(x, y);
//=> true

y[1]['c']['d'] = 42;

_.isEqual(x, y);
//=> false
```

The implementation of deepClone isn't terribly interesting except for the fact that Java-Script's everything-is-an-object foundation really allows the recursive solution to be compact and elegant. In the next section, I'll re-implement depthSearch using mutual recursion, but one that actually does something.

Walking Nested Arrays

Walking nested objects like in deepClone is nice, but not frequently needed. Instead, a far more common occurrence is the need to traverse an array of nested arrays. Very often you'll see the following pattern:

```
doSomethingWithResult(_.map(someArray, someFun));
```

The result of the call to _.map is then passed to another function for further processing. This is common enough to warrant its own abstraction, I'll call it visit, implemented here:

```
function visit(mapFun, resultFun, array) {
  if (_.isArray(array))
    return resultFun(_.map(array, mapFun));
  else
    return resultFun(array);
}
```

The function visit takes two functions in addition to an array to process. The map Fun argument is called on each element in the array, and the resulting array is passed to resultFun for final processing. If the thing passed in array is not an array, then I just run the resultFun on it. Implementing functions like this is extremely useful in light of partial application because one or two functions can be partially applied to form a plethora of additional behaviors from `visit`. For now, just observe how `visit` is used:

```
visit(_.identity, _.isNumber, 42);
//=> true

visit(_.isNumber, _.identity, [1, 2, null, 3]);
//=> [true, true, false, true]

visit(function(n) { return n*2 }, rev, _.range(10));
//=> [18, 16, 14, 12, 10, 8, 6, 4, 2, 0]
```

Using the same principle behind `flat`, I can use `visit` to implement a mutually recursive version of `depthSearch` called `postDepth`:[7]

```
function postDepth(fun, ary) {
  return visit(partial1(postDepth, fun), fun, ary);
}
```

The reason for the name `postDepth` is that the function performs a depth-first traversal of any array performing the `mapFun` on each element *after* expanding its children. A related function, `preDepth`, performs the `mapFun` call *before* expanding an element's children and is implemented as follows:

```
function preDepth(fun, ary) {
  return visit(partial1(preDepth, fun), fun, fun(ary));
}
```

There's plenty of `fun` to go around in the case of pre-order depth-first search, but the principle is sound; just perform the function call before moving onto the other elements in the array. Let's see `postDepth` in action:

```
postDepth(_.identity, influences);
//=> [['Lisp','Smalltalk'], ['Lisp','Scheme'], ...
```

Passing the `_.identity` function to the `*Depth` functions returns a copy of the `influ ences` array. The execution scheme of the mutually recursive functions `evenSteven`, `oddJohn`, `postDepth` and `visit` is itself a graph-like model, as shown in Figure 6-6.

---

7. The `JSON.parse` method takes an optional "reviver" function and operates similarly to `postDepth`. That is, after a form is parsed, `JSON.parse` passes to the reviver the associated key with the parsed data, and whatever the reviver returns becomes the new value. People have been known to use the reviver for numerous reasons, but perhaps the most common is to generate `Date` objects from date-encoded strings.

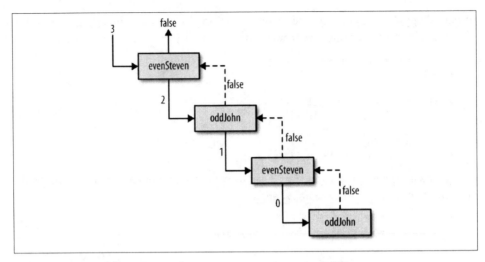

Figure 6-6. Mutually recursive functions execute in a graph-like way

What if I want to capitalize every instance of Lisp? There's a function to do that:

```
postDepth(function(x) {
  if (x === "Lisp")
    return "LISP";
  else
    return x;
}, influences);

//=> [['LISP','Smalltalk'], ['LISP','Scheme'], ...
```

So the rule is that if I want to change a node, then I do something with it and return the new value; otherwise, I just return the node. Of course, the original array is never modified:

```
influences;
//=> [['Lisp','Smalltalk'], ['Lisp','Scheme'], ...
```

What if I want to build an array of all of the languages that another language has influenced? I could perform this act as follows:

```
function influencedWithStrategy(strategy, lang, graph) {
  var results = [];

  strategy(function(x) {
    if (_.isArray(x) && _.first(x) === lang)
      results.push(second(x));

    return x;
  }, graph);
```

```
    return results;
  }
```

The function influencedWithStrategy takes one of the depth-first searching functions and walks the graph, building an array of influenced languages along the way:

```
influencedWithStrategy(postDepth, "Lisp", influences);
//=> ["Smalltalk", "Scheme"]
```

Again, while I mutated an array to build the results, the action was confined to the internals of the influencedWithStrategy function localizing its effects.

Too Much Recursion!

As I mentioned in the earlier section about tail-recursion, current JavaScript engines do not optimize recursive calls, even if they technically could. Therefore, when using or writing recursive functions, you'll occasionally run into the following error:

```
evenSteven(100000);
// Too much recursion (or some variant)
```

The problem with this error (called "blowing the stack") is that the mutual-recursive nature of evenSteven and oddJohn causes each function to be called thousands of times before either one reaches zero. Because most JavaScript *implementations* have a limit on the number of recursive calls, functions like these can "blow the stack" fairly easily (Zakas 2010).

In this section, I'll talk briefly about a control structure called a *trampoline* that helps eliminate these types of errors. The basic principle is that instead of a deeply nested recursive call, a trampoline flattens out the calls. However, before getting into that, let me explore how I could manually fix the operation of evenSteven and oddJohn to not blow the stack with recursive calls. One possible way is to return a function that wraps the call to the mutually recursive function, instead of calling it directly. I can use parti al1 as follows to achieve just that:

```
function evenOline(n) {
  if (n === 0)
    return true;
  else
    return partial1(oddOline, Math.abs(n) - 1);
}

function oddOline(n) {
  if (n === 0)
    return false;
  else
    return partial1(evenOline, Math.abs(n) - 1);
}
```

As shown, instead of calling the mutually recursive function in the body of either evenOline and oddOline, a function wrapping those calls is returned instead. Calling either function with the termination case works as you'd expect:

```
evenOline(0);
//=> true

oddOline(0);
//=> false
```

Now I can manually flatten the mutual recursion via the following:

```
oddOline(3);
//=> function () { return evenOline(Math.abs(n) - 1) }

oddOline(3)();
//=> function () { return oddOline(Math.abs(n) - 1) }

oddOline(3)()();
//=> function () { return evenOline(Math.abs(n) - 1) }

oddOline(3)()()();
//=> true

oddOline(200000001)()()(); //... a bunch more ()s
//=> true
```

I suppose you could release these functions in a user-facing API, but I suspect that your clients would be less than happy to use them. Instead, you might want to supply another function, trampoline, that performs the flattening calls programmatically:

```
function trampoline(fun /*, args */) {
  var result = fun.apply(fun, _.rest(arguments));

  while (_.isFunction(result)) {
    result = result();
  }

  return result;
}
```

All that trampoline does is repeatedly call the return value of a function until it's no longer a function. You can see it in action here:

```
trampoline(oddOline, 3);
//=> true

trampoline(evenOline, 200000);
//=> true

trampoline(oddOline, 300000);
//=> false
```

```
trampoline(evenOline, 200000000);
// wait a few seconds
//=> true
```

Because of the indirectness of the call chain, the use of a trampoline adds some overhead to mutually recursive functions. However, slow is usually better than exploding. Again, you might not want to force your users to use trampoline just to avoid stack explosions. Instead, it can be hidden entirely with a functional facade:

```
function isEvenSafe(n) {
  if (n === 0)
    return true;
  else
    return trampoline(partial1(oddOline, Math.abs(n) - 1));
}

function isOddSafe(n) {
  if (n === 0)
    return false;
  else
    return trampoline(partial1(evenOline, Math.abs(n) - 1));
}
```

And these functions are used normally:

```
isOddSafe(2000001);
//=>true

isEvenSafe(2000001);
//=> false
```

Generators

Extrapolating from the nature of a trampoline, I'll end this section by showing a couple of examples of the infinite. Using recursion, I can demonstrate how to build and process infinite streams of "lazy" data, and likewise call mutual functions until the heat death of the sun. By lazy, I only mean that portions of a structure are not calculated until needed. By contrast, consider the use of the cycle function defined earlier in this chapter:

```
_.take(cycle(20, [1,2,3]), 11);
//=> [1, 2, 3, 1, 2, 3, 1, 2, 3, 1, 2]
```

In this call, the array created by cycle is definitely not lazy, because it is fully constructed before being passed to _.take. Even though _.take only needed 11 elements from the cycled array, a full 60 elements were generated. This is quite inefficient, but alas, the default in Underscore and JavaScript itself.

However, a basic (and some would say base) way to view an array is that it consists of the first cell followed by the rest of the cells. The fact that Underscore provides a _.first and _.rest hints at this view. An infinite array can likewise be viewed as a "first" or "head," and a "rest" or "tail." However, unlike a finite array, the tail of an infinite array may or may not yet exist. Breaking out the head and tail view into an object might help to conceptualize this view (Houser 2013):

```
{head: aValue, tail: ???}
```

The question arises: what should go into the tail position of the object? The simple answer, taken from what was shown in odd0line, is that a function that calculates the tail *is* the tail. Not only is the tail a normal function, it's a recursive function.

The head/tail object requires some maintenance, and is built using two functions: (1) a function to calculate the value at the current cell, and (2) another function to calculate the "seed" value for the next cell. In fact, the type of structure built in this way is a weak form of what is known as a generator, or a function that returns each subsequent value on demand. Keeping all of this in mind, the implementation of generator is as follows:[8]

```
function generator(seed, current, step) {
  return {
    head: current(seed),
    tail: function() {
      console.log("forced");
      return generator(step(seed), current, step);
    }
  };
}
```

As shown, the current parameter is a function used to calculate the value at the head position and step is used to feed a value to the recursive call. The key point about the tail value is that it's wrapped in a function and not "realized" until called. I can implement a couple of utility functions useful for navigating a generator:

```
function genHead(gen) { return gen.head }
function genTail(gen) { return gen.tail() }
```

The genHead and genTail functions do exactly what you think—they return the head and tail. However, the tail return is "forced." Allow me to create a generator before demonstrating its use:

```
var ints = generator(0, _.identity, function(n) { return n+1 });
```

Using the generator function, I can define the full range of integers. Now, using the accessor functions, I can start plucking away at the front:

```
genHead(ints);
//=> 0

genTail(ints);
```

---

8. The call to console.log is for demonstrative purposes only.

```
// (console) forced
//=> {head: 1, tail: function}
```

The call to genHead did not force the tail of ints, but a call to genTail did, as you might have expected. Executing nested calls to genTail will likewise force the generator to a depth equal to the number of calls:

```
genTail(genTail(ints));
// (console) forced
// (console) forced
//=> {head: 2, tail: function}
```

This is not terribly exciting, but using just these two functions I can build a more powerful accessor function like genTake, which builds an array out of the first n entries in the generator:

```
function genTake(n, gen) {
  var doTake = function(x, g, ret) {
    if (x === 0)
      return ret;
    else
      return partial(doTake, x-1, genTail(g), cat(ret, genHead(g)));
  };

  return trampoline(doTake, n, gen, []);
}
```

As shown, genTake is implemented using a trampoline, simply because it makes little sense to provide a function to traverse an infinite structure that explodes with a "Too much recursion" error for an unrelated reason. Using genTake is shown here:

```
genTake(10, ints);
// (console) forced x 10
//=> [0, 1, 2, 3, 4, 5, 6, 7, 8, 9]

genTake(100, ints);
// (console) forced x 100
//=> [0, 1, 2, 3, 4, 5, 6, ..., 98, 99]

genTake(1000, ints);
// (console) forced x 1000
//=> Array[1000]

genTake(10000, ints);
// (console) forced x 10000
// wait a second
//=> Array[10000]

genTake(100000, ints);
// (console) forced x 100000
// wait a minute
//=> Array[100000]
```

```
genTake(1000000, ints);
// (console) forced x 1000000
// wait an hour
//=> Array[1000000]
```

While not necessarily the fastest puppy in the litter, it's interesting to see how the "trampoline principle" works to define structures of infinite size, without blowing the stack, and while calculating values on demand. There is one fatal flaw with generators created with generator: while the tail cells are not calculated until accessed, they are calculated *every* time they are accessed:

```
genTake(10, ints);
// (console) forced x 10
//=> [0, 1, 2, 3, 4, 5, 6, 7, 8, 9]
```

Knowing that I already called genTake to calculate the first 10 entries, it would have been nice to avoid performing the same actions again, but building a full-fledged generator is outside the scope of this book.[9]

Of course there is no free lunch, even when using trampolines. While I've managed to avoid exploding the call stack, I've just transferred the problem to the heap. Fortunately, the heap is orders of magnitude larger than the JavaScript call stack, so you're far less likely to run into a problem of memory consumption when using a trampoline.

Aside from the direct use of a trampoline, the idea of "trampolineness" is a general principle worth noting in JavaScript seen in the wild—something I'll discuss presently.

The Trampoline Principle and Callbacks

Asynchronous JavaScript APIs—like setTimeout and the XMLHttpRequest library (and those built on it like jQuery's $.ajax)—have an interesting property relevant to the discussion of recursion. You see, asynchronous libraries work off of an event loop that is non-blocking. That is, if you use an asynchronous API to schedule a function that might take a long time, then the browser or runtime will not block waiting for it to finish. Instead, each asynchronous API takes one or more "callbacks" (just functions or closures) that are invoked when the task is complete. This allows you to perform (effectively) concurrent tasks, some immediate and some long-running, without blocking the operation of your application.[10]

---

9. The ECMAScript.next activity is working through a design for generators in a future version of JavaScript. More information can be found at ECMA script's website (*http://bit.ly/10Py5VY*).

10. There are caveats here. Of course you can still block your application any number of ways, but if used correctly, the event architecture of JavaScript will help you to avoid doing so.

An interesting feature of non-blocking APIs is that calls return immediately, before any of the callbacks are ever called. Instead, those callbacks occur in the not-too-distant future:[11]

```
setTimeout(function() { console.log("hi") }, 2000);
//=> returns some value right away
// ... about 2 seconds later
// hi
```

A truly interesting aspect of the immediate return is that JavaScript cleans up the call stack on every new tick of the event loop. Because the asynchronous callbacks are always called on a new tick of the event loop, even recursive functions operate with a clean slate! Observe the following:

```
function asyncGetAny(interval, urls, onsuccess, onfailure) {
  var n = urls.length;

  var looper = function(i) {
    setTimeout(function() {
      if (i >= n) {
        onfailure("failed");
        return;
      }

      $.get(urls[i], onsuccess)
        .always(function() { console.log("try: " + urls[i]) })
        .fail(function() {
          looper(i + 1);
        });
    }, interval);
  }

  looper(0);
  return "go";
}
```

You'll notice that when the call to jQuery's asynchronous $.get function fails, a recursive call to looper is made. This call is no different (in principle) than any other mutually recursive call, except that each invocation occurs on a different event-loop tick and starts with a clean stack. For the sake of completeness, the use of asyncGetAny is as follows:[12]

```
var urls = ['http://dsfgfgs.com', 'http://sghjgsj.biz', '_.html', 'foo.txt'];

asyncGetAny(2000,
```

11. Next Sunday, A.D.

12. I'm using the jQuery promise-based interface to perform the GET and to fluently build the always and fail handlers. Because of the nature of the concurrent execution, there is no guarantee that the console printing will occur before or after the GET result. I show them in order for the sake of expediency. I'll talk a little more about jQuery promises in Chapter 8.

```
    urls,
    function(data) { alert("Got some data") },
    function(data) { console.log("all failed") });
//=> "go"

// (console after 2 seconds) try: http://dsfgfgs.com
// (console after 2 seconds) try: http://sghjgsj.biz
// (console after 2 seconds) try: _.html

// an alert box pops up with 'Got some data' (on my computer)
```

There are better resources for describing asynchronous programming in JavaScript than this book, but I thought it worth mentioning the unique properties of the event loop and recursion. While tricky in practice, using the event loop for maximum benefit can make for highly efficient JavaScript applications.

Recursion Is a Low-Level Operation

This chapter has dealt extensively with recursion, creating recursive functions, and reasoning in the face of recursion. While this information is potentially useful, I should make one caveat to the entire discussion: recursion should be seen as a low-level operation and avoided if at all possible. The better path is to take a survey of the available higher-order functions and plug them together to create new functions. For example, my implementation of influencedWithStrategy, while clever in its way, was completely unnecessary. Instead, I should have known that functions already available could be mixed to produce the desired effect. First, I can create two auxiliary functions:

```
var groupFrom = curry2(_.groupBy)(_.first);
var groupTo   = curry2(_.groupBy)(second);
```

Because I'm using a simple nested array for my graph representation, creating new functions to operate on it is as simple as reusing existing array functions. I can explore the operation of groupFrom and groupTo here:

```
groupFrom(influences);
//=> {Lisp:[["Lisp", "Smalltalk"], ["Lisp", "Scheme"]],
//    Smalltalk:[["Smalltalk", "Self"]],
//    Scheme:[["Scheme", "JavaScript"], ["Scheme", "Lua"]],
//    Self:[["Self", "Lua"], ["Self", "JavaScript"]]}

groupTo(influences);
//=> {Smalltalk:[["Lisp", "Smalltalk"]],
//    Scheme:[["Lisp", "Scheme"]],
//    Self:[["Smalltalk", "Self"]],
//    JavaScript:[["Scheme", "JavaScript"], ["Self", "JavaScript"]],
//    Lua:[["Scheme", "Lua"], ["Self", "Lua"]]}
```

These are definitely fun functions (ha!), but they're not sufficient. Instead, a function—influenced—squares the circle in implementing my desired behavior:

```
function influenced(graph, node) {
  return _.map(groupFrom(graph)[node], second);
}
```

And this is, effectively, the same as my recursive influencedWithStrategy function:

```
influencedWithStrategy(preDepth, 'Lisp', influences);
//=> ["Smalltalk", "Scheme"]

influenced(influences, 'Lisp');
//=>["Smalltalk", "Scheme"]
```

Not only does the implementation of influences require far less code, but it's also conceptually simpler. I already know what _.groupBy, _.first, second, and _.map do, so to understand the implementation of influenced is to understand only how the data transforms from one function to the other. This is a huge advantage of functional programming—pieces fitting together like Lego blocks, data flowing and transforming along a pipeline of functions to achieve the desired final data form.

This is beautiful programming.

Summary

This chapter dealt with recursion, or functions that call themselves either directly or through other functions. Self-calling functions were shown as powerful tools used to search and manipulate nested data structures. For searching, I walked through tree-walking examples (no pun intended) using the visit function, which called out to depth-first searching functions.

Although the tree searching was a powerful technique, there are fundamental limitations in JavaScript that bound the number of recursive calls that can happen. However, using a technique called trampolining, I showed how you can build functions that call one another indirectly through an array of closures.

Finally, I felt the need to take a step back and make the point that recursion should be used sparingly. Very often, recursive functions are more confusing and less direct than higher-order or composed functions. The general consensus is to use function composition first and move to recursion and trampolines only if needed.

In the next chapter, I will cover a topic often at odds with functional programming—mutation, or the act of modifying variables in place—and how to limit or even outright avoid it.

CHAPTER 7

Purity, Immutability, and Policies for Change

This chapter marks the point when a fully functional and practical style is explored. Functional programming is not just about functions; it's also a way of thinking about how to build programs to minimize the complexities inherent in the creation of software. One way of reducing the complexity is to reduce or eliminate (ideally) the footprint of state change taking place in our programs.

Purity

Imagine that you needed a function that, when given a number, returned a (pseudo) random number greater than 0 and up to and including the number itself. Underscore's `_.random` function is almost correct, but it defaults to including zero. Therefore, as a first approximation, you might write something like this:

```
var rand = partial1(_.random, 1);
```

Using `rand` is as simple as the following:

```
rand(10);
//=> 7

repeatedly(10, partial1(rand, 10));
//=> [2, 6, 6, 7, 7, 4, 4, 10, 8, 5]

_.take(repeatedly(100, partial1(rand, 10)), 5);
//=> [9, 6, 6, 4, 6]
```

You can use `rand` as the basis for a generator for random lowercase ASCII strings-with-numbers of a certain length as follows:

```
function randString(len) {
  var ascii = repeatedly(len,  partial1(rand, 26));
```

```
    return _.map(ascii, function(n) {
      return n.toString(36);
    }).join('');
  }
```

And here's the use of randString:

```
randString(0);
//=> ""

randString(1);
//=> "f"

randString(10);
//=> "k52k7bae8p"
```

Building the randString function is just like what I've shown throughout the course of this book. Plugging functions into functions to build higher-level capabilities has been what I've been building up to all this time, right? While randString technically fits this definition, there is one big difference in the way that randString is constructed from the way that the previous functions were. Can you see it? The answer lies in another question. Can you test it?

The Relationship Between Purity and Testing

How would you test the function randString? That is, if you were using something like Jasmine[1] to build a spec for the randString function, how would you complete the following code fragment?

```
describe("randString", function() {
  it("builds a string of lowercase ASCII letters/digits", function() {
    expect(randString()).to???(???);
  });
});
```

What validation function and value could you put into the parts labeled ??? to make the specification pass? You could try to add a given string, but that would be a waste of time, given that the whole point is to generate randomness. It may start to be clear now that the problem with randString is that there is no way to predict what the result of a call will be. This condition is very different from a function like _.map, where every call is determinable from the arguments presented to it:

```
describe("_.map", function() {
  it("should return an array made from...", function(){
    expect(.map([1,2,3], sqr)).toEqual([1, 4, 9]);
```

---

1. Jasmine (*http://pivotal.github.com/jasmine/*) is a lovely test framework that I personally use and highly recommend.

```
        });
    });
    {
        expect(_.map([1,2,3], sqr)).toEqual([1, 4, 9]);
    });
});
```

The operation of _.map as just described is know as "pure." A pure function adheres to the following properties:

- Its result is calculated only from the values of its arguments.
- It cannot rely on data that changes external to its control.
- It cannot change the state of something external to its body.

In the case of randString, the first rule of purity is violated because it doesn't take any arguments to use in a calculation. The second rule is violated because its result is entirely based on JavaScript's random number generator, which is a black-box taking no input arguments and producing opaque values. This particular problem is a problem at the language level and not at the level of generating randomness. That is, you could create a random number generator that was pure by allowing the caller to supply a "seed" value.

Another example of a function that breaks rule #1 is as follows:

```
PI = 3.14;

function areaOfACircle(radius) {
    return PI * sqr(radius);
}

areaOfACircle(3);
//=> 28.26
```

You probably already see where the problem lies, but for the sake of completeness, assume that within a web page, another library is loaded with the following code fragment:

```
// ... some code

PI = "Magnum";

// ... more code
```

What is the result of calling areaOfACircle? Observe:

```
areaOfACircle(3);
//=> NaN
```

Whoops!

This kind of problem is especially nasty in JavaScript because of its ability to load arbitrary code at runtime that can easily change objects and variables. Therefore, to write functions that rely on data outside of its control is a recipe for confusion. Typically, when you attempt to test functions that rely on the vagaries of external conditions, all test cases *must* set up those same conditions for the very purpose of testing. Observing a functional style that adheres to a standard of purity wherever possible will not only help to make your programs easier to test, but also easier to reason about in general.

Separating the Pure from the Impure

Because JavaScript's `Math.rand` method is impure by design, any function that uses it is likewise impure and likely more difficult to test. Pure functions are tested by building a table of input values and output expectations. Other methods and functions within JavaScript that infect code with impurity are `Date.now`, `console.log`, `this`, and use of global variables (this is not a comprehensive list). In fact, because JavaScript passes object references around, every function that takes an object or array is potentially subject to impurity. I'll talk later in this section about how to alleviate these kinds of problems, but the gist of this is that while JavaScript can never be completely pure (nor would we want that), the effects of change can be minimized.

While the `randString` function is undoubtedly impure as written, there are ways to restructure the code to separate the pure from the impure parts. In the case of `rand String`, the delineation is fairly clear: there is a character generation part, and a part that joins the characters together. To separate the pure from the impure, then, is as simple as creating two functions:

```
function generateRandomCharacter() {
  return rand(26).toString(36);
}

function generateString(charGen, len) {
  return repeatedly(len, charGen).join('');
}
```

Changing the implementation to `generateString` (which explicitly takes a function intended for character generation) allows the following patterns of usage:

```
generateString(generateRandomCharacter, 20);
//=> "2lfhjo45n2nfnpbf7m7e"
```

Additionally, because `generateString` is a higher-order function, I can use `partial` to compose the original, impure version of `randomString`:

```
var composedRandomString = partial1(generateString, generateRandomCharacter);

composedRandomString(10);
//=> "j18obij1jc"
```

Now that the pure part is encapsulated within its own function, it can be tested independently:

```
describe("generateString", function() {
  var result = generateString(always("a"), 10);

  it("should return a string of a specific length", function() {
    expect(result.constructor).toBe(String);
    expect(result.length).toBe(10);
  });

  it("should return a string congruent with its char generator", function() {
    expect(result).toEqual("aaaaaaaaaa");
  });
});
```

There's still a problem testing the validity of the impure generateRandomCharacter function, but it's nice to have a handle on a generic, easily testable capability like gener ateString.

Property-Testing Impure Functions

If a function is impure, and its return value is subject to conditions outside of its control, then how can it be tested? Assuming that you've managed to reduce the impure part to its bare minimum, like with generateRandomCharacter, then the matter of testing is somewhat easier. While you cannot test the return value for specific values, you can test it for certain characteristics. In the example of generateRandomCharacter, I could test for the following characteristics:

- ASCII-ness
- Digit-ness
- String-ness
- Character-ness
- Lowercase-ness

To check each of these characteristics requires a lot of data, however:

```
describe("generateRandomCharacter", function() {
  var result = repeatedly(10000, generateRandomCharacter);

  it("should return only strings of length 1", function() {
    expect(_.every(result, _.isString)).toBeTruthy();
    expect(_.every(result, function(s) { return s.length === 1 })).toBeTruthy();
  });

  it("should return a string of only lowercase ASCII letters or digits", function()
  {
    expect(_.every(result, function(s) {
      return /[a-z0-9]/.test(s) })).toBeTruthy();
```

```
      expect(_.any(result, function(s) { return /[A-Z]/.test(s) })).toBeFalsy();
    });
  });
```

Testing the characteristics of only 10000 results of calls to generateRandomCharacter is not enough for full test coverage. You can increase the number of iterations, but you'll never be fully satisfied. Likewise, it would be nice to know that the characters generated fall within certain bounds. In fact, there is a limitation in my implementation that restricts it from generating every possible legal lowercase ASCII character, so what have I been testing? I've been testing the incorrect solution. Solving the problem of creating the wrong thing is a philosophical affair, far outside the depth of this book. For the purposes of random password generation this might be a problem, but for the purposes of demonstrating the separation and testing of impure pieces of code, my implementation should suffice.

Purity and the Relationship to Referential Transparency

Programming with pure functions may seem incredibly limiting. JavaScript, as a highly dynamic language, allows the definition and use of functions without a strict adherence to the types of their arguments or return value. Sometimes this loose adherence proves problematic (e.g., true + 1 === 2), but other times you know exactly what you're doing and can take advantage of the flexibility. Very often, however, JavaScript programmers equate the ability of JavaScript to allow free-form mutation of variables, objects, and array slots as essential to dynamism. However, when you exercise a libertarian view of state mutation, you're actually limiting your possibilities in composition, complicating your ability to reason through the effects of any given statement, and making it more difficult to test your code.

Using pure functions, on the other hand, allows for the easy composition of functions and makes replacing any given function in your code with an equivalent function, or even the expected value, trivial. Take, for example, the use of the nth function to define a second function from Chapter 1:

```
function second(a) {
  return nth(a, 1);
}
```

The nth function is a pure function. That is, it will adhere to the following for any given array argument. First, it will always return the same value given some array value and index value:

```
nth(['a', 'b', 'c'], 1);
//=> 'b'

nth(['a', 'b', 'c'], 1);
// 'b'
```

You could run this call a billion times and as long as nth receives the array ['a', 'b', 'c'] and the number 1, it will always return the string 'b', regardless of the state of anything else in the program. Likewise, the nth function will never modify the array given to it:

```
var a = ['a', 'b', 'c'];

nth(a, 1);
//=> 'b'

a === a;
//=> true

nth(a, 1);
//=> 'b'

_.isEqual(a, ['a', 'b', 'c']);
//=> true
```

The one limiting factor, and it's one that we've got to live with in JavaScript, is that the nth function might return something that's impure, such as an object, an array, or even an impure function:

```
nth([{a: 1}, {b: 2}], 0);
//=> {a: 1}

nth([function() { console.log('blah') }], 0);
//=> function ...
```

The only way to rectify this problem is to observe a strict adherence to the use and definition of pure functions that do not modify their arguments, nor depend on external values, except where such effects have been minimized explicitly. Realizing that some discipline is required to maintain functional purity, we will be rewarded with programming options. In the case of second, I can replace the definition of nth with something equivalent and not miss a beat:[2]

```
function second(a) {
  return a[1];
}
```

Or maybe:

```
function second(a) {
  return _.first(_.rest(a));
}
```

2. That's not exactly true because nth checks array bounds and throws an error when an index exceeds the array's length. When changing underlying implementations, be aware of the tangential effects of the change in addition to gains in raw speed.

In either of these cases, the behavior of second has not changed. Because nth was a pure function, its replacement in this case was trivial. In fact, because the nth function is pure, it could conceivably be replaced with the value of its result for a given array and still maintain program consistency:

```
function second() {
  return 'b';
}

second(['a', 'b', 'c'], 1);
//=> 'b'
```

The ability to freely swap new functions without the confusion brought on by the balancing act of mutation is a different way to look at freedom in program composition. A related topic to purity and referential transparency is the idea of idempotence, explained next.

Purity and the Relationship to Idempotence

With the growing prevalence of APIs and architectures following a RESTful style, the idea of idempotence has recently thrust itself into the common consciousness. Idempotence is the idea that executing an activity numerous times has the same effect as executing it once. Idempotence in functional programming is related to purity, but different enough to bear mention. Formally, a function that is idempotent should make the following condition true:

```
someFun(arg) == _.compose(someFun, someFun)(arg);
```

In other words, running a function with some argument should be the same as running that same function twice in a row with the same argument as in someFun(some Fun(arg)). Looking back on the second function, you can probably guess that it's not idempotent:

```
var a = [1, [10, 20, 30], 3];

var secondTwice = _.compose(second, second);

second(a) === secondTwice(a);
//=> false
```

The problem, of course, is that the bare call to second returns the array [10, 20, 30], and the call to secondTwice returns the nested value 20. The most straightforward idempotent function is probably Underscore's _.identity function:

```
var dissociativeIdentity = _.compose(_.identity, _.identity);

_.identity(42) === dissociativeIdentity(42);
//=> true
```

JavaScript's Math.abs method is also idempotent:

```
Math.abs(Math.abs(-42));
//=> 42
```

You need not sacrifice dynamism by adhering to a policy of pure functions. However, bear in mind that any time that you explicitly change a variable, be it encapsulated in a closure, directly or even in a container object (later this chapter), you introduce a time-sensitive state. That is, at any given tick of the program execution, the total state of the program is dependent on the subtle change interactions occurring. While you may not be able to eliminate all state change in your programs, it's a good idea to reduce it as much as possible. I'll get into isolated change later in this chapter, but first, related to functional purity is the idea of immutability, or the lack of explicit state change, which I'll cover next.

Immutability

Very few data types in JavaScript are immutable by default. Strings are one example of a data type that cannot be changed:

```
var s = "Lemongrab";

s.toUpperCase();
//=> "LEMONGRAB"

s;
//=> "Lemongrab"
```

It's a good thing that strings are immutable because scenarios like the following might occur, wreaking mass confusion:[3]

```
var key = "lemongrab";
var obj = {lemongrab: "Earl"};

obj[key] === "Earl";
//=> true

doSomethingThatMutatesStrings(key);

obj[key];
//=> undefined

obj["lemonjon"];
//=> "Earl"
```

This would be an unfortunate sequence of events. You'd likely find the problem with some digging, but if there was a widespread culture of string mutating, then these kinds

---

3. The Ruby programming language allows string mutation, and prior to version 1.9 fell victim to this kind of trap. However, Ruby 1.9 Hash objects copy string keys and are therefore shielded. Unfortunately, it still allows mutable objects as keys, so mutating those can and will break Hash lookups.

of problems would pop up far more frequently than you'd like. Thankfully, that strings in JavaScript are immutable eliminates a whole class of nasty problems. However, the following mutation *is* allowed in JavaScript:[4]

```
var obj = {lemongrab: "Earl"};

(function(o) {
  _.extend(o, {lemongrab: "King"});
})(obj);

obj;
//=> {lemongrab: "King"}
```

While we're happy that strings are immutable, we tend not to blink an eye over the fact that JavaScript objects are mutable. In fact, much of JavaScript has been built to take advantage of mutability. However, as JavaScript gains more acceptability in industry, larger and larger programs will be written using it. Imagine a depiction of the dependencies created by points of mutation within a very small program as shown in Figure 7-1.

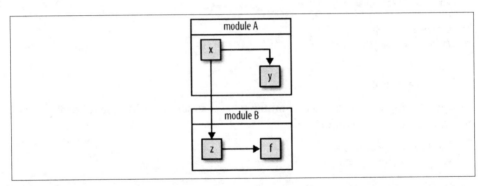

Figure 7-1. Even in small programs, the "web of mutation" is tangled, but it may be manageable

However, as the program grows, the "web of mutation" likewise grows, gaining more and more edges from one change dependency to the next, as shown in Figure 7-2.

---

4. Underscore's extend function fooled me once, but really it was my own prejudices that allowed me to assume that it was a pure function. Once I learned that it was not, I realized a fun way to take advantage of that fact, as you'll see in Chapter 9.

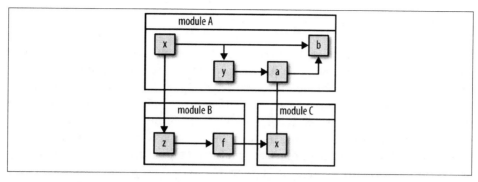

Figure 7-2. As programs grow, so grows the "web of mutation"

This state of affairs cannot be easily maintained. If every change affecting the web of mutation causes widespread disturbances in the delicate relationships between the states and their dependents, then *any* change affects the whole.[5] In functional programming, the ideal situation is that there is *never* mutation, and if you start with a policy of immutability, you'd be surprised how far you can get. In this section, I'll discuss the virtues of immutability and how to observe its dictum.

If a Tree Falls in the Woods, Does It Make a Sound?

Throughout this book, you'll notice that I've often used mutable arrays and objects within the implementations of many functions. To illustrate what I mean, observe the implementation of a function, skipTake, that when given a number n and an array, returns an array containing every nth element:

```
function skipTake(n, coll) {
  var ret = [];
  var sz = _.size(coll);

  for(var index = 0; index < sz; index += n) {
    ret.push(coll[index]);
  }

  return ret;
}
```

The use of skipTake is as follows:

```
skipTake(2, [1,2,3,4]);
//=> [1, 3]
```

5. That's not to say that all JavaScript programs work that way. In the past few years, there has been a growing focus on discipline in design. One article of particular note along this theme is "Don't Modify Objects You Don't Own" (Zakas 2010).

```
    skipTake(3, _.range(20));
    //=> [0, 3, 6, 9, 12, 15, 18]
```

Within the implementation of skipTake, I very deliberately used an array coupled with an imperative loop performing an Array#push. There are ways to implement skip Take using functional techniques, therefore requiring no explicit mutation. However, the for loop implementation is small, straightforward, and fast. More importantly, the use of this imperative approach is completely hidden from the users of the skipTake function. The advantage of viewing the function as the basic unit of abstraction is that within the confines of any given function, implementation details are irrelevant as long as they do not "leak out." By "leak out" I mean that you can use a function as a boundary for local state mutation, shielding change from the sight of external code.

Whether I used _.foldRight or while within skipTake is irrelevant to the users of the function. All that they know, or care about, is that they will get a new array in return and that the array that they passed in will not be molested.

> If a tree falls in the woods, does it make a sound?
>
> If a pure function mutates some local data in order to produce an immutable return value, is that ok?
>
> —Rich Hickey at *http://clojure.org/tran sients*

As it turns out, the answer is yes.[6]

Immutability and the Relationship to Recursion

If you've read as many books on functional programming as me (or even two), then an interesting pattern emerges. In almost every case, the topic of recursion and recursive techniques is covered. There are many reasons why this is the case, but one important reason relates to purity. In many functional programming languages, you cannot write a function like summ using local mutation:

```
function summ(array) {
  var result = 0;
  var sz = array.length;

  for (var i = 0; i < sz; i++)
    result += array[i];

  return result;
}
```

6. The function is a convenient boundary for hiding mutation, but its not the only one. As I'll show in Chapter 8, there are larger boundaries available to hide mutation. Historically, objects have served as nice boundaries to hide mutations, and even whole libraries and systems have been written to leverage the inherent speed of mutation while still presenting a nicely functional public facade.

```
summ(_.range(1,11));
//=> 55
```

The problem is that the function summ mutates two local variables: i and result. However, in traditional functional languages, local variables are not actually variables at all, but are instead immutable and cannot change. The only way to modify the value of a local is to change it via the call stack, and this is exactly what recursion does. Below is a recursive implementation of the same function:

```
function summRec(array, seed) {
  if (_.isEmpty(array))
    return seed;
  else
    return summRec(_.rest(array), _.first(array) + seed);
}

summRec([], 0);
//=> 0

summRec(_.range(1,11), 0);
//=> 55
```

When using recursion, state is managed via the function arguments, and change is modeled via the arguments from one recursive call to the next.[7] JavaScript allows this kind of recursive state management, with recursion depth limits as mentioned in Chapter 6, but it also allows for the mutation of local variables. So why not use the one that's faster all the time? As I'll discuss in the next section, there are also caveats to mutating local state.

Defensive Freezing and Cloning

Because JavaScript passes arrays and objects by reference, nothing is truly immutable. Likewise, because JavaScript object fields are always visible, there is no easy way to make them immutable (Goetz 2005). There are ways to hide data using encapsulation to avoid accidental change, but at the topmost level, all JavaScript objects are mutable, unless they are frozen.

Recent versions of JavaScript provide a method, Object#freeze, that when given an object or array, will cause all subsequent mutations to fail. In the case where strict mode is used, the failure will throw a TypeError; otherwise, any mutations will silently fail. The freeze method works as follows:

```
var a = [1, 2, 3];

a[1] = 42;
```

---

7. In other words, the state change in a recursive function is modeled in the stack much like I used a stack to change dynamic values way back in Chapter 3.

```
a;
//=> [1, 42, 3]

Object.freeze(a);
```

A normal array is mutable by default, but after the call to `Object#freeze`, the following occurs:

```
a[1] = 108;

a;
//=> [1, 42, 3]
```

That is, mutations will no longer take effect. You can also use the `Object#isFrozen` method to check if a is indeed frozen:

```
Object.isFrozen(a);
//=> true
```

There are two problems with using `Object#freeze` to ensure immutability:

- Unless you have complete control over the codebase, it might cause subtle (and not so subtle) errors to occur.
- The `Object#freeze` method is shallow.

Regarding the willy-nilly freezing of objects, while it might be a good idea to practice pervasive immutability, not all libraries will agree. Therefore, freezing objects and passing them around to random APIs might cause trouble. However, the deeper (ha!) problem is that `Object#freeze` is a shallow operation. That is, a freeze will only happen at the topmost level and will not traverse nested objects. Observe:

```
var x = [{a: [1, 2, 3], b: 42}, {c: {d: []}}];

Object.freeze(x);

x[0] = "";

x;
//=> [{a: [1, 2, 3], b: 42}, {c: {d: []}}];
```

As shown, attempting to mutate the array a fails to make a modification. However, mutating within a's nested structures indeed makes a change:

```
x[1]['c']['d'] = 100000;

x;
//=> [{a: [1, 2, 3], b: 42}, {c: {d: 100000}}];
```

To perform a deep freeze on an object, I'll need to use recursion to walk the data structure, much like deepClone in Chapter 6:

```
function deepFreeze(obj) {
  if (!Object.isFrozen(obj))
    Object.freeze(obj);

  for (var key in obj) {
    if (!obj.hasOwnProperty(key) || !_.isObject(obj[key]))
      continue;

    deepFreeze(obj[key]);
  }
}
```

The deepFreeze function then does what you might expect:

```
var x = [{a: [1, 2, 3], b: 42}, {c: {d: []}}];

deepFreeze(x);

x[0] = null;

x;
//=> [{a: [1, 2, 3], b: 42}, {c: {d: []}}];

x[1]['c']['d'] = 42;

x;
//=> [{a: [1, 2, 3], b: 42}, {c: {d: []}}];
```

However, as I mentioned before, freezing arbitrary objects might introduce subtle bugs when interacting with third-party APIs. Your options are therefore limited to the following:

- Use _.clone if you know that a shallow copy is appropriate
- Use deepClone to make copies of structures
- Build your code on pure functions

Throughout this book, I've chosen the third option, but as you'll see in Chapter 8, I'll need to resort to using deepClone to ensure functional purity. For now, let's explore the idea of preserving immutability for the sake of purity in functional and object-centric APIs.

Observing Immutability at the Function Level

With some discipline and adherence to the following techniques, you can create immutable objects and pure functions.

Many of the functions implemented in this book, and indeed in Underscore, share a common characteristic: they take some collection and build another collection from it. Consider, for example, a function, freq, that takes an array of numbers or strings and returns an object of its elements keyed to the number of times they occur, implemented here:

```
var freq = curry2(_.countBy)(_.identity);
```

Because I know that the function _.countBy is a nondestructive operation (i.e., doesn't mutate the input array), then the composition of it and _.identity should form a pure function. Observe:

```
var a = repeatedly(1000, partial1(rand, 3));
var copy = _.clone(a);

freq(a);
//=> {1: 498, 2: 502}
```

Counting the frequencies of what is effectively a coin toss verifies that the result is almost a 50/50 split. Equally interesting is that the operation of freq did not harm the original array a:

```
_.isEqual(a, copy);
//=>true
```

Observing a policy of purity in function implementation helps to eliminate the worry of what happens when two or more functions are composed to form new behaviors. If you compose pure functions, what comes out are pure functions.

Because my implementation of skipTake was also pure, even though it used mutable structures internally, it too can be composed safely:

```
freq(skipTake(2, a));
//=> {1: 236, 2: 264}

_.isEqual(a, copy);
//=> true
```

Sometimes, however, there are functions that do not want to cooperate with a plan of purity and instead change the contents of objects with impunity. For example, the _.extend function merges some number of objects from left to right, resulting in a single object, as follows:

```
var person = {fname: "Simon"};

_.extend(person, {lname: "Petrikov"}, {age: 28}, {age: 108});
//=> {age: 108, fname: "Simon", lname: "Petrikov"}
```

The problem of course is that _.extend mutates the first object in its argument list:

```
person;
//=> {age: 108, fname: "Simon", lname: "Petrikov"}
```

So _.extend is off the list of functions useful for composition, right? Well, no. The beauty of functional programming is that with a little bit of tweaking you can create new abstractions. That is, rather than using object "extension," perhaps object "merging" would be more appropriate:

```
function merge(/*args*/) {
   return _.extend.apply(null, construct({}, arguments));
}
```

Instead of using the first argument as the target object, I instead stick a local empty object into the front of `_.extend`'s arguments and mutate that instead. The results are quite different, but probably as you'd expect:

```
var person = {fname: "Simon"};

merge(person, {lname: "Petrikov"}, {age: 28}, {age: 108})
//=> {age: 108, fname: "Simon", lname: "Petrikov"}

person;
//=> {fname: "Simon"};
```

Now the merge function can be composed with other pure functions perfectly safely— from hiding mutability you can achieve purity. From the caller's perspective, nothing was ever changed.

Observing Immutability in Objects

For JavaScript's built-in types and objects there is very little that you can do to foster pervasive immutability except pervasive freezing—or rabid discipline. Indeed, with your own JavaScript objects, the story of discipline becomes more compelling. To demonstrate, I'll define a fragment of a `Point` object with its constructor defined as follows:

```
function Point(x, y) {
   this._x = x;
   this._y = y;
}
```

I could probably resort to all kinds of closure encapsulation tricks[8] to hide the fact that `Point` instances do not have publicly accessible fields. However, I prefer a more simplistic approach to defining object constructors with the "private" fields marked in a special way (Bolin 2010).

---

8. I use this technique in Chapter 8 to implement `createPerson`.

As I'll soon show, an API will be provided for manipulating points that will not expose such implementation details. However, for now, I'll implement two "change" methods, withX and withY, but I'll do so in a way that adheres to a policy of immutability:[9]

```
Point.prototype = {
  withX: function(val) {
    return new Point(val, this._y);
  },
  withY: function(val) {
    return new Point(this._x, val);
  }
};
```

On Point's prototype, I'm adding the two methods used as "modifiers," except in both cases nothing is modified. Instead, both withX and withY return fresh instances of Point with the relevant field set. Here's the withX method in action:

```
var p = new Point(0, 1);

p.withX(1000);
//=> {_x: 1000, _y: 1}
```

Calling withX in this example returns an instance of the Point object with the _x field set to 1000, but has anything been changed? No:

```
p;
//=> {_x: 0, _y: 1}
```

As shown, the original p instance is the same old [0,1] point that was originally constructed. In fact, immutable objects by design should take their values at construction time and never change again afterward. Additionally, all operations on immutable objects should return new instances. This scheme alleviates the problem of mutation, and as a side effect, allows a nice chaining API for free:

```
(new Point(0, 1))
  .withX(100)
  .withY(-100);

//=> {_x: 100, _y: -100}
```

So the points to take away are as follows:

- Immutable objects should get their values at construction time and never again change

---

9. Note that I excluded a constructor property, a la Point.prototype = {constructor: Point, ...}. While not strictly required for this example, it's probably best to adhere to a semblence of best pratice in production code.

- Operations on immutable objects return fresh objects[10]

Even when observing these two rules you can run into problems. Consider, for example, the implementation of a Queue type that takes an array of elements at construction time and provides (partial) queuing logic to access them:[11]

```
function Queue(elems) {
  this._q = elems;
}

Queue.prototype = {
  enqueue: function(thing) {
    return new Queue(cat(this._q, [thing]));
  }
};
```

As with Point, the Queue object takes its seed values at the time of construction. Additionally, Queue provides an enqueue method that is used to add the elements used as the seed to a new instance. The use of Queue is as follows:

```
var seed = [1, 2, 3];

var q = new Queue(seed);

q;
//=> {_q: [1, 2, 3]}
```

At the time of construction, the q instance receives an array of three elements as its seed data. Calling the enqueue method returns a new instance as you might expect:

```
var q2 = q.enqueue(108);
//=> {_q: [1, 2, 3, 108]}
```

And in fact, the value of q seems correct:

```
q;
//=> {_q: [1, 2, 3]}
```

However, all is not sunny in Philadelphia:

```
seed.push(10000);

q;
//=> {_q: [1, 2, 3, 1000]}
```

Whoops!

---

10. There are ways to create immutable objects that share elements from one instance to another to avoid copying larger structures entirely. However, this approach is outside the scope of this book.

11. Again, I intentionally excluded setting the constructor to avoid cluttering the example.

That's right, mutating the original seed changes the Queue instance that it seeded on construction. The problem is that I used the reference directly at the time of construction instead of creating a defensive clone. This time I'll implement a new object SaferQueue that will avoid this pitfall:

```
var SaferQueue = function(elems) {
  this._q = _.clone(elems);
}
```

A deepClone is probably not necessary because the purpose of the Queue instance is to provide a policy for element adding and removal rather than a data structure. However, it's still best to maintain immutability at the level of the elements set, which the new enqueue method does:

```
SaferQueue.prototype = {
  enqueue: function(thing) {
    return new SaferQueue(cat(this._q, [thing]));
  }
};
```

Using the immutability-safe cat function will eliminate a problem of sharing references between one SaferQueue instance and another:

```
var seed = [1,2,3];
var q = new SaferQueue(seed);

var q2 = q.enqueue(36);
//=> {_q: [1, 2, 3, 36]}

seed.push(1000);

q;
//=> {_q: [1, 2, 3]}
```

I don't want to lie and say that everything is safe. As mentioned before, the q instance has a public field _q that I could easily modify directly:

```
q._q.push(-1111);

q;
//=> {_q: [1, 2, 3, -1111]}
```

Likewise, I could easily replace the methods on SaferQueue.prototype to do whatever I want:

```
SaferQueue.prototype.enqueue = sqr;

q2.enqueue(42);
//=> 1764
```

Alas, JavaScript will only provide so much safety, and the burden is therefore on us to adhere to certain strictures to ensure that our programming practices are as safe as possible.[12]

Objects Are Often a Low-Level Operation

One final point before moving on to controlled mutation is that while the use of bare new and object methods is allowed, there are problems that could crop up because of them:

```
var q = SaferQueue([1,2,3]);

q.enqueue(32);
// TypeError: Cannot call method 'enqueue' of undefined
```

Whoops. I forgot the new. While there are ways to avoid this kind of problem and either allow or disallow the use of new to construct objects, I find those solutions more boilerplate than helpful. Instead, I prefer to use constructor functions, like the following:

```
function queue() {
  return new SaferQueue(_.toArray(arguments));
}
```

Therefore, whenever I need a queue I can just use the construction function:

```
var q = queue(1,2,3);
```

Further, I can use the invoker function to create a function to delegate to enqueue:

```
var enqueue = invoker('enqueue', SaferQueue.prototype.enqueue);

enqueue(q, 42);
//=> {_q: [1, 2, 3, 42]}
```

Using functions rather than bare method calls gives me a lot of flexibility including, but not limited to, the following:

- I do not need to worry as much about the actual types.
- I can return types appropriate for certain use cases. For example, small arrays are quite fast at modeling small maps, but as maps grow, an object may be more appropriate. This change-over can occur transparently based on programmatic use.
- If the type or methods change, then I need only to change the functions and not every point of use.
- I can add pre- and postconditions on the functions if I choose.

---

12. There are a growing number of JavaScript.next languages that were created because of the inconsistencies and reliance on convention with JavaScript.

- The functions are composable.

Using functions in this way is not a dismissal of object-programming (in fact, it's complementary). Instead, it pushes the fact that you're dealing with objects at all into the realm of implementation detail. This allows you and your users to work in functional abstractions and allows implementers to focus on the matter of making changes to the underlying machinery without breaking existing code.

Policies for Controlling Change

Let's be realistic. While it's wonderful if you can eliminate all unnecessary mutations and side effects in your code, there will come a time when you'll absolutely need to change some state. My goal is to help you think about ways to reduce the footprint of such changes. For example, imagine a small program represented as a dependency graph between the places where an object is created and subsequently mutated over the course of the program's lifetime.

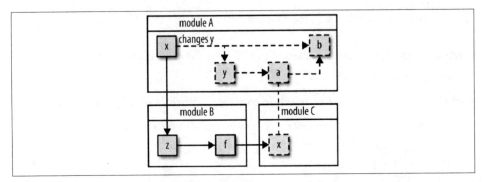

Figure 7-3. A web of mutation makes any change potentially global in its effects

Figure 7-3 should look familiar, since I talked about it earlier in this chapter. When you pass around mutable objects and modify them within one function to another method to a global scope, you've effectively lifted the effect of any change relevant to your changed object to affecting the program as a whole. What happens if you add a function that expects a certain value? What happens if you remove a method that makes a subtle mutation? What happens if you introduce concurrency via JavaScript's asynchronous operations? All of these factors work to subvert your ability to make changes in the future. However, what would it be like if change occurred only at a single point, as shown in Figure 7-4?

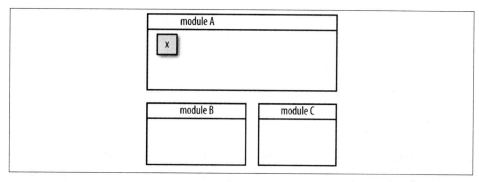

Figure 7-4. If you absolutely need to manage state, then the ideal situation is to isolate it within a single place

This is a section about isolating change to single points of mutation and strategies for achieving a compromise between the need to maintain state and to reduce complexity. The way to control the scope of change is to isolate the thing that changes. That is, rather than taking a random object and changing it in-place, a better strategy might be to hold the object in a container and change that instead. That is:

```
var container = contain({name: "Lemonjon"});

container.set({name: "Lemongrab"});
```

versus:

```
var being = {name: "Lemonjon"};

being.name = "Lemongrab";
```

While this simplistic level of indirection allows you to more easily find the place where a given value changes, it really doesn't gain much over the in-place mutation scheme. But I can take this line of thinking one step further and restrict change to occur as the result of a function call:

```
var container = contain({name: "Lemonjon"});

container.update(merge, {name: "Lemongrab"});
```

The idea behind this thinking is two-fold. First, rather than replacing the value directly, as with the fictional `container#set` method, change now occurs as the result of a function call given the current value of the container and some number of arguments. Second, by adding this functional level of indirection, change can occur based on any conceivable function, even those with domain-specific constraint checkers attached. By contrast, consider how difficult it would be to check value constraints when objects are mutated in-place, potentially at various points within your programs.

I can now show a very simple implementation of a container type:

```
function Container(init) {
  this._value = init;
};
```

Using this `Container` type is as follows:

```
var aNumber = new Container(42);

aNumber;
//=> {_value: 42}
```

However, there's more left to implement, namely the update method:

```
Container.prototype = {
  update: function(fun /*, args */) {
    var args = _.rest(arguments);
    var oldValue = this._value;

    this._value = fun.apply(this, construct(oldValue, args));

    return this._value;
  }
};
```

The thinking behind the `Container#update` method is simple: take a function and some arguments and set the new value based on a call with the existing (i.e., "old") value. Observe how this operates:

```
var aNumber = new Container(42);

aNumber.update(function(n) { return n + 1 });
//=> 43

aNumber;
//=> {_value: 43}
```

And an example that takes multiple arguments:

```
aNumber.update(function(n, x, y, z) { return n / x / y / z }, 1, 2, 3);
//=> 7.166666666666667
```

And an example showing the use of a constrained function:

```
aNumber.update(_.compose(megaCheckedSqr, always(0)));
// Error: arg must not be zero
```

This is just the beginning. In fact, in Chapter 9 I'll extend the implementation of Container using the idea of "protocol-based extension." However, for now, the seeds for reducing the footprint of mutation have been sown.

Summary

The chapter started by outlining and diving into functional purity, summarized as a function that does not change, return, or rely on any variable outside of its own control. While I spent a lot of time talking about functions that make no changes to their arguments, I did mention that if you need to mutate a variable internally then that was OK. As long as no one knows you've mutated a variable then does it matter? I'd say no.

The next part of the chapter talked about the related topic of immutability. Immutable data is often thwarted by JavaScript because changeable variables are the default. However, by observing certain change patterns in your program, you can get as close to immutable as possible. Again, what your callers don't know won't hurt them. Observing immutability and purity was shown to help you not only reason about your program at large, but also at the level of the unit test. If you can reason clearly about a function in isolation, then you can more easily reason about composed functions.

In the next chapter, I will cover the notion of functional "pipeline." This is very related to function composition with `_.compose`, but diving deeper into the abstraction and safety possibilities is worth devoting a chapter.

CHAPTER 8

Flow-Based Programming

This chapter continues the discussion of functional style by showing how functions, together with purity and isolated change, can compose to offer a fairly fluent programming style. The idea of snapping functional blocks together will be discussed herein and demonstrated with relevant examples.

Chaining

If you recall, in the implementation of `condition1` from Chapter 5, I resorted to using the following lines of code:

```
// ...
    var errors = mapcat(function(isValid) {
      return isValid(arg) ? [] : [isValid.message];
    }, validators);
// ...
```

The reason for this bit of trickery was that while the final result needed to be an array of error strings, each intermediate step could be either an array of suberror messages or nothing at all. Another reason was that I wanted to combine disparate behaviors, each with different return types. It would be much easier to compose these behaviors if the return value of one was of a form agreeable to the input arguments to the other. Take, for example, the following code:

```
function createPerson() {
  var firstName = "";
  var lastName = "";
  var age = 0;

  return {
    setFirstName: function(fn) {
      firstName = fn;
      return this;
    },
```

```
    setLastName: function(ln) {
      lastName = ln;
      return this;
    },
    setAge: function(a) {
      age = a;
      return this;
    },
    toString: function() {
      return [firstName, lastName, age].join(' ');
    }
  };
}

createPerson()
  .setFirstName("Mike")
  .setLastName("Fogus")
  .setAge(108)
  .toString();

//=> "Mike Fogus 108"
```

The "magic" that allows method chains is that each method in the chain returns the same host object reference (Stefanov 2010). The chaining of methods via common return value is effectively a design pattern in JavaScript finding its way into jQuery and even Underscore. In fact, three useful functions in Underscore are _.tap, _.chain, and _.value. If you recall from Chapter 2, I used these functions to implement the lyric Segment function used to build a "99 bottles" song generator. However, in that implementation I glossed over just how these functions operate.

The _.chain function is the most hardcore of the three, allowing you to specify an object as an implicit target to repeated Underscore functions pretending to be methods. A simple example works best to start understanding _.chain:

```
_.chain(library)
  .pluck('title')
  .sort();

//=> _
```

Um. What?[1]

Thankfully, there is a good explanation for why the Underscore object was returned. You see, the _.chain function takes some object and wraps it in another object that contains modified versions of all of Underscore's functions. That is, where a function like _.pluck has a call signature like function pluck(array, propertyName) by

---

1. If you're using a minified version of Underscore, you might actually see a differently named object here. That is only the result of renaming by the chosen minification tool.

default, the modified version found in the wrapper object used by _.chain looks like function pluck(propertyName). Underscore uses a lot of interesting trickery to allow this to happen, but the result is that what passes from one wrapper method call to the next is the wrapper object and *not* the target object itself. Therefore, whenever you want to end the call to _.chain and extract the final value, the _.value function is used:

```
_.chain(library)
 .pluck('title')
 .sort()
 .value();

//=> ["Joy of Clojure", "SICP", "SICP"]
```

With the use of _.result, you take a value from the world of the wrapper object and bring it into the "real world." This notion will pop up again a couple of sections from now. When using the _.chain function, you might receive results for any number of buggy reasons. Imagine the following scenario:

```
var TITLE_KEY = 'titel';

// ... a whole bunch of code later

_.chain(library)
 .pluck(TITLE_KEY)
 .sort()
 .value();

//=> [undefined, undefined, undefined]
```

Because the code is compact, the problem is obvious—I misspelled "title." However, in a large codebase you're likely to start debugging closer to the point of failure. Unfortunately, with the presence of the _.chain call, there is seemingly no easy way to *tap into* the chain to inspect intermediate values. Not so. In fact, Underscore provides a _.tap function that, given an object and a function, calls the function with the object and returns the object:

```
_.tap([1,2,3], note);
;; NOTE: 1,2,3
//=> [1, 2, 3]
```

Passing the note function[2] to Underscore's tap shows that indeed the function is called and the array returned. As you might suspect, _.tap is also available in the wrapper object used by _.chain, and therefore can be used to inspect intermediate values, like so:

```
_.chain(library)
 .tap(function(o) {console.log(o)})
 .pluck(TITLE_KEY)
 .sort()
```

---

2. The note function was defined all the way back in Chapter 1.

```
  .value();

// [{title: "SICP" ...
//=> [undefined, undefined, undefined]
```

Nothing seems amiss in the form of the library table, but what about if I move the tap to a different location:

```
_.chain(library)
 .pluck(TITLE_KEY)
 .tap(note)
 .sort()
 .value();

// NOTE:  ,,
//=> [undefined, undefined, undefined]
```

Now wait a minute; the result of the pluck is an odd looking array. At this point, the tap has pointed to the location of the problem: the call to _.pluck. Either there is a problem with TITLE_KEY or a problem with _.pluck itself. Thankfully, the problem lies in the code under my control.

The use of _.chain is very powerful, especially when you want to fluently describe a sequence of actions occurring on a single target. However, there is one limitation of _chain—it's not lazy. What I mean by what is hinted at in the following code:

```
_.chain(library)
 .pluck('title')
 .tap(note)
 .sort();

// NOTE: SICP,SICP,Joy of Clojure
//=> _
```

Even though I never explicitly asked for the wrapped value with the _.value function, all of the calls in the chain were executed anyway. If _.chain were lazy, then none of the calls would have occurred *until* the call to _.value.

A Lazy Chain

Taking a lesson from the implementation of trampoline from Chapter 6, I can implement a lazy variant of _.chain that will not run any target methods until a variant of _.value is called:

```
function LazyChain(obj) {
  this._calls  = [];
  this._target = obj;
}
```

The constructor for the LazyChain object is simple enough; it takes a target object like _.chain and sets up an empty call array. While the operation of trampoline from Chapter 6 operated on an implicit chain of calls, LazyChain works with an explicit array of...something. However, the question remains as to what it is that I put into the _calls array. The most logical choice is, of course, functions, as shown below:

```
LazyChain.prototype.invoke = function(methodName /*, args */) {
  var args = _.rest(arguments);

  this._calls.push(function(target) {
    var meth = target[methodName];

    return meth.apply(target, args);
  });

  return this;
};
```

The LazyChain#invoke method is fairly straightforward, but I could stand to walk through it. The arguments to LazyChain#invoke are a method name in the form of a string, and any additional arguments to the method. What LazyChain#invoke does is to "wrap" up the actual method call in a closure and push it onto the _calls array. Observe what the _calls array looks like after a single invocation of LazyChain#invoke here:

```
new LazyChain([2,1,3]).invoke('sort')._calls;
//=> [function (target) { ... }]
```

As shown, the only element in the _calls array after adding one link to the lazy chain is a single function that corresponds to a deferred Array#sort method call on the array [2,1,3].

A function that wraps some behavior for later execution is typically called a *thunk*[3] (see Figure 8-1). The thunk that's stored in _calls expects some intermediate target that will serve as the object receiving the eventual method call.

3. The term "thunk" has roots extending all the way back to ALGOL.

Figure 8-1. A thunk is a function waiting to be called

While thunks are not always functions in every programming language that supports them, in JavaScript it makes sense to implement them as such because functions are readily available.

Since the thunk is waiting to be called, why don't I just call it to see what happens:

```
new LazyChain([2,1,3]).invoke('sort')._calls[0]();

// TypeError: Cannot read property 'sort' of undefined
```

Well, that was less than satisfying. The problem is that directly calling the thunk is not enough to make it execute properly. If you'll recall, the thunk expected a `target` object to execute its closed-over method on. To make it work, I would need to somehow pass the original array as an argument to the thunk, as shown in Figure 8-2.

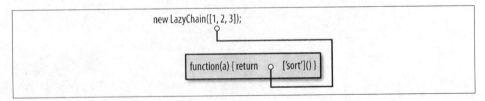

Figure 8-2. To make the LazyChain work, I have to find a way to loop the original object back into the call

I could satisfy the argument lookback manually by pasting the array into the thunk call as in the following:

```
new LazyChain([2,1,3]).invoke('sort')._calls[0]([2,1,3]);

//=> [1, 2, 3]
```

Placing the argument directly into the thunk call seems not only like cheating, but also like a terrible API. Instead, I can use the _.reduce function to provide the loopback argument not only to the initial thunk, but also every intermediate call on the _calls array:

```
LazyChain.prototype.force = function() {
  return _.reduce(this._calls, function(target, thunk) {
    return thunk(target);
  }, this._target);
};
```

The LazyChain#force function is the execution engine for the lazy chaining logic. As shown in Figure 8-3, the use of _.reduce nicely provides the same kind of trampolining logic as demonstrated in Chapter 6. Starting with the initial target object, the thunk calls are called, one by one, with the result of the previous call.

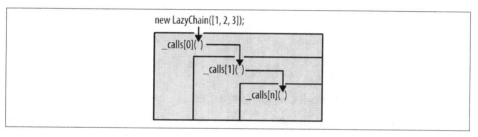

Figure 8-3. Using reduce allows me to pass the intermediate result forward into each thunk

Now that LazyChain#force is in place, observe what happens when it is used to "terminate" a lazy chain:

```
new LazyChain([2,1,3]).invoke('sort').force();

//=> [1, 2, 3]
```

Excellent! The logic seems sound, but what happens when more links are added to the chain? Observe:

```
new LazyChain([2,1,3])
  .invoke('concat', [8,5,7,6])
  .invoke('sort')
  .invoke('join', ' ')
  .force();

//=> "1 2 3 5 6 7 8"
```

I can chain as long as I want while remaining mindful of the way that the types change from one link to the next. I mentioned earlier that LazyChain was lazy in its execution. While you might see how that is indeed the case because thunks are stored in the _calls array and never executed until LazyChain#force, it's still better to show it actually being lazy. First, let me implement a lazy version of _.tap that works with LazyChain instances:

```
LazyChain.prototype.tap = function(fun) {
  this._calls.push(function(target) {
    fun(target);
    return target;
  });

  return this;
}
```

The operation of LazyChain#tap is similar to LazyChain#invoke because the actual work (i.e., calling a function and returning the target) is wrapped in a thunk. I show how tap works below:

```
new LazyChain([2,1,3])
  .invoke('sort')
  .tap(alert)
  .force();

// alert box pops up
//=> "1,2,3"
```

But what happens if I never call LazyChain#force?

```
var deferredSort = new LazyChain([2,1,3])
  .invoke('sort')
  .tap(alert);

deferredSort;
//=> LazyChain
```

Nothing happens! I can hold onto deferredSort as long as I want and it'll never execute until I explicitly invoke it:

```
// ... in the not too distant future

deferredSort.force();

// alert box pops up
//=> [1, 2, 3]
```

This operation is very similar to the way that something like jQuery promises work. Before I talk a little bit about promises, however, I want to explore an easy extension to LazyChain that allows me to, well, chain lazy chains to other lazy chains. That is, keeping in mind that at the heart of a LazyChain is just an array of thunks, I can change the constructor to concatenate the arrays when presented with another LazyChain as its argument:

```
function LazyChainChainChain(obj) {
  var isLC = (obj instanceof LazyChain);

  this._calls  = isLC ? cat(obj._calls, []) : [];
  this._target = isLC ? obj._target : obj;
}
```

```
LazyChainChainChain.prototype = LazyChain.prototype;
```

That is, if the argument to the constructor is another LazyChain instance, then just steal its call chain and target object. Observe the chaining of chains:

```
new LazyChainChainChain(deferredSort)
  .invoke('toString')
  .force();
```

```
// an alert box pops up
//=> "1,2,3"
```

Allowing chains to compose in this way is a very powerful idea. It allows you to build up a library of discrete behaviors without worrying about the final result. There are other ways to enhance LazyChain, such as caching the result and providing an interface that does not rely on strings, but I leave that as an exercise for the reader.

Promises

While LazyChain and LazyChainChainChain are useful for packaging the description of a computation for later execution, jQuery[4] provides something called a *promise* that works similarly, but slightly differently. That is, jQuery promises are intended to provide a fluent API for sequencing asynchronous operations that run concurrent to the main program logic.

First, the simplest way to look at a promise is that it represents an unfulfilled activity. As shown in the following code, jQuery allows the creation of promises via $.Deferred:

```
var longing = $.Deferred();
```

I can now grab a promise from the Deferred:

```
longing.promise();
//=> Object
```

The object returned is the handle to the unfulfilled action:

```
longing.promise().state();
//=> "pending"
```

---

4. Other JavaScript libraries that offer promises similar to jQuery's include, but are not limited to: Q, RSVP.js, when.js, and node-promises.

As shown, the promise is in a holding pattern. The reason for this is of course that the promise was never fulfilled. I can do so simply by resolving it:

```
longing.resolve("<3");

longing.promise().state();
//=> "resolved"
```

At this point, the promise has been fulfilled and the value is accessible:

```
longing.promise().done(note);
// NOTE: <3
//=> <the promise itself>
```

The `Deferred#done` method is just one of many useful chaining methods available in the promise API. I will not go into depth about jQuery promises, but a more complicated example could help to show how they differ from lazy chains. One way to build a promise in jQuery is to use the `$.when` function to start a promise chain, as shown here:

```
function go() {
  var d = $.Deferred();

  $.when("")
   .then(function() {
     setTimeout(function() {
       console.log("sub-task 1");
     }, 5000)
   })
   .then(function() {
     setTimeout(function() {
       console.log("sub-task 2");
     }, 10000)
   })
   .then(function() {
     setTimeout(function() {
       d.resolve("done done done done");
     }, 15000)
   })

  return d.promise();
}
```

The promise chain built in the go function is very simple-minded. That is, all I've done is to tell jQuery to kick off three asynchronous tasks, each delayed by increasingly longer timings. The `Deferred#then` methods each take a function and execute them immediately. Only in the longest-running task is the `Deferred` instance resolved. Running go illustrates this example:

```
var yearning = go().done(note);
```

I tacked on a done call to the promise that will get called whenever the promise is resolved. However, immediately after running go, nothing appears to have happened.

That's because due to the timeouts in the subtasks, the console logging has not yet occurred. I can check the promise state using the aptly named `state` method:

```
yearning.state();
//=> "pending"
```

As you might expect, the state is still pending. After a few seconds, however:

```
// (console) sub-task 1
```

The timeout of the first subtask triggers and a notification is printed to the console.

```
yearning.state();
//=> "pending"
```

Of course, because the other two actions in the original promise chain are awaiting timeouts, the state is still pending. However, again waiting for some number of seconds to pass shows the following:

```
// (console) sub-task 2

// ... ~5 seconds later

// NOTE: done done done done
```

Eventually, the final link in the deferred chain is called, and the done notification is printed by the `note` function. Checking the state one more time reveals the following:

```
yearning.state();
//=> "resolved"
```

Of course, the promise has been resolved because the final subtask ran and called `resolve` on the original `Deferred` instance. This sequence of events is very different from that presented using `LazyChain`. That is, a `LazyChain` represents a strict sequence of calls that calculate a value. Promises, on the other hand, also represent a sequence of calls, but differ in that once they are executed, the value is available on demand.

Further, jQuery's promise API is meant to define aggregate tasks composed of some number of asynchronous subtasks. The subtasks themselves execute, as possible, concurrently. However, the aggregate task is not considered completed until every subtask has finished *and* a value is delivered to the promise via the `resolve` method.

A lazy chain also represents an aggregate task composed of subtasks, but they, once forced, are always run one after the other. The difference between the two can be summarized as the difference between aggregating highly connected tasks (`LazyChain`) versus loosely related (`Deferred`) tasks.

Most of jQuery's asynchronous API calls now return promises, so the result of an async call is chainable according to the promise API. However, the complete specification of this API is outside the scope of this book.

Pipelining

Chaining is a useful pattern for creating fluent APIs built around objects and method calls, but is less useful for functional APIs. The Underscore library is built for chaining via _.chain, as most functions take a collection as the first argument. By contrast, the functions in this book take functions as their first argument. This choice was explicit, to foster partial application and currying.

There are various downsides to method chaining including tight-coupling of object set and get logic (which Fowler refers to as command/query separation [2010]) and awkward naming problems. However, the primary problem is that very often method chains mutate some common reference from one call to the rest, as shown in Figure 8-4. Functional APIs, on the other hand, work with values rather than references and often subtly (and sometimes not so subtly) transform the data, returning the new result.

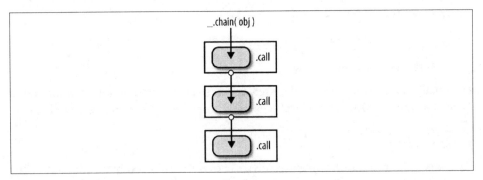

Figure 8-4. Chained method calls work to mutate a common reference

In this section, I'll talk about function pipelines and how to use them to great effect. In an ideal world, the original data presented to a function should remain the same after the call. The chain of calls in a functional code base are built from expected data values coming in, nondestructive transformations, and new data returned—strung end to end, as shown in Figure 8-5.

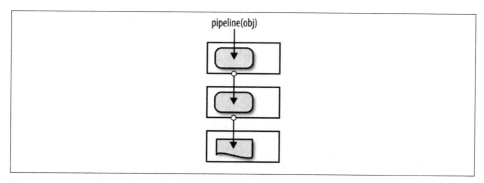

Figure 8-5. Pipelined functions work to transform data

A "faux" API for such a pipeline of transformations can look like the following:

```
pipeline([2, 3, null, 1, 42, false]
    , _.compact
    , _.initial
    , _.rest
    , rev);

//=> [1, 3]
```

The sequence of this pipeline call could be described as follows:

1. Take the array [2, 3, null, 1, 42, false] and pass it to the _.compact function.
2. Take the result of _.compact and pass it to _.initial.
3. Take the result of _.initial and pass it to _.rest.
4. Take the result of _.rest and pass it to rev.

In other words, the pipeline looks like the following if written out as nested calls:

```
rev(_.rest(_.initial(_.compact([2, 3, null, 1, 42, false]))));

//=> [1, 3]
```

This description should start setting off alarms bells in you brain. That's because this description is almost the same as the description of LazyChain#force. The same result/ call weaving is prevalent in both algorithms. Therefore, the implementation of pipe line should look very similar to LazyChain#force, and indeed it is:

```
function pipeline(seed /*, args */) {
  return _.reduce(_.rest(arguments),
                  function(l,r) { return r(l); },
                  seed);
};
```

The use of _.reduce makes pipeline almost trivial, however, with a seemingly small amount of code comes great power. Before I dig into this power, look at a few examples of pipeline in action:

```
pipeline();
//=> undefined

pipeline(42);
//=> 42

pipeline(42, function(n) { return -n });
//=> -42
```

The first argument to pipeline serves as the seed value, or in other words, the value that starts as the argument to the first function. The result of each subsequent function call is then fed into the next function until all are exhausted.[5]

Pipelines are somewhat similar to lazy chains, except they are not lazy and they work against values rather than mutable references.[6] Instead, pipelines are more akin to functions created using _.compose. The act of making a pipeline lazy is simply the act of encapsulating it within a function (or thunk if you prefer):

```
function fifth(a) {
  return pipeline(a
    , _.rest
    , _.rest
    , _.rest
    , _.rest
    , _.first);
}
```

And now the act of forcing a pipeline is just to feed it a piece of data:

```
fifth([1,2,3,4,5]);
//=> 5
```

A very powerful technique is to use the abstraction built via a pipeline and insert it into another pipeline. They compose thus:

```
function negativeFifth(a) {
  return pipeline(a
    , fifth
    , function(n) { return -n });
}

negativeFifth([1,2,3,4,5,6,7,8,9]);
//=> -5
```

5. If you want to be truly fancy, then you can call pipeline by its proper name: the thrush combinator. I'll avoid that temptation, however.

6. I guess, based on these vast differences, you could say that they are not similar at all.

This is interesting as an illustrative example, but it might be more compelling to show how it could be used to create fluent APIs. Recall the implementation of the relational algebra operators as, project, and restrict from Chapter 2. Each function took as its first argument a table that it used to generate a new table, "modified" in some way. These functions seem perfect for use in a pipeline such as one to find all of the first edition books in a table:

```
function firstEditions(table) {
  return pipeline(table
    , function(t) { return as(t, {ed: 'edition'}) }
    , function(t) { return project(t, ['title', 'edition', 'isbn']) }
    , function(t) { return restrict(t, function(book) {
        return book.edition === 1;
      });
    });
}
```

And here's the use of firstEditions:

```
firstEditions(library);

//=> [{title: "SICP", isbn: "0262010771", edition: 1},
//     {title: "Joy of Clojure", isbn: "1935182641", edition: 1}]
```

For processing and extracting elements from the table, the relational operators worked well, but with pipeline, I can make it nicer to deal with.

The problem is that the pipeline expects that the functions embedded within take a single argument. Since the relational operators expect two, an adapter function needs to wrap them in order to work within the pipeline. However, the relational operators were designed very specifically to conform to a consistent interface: the table is the first argument and the "change" specification is the second. Taking advantage of this consistency, I can use curry2 to build curried versions of the relational operators to work toward a more fluent experience:

```
var RQL = {
  select: curry2(project),
  as: curry2(as),
  where: curry2(restrict)
};
```

I've decided to namespace the curried functions inside of an object RQL (standing for *relational query language*) and change the names in two of the circumstances to more closely mimic the SQL operators. Now that they are curried, implementing an improved version of firstEditions reads more more cleanly:

```
function allFirstEditions(table) {
  return pipeline(table
    , RQL.as({ed: 'edition'})
    , RQL.select(['title', 'edition', 'isbn'])
    , RQL.where(function(book) {
```

```
        return book.edition === 1;
    }));
}
```

Aside from being easier to read,[7] the new `allFirstEditions` function will work just as well:

```
allFirstEditions(table);

//=> [{title: "SICP", isbn: "0262010771", edition: 1},
//    {title: "Joy of Clojure", isbn: "1935182641", edition: 1}]
```

The use of pipelines in JavaScript, coupled with currying and partial application, works to provide a powerful way to compose functions in a fluent manner. In fact, the functions created in this book were designed to work nicely in pipelines. As an added advantage, functional programming focuses on the transformation of data as it flows from one function to the next, but this fact can often be obscured by indirection and deep function nesting. Using a pipeline can work to make the data flow more explicit. However, pipelines are not appropriate in all cases. In fact, I would rarely use a pipeline to perform side-effectful acts like I/O, Ajax calls, or mutations because they very often return nothing of value.

The data going into a pipeline should be the same after the pipeline has completed. This helps ensure that the pipelines are composable. Is there a way that I can compose impure functions along a pipeline-like structure? In the next section, I'll talk a bit about a way to perform side effects in a composable and fluent way, building on the lessons learned while exploring chains and pipelines.

Data Flow versus Control Flow

In the `lazyChain` example, I separated out the execution specification (via `.invoke`) from the execution logic (via `.force`). Likewise, with the `pipeline` function, I juxtaposed numerous pure functions to achieve the equivalent of a serial processing pipeline. In both the cases of `lazyChain` and `pipeline`, the value moving from one node in the call sequence to the next was stable. Specifically, `lazyChain` always returned some LazyChain-like object up until the point `force` was called. Likewise, while at any point in the `pipeline` the intermediate type could change, the change was known prior to composition to ensure the proper values were fed from one stage to the next. However, what if we want to compose functions that were not necessarily meant to compose?

In this final section of this chapter, I'll talk about a technique for composing functions of incongruous return types using a new kind of lazy pipeline called `actions` (Stan 2011).

---

7. I'm of the opinion that code should be written for readers.

If you imagine a function as a box of indeterminate behavior taking as input data of some "shape" and outputting data of some other shape (possibly the same shape), then Figure 8-6 might be what you'd picture.[8]

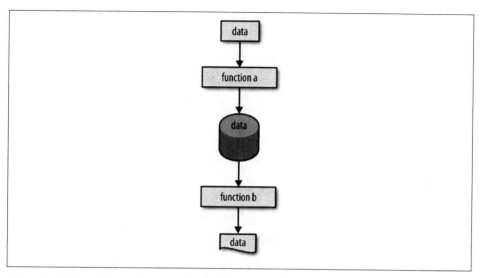

Figure 8-6. Function a takes a rectangular shaped thing and returns a database shaped thing; function b takes a database shaped thing and returns a document shaped thing

Therefore, the reason that a lazy chain works properly is that the shape from one chained method call to the next is consistent and only changes[9] when force is called. Figure 8-7 illustrates this fact.

8. By shape in this circumstance, I'm simply referring to the idea that the shape of an array of strings would be very different than the shape of a floating-point number, which in turn is different than an object of strings to arrays. You can substitute shape for "type" or "structure," if you prefer, but I'll stick to shape because the pictures look prettier. The idea of visualizing shapes was inspired by the amazing Alan Dipert (Dipert 2012).

9. Although there is no reason that the result of force couldn't be yet another lazy chain; but I digress.

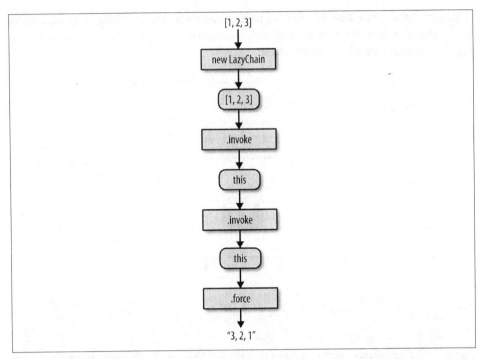

Figure 8-7. The shape flowing between calls in a lazy chain is stable, only (potentially) changing when force is called

Similarly, the shape between the nodes of a pipeline or a composed function, while not as stable as a common object reference, is designed to change in accordance with the needs of the next node, as shown in Figure 8-8.

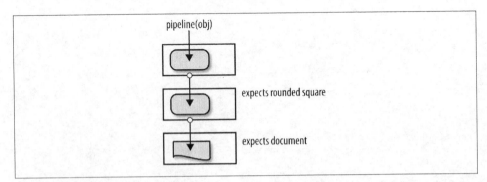

Figure 8-8. The shape flowing between calls in a pipeline or compose is designed to change in expected ways

The problem is that if the shapes do not align, then neither `pipeline`, `_.compose`, nor `lazyChain` will operate as expected:

```
pipeline(42
  , sqr
  , note
  , function(n) { return -n });

// NOTE: 1764
//=> NaN
```

Not cool. The reason that failed was because the shape of the type changed in midstream to `undefined` (from `note`).

In fact, if you want to achieve the correct effect, then you'd need to do so manually:

```
function negativeSqr(n) {
  var s = sqr(n);
  note(n);
  return -s;
}

negativeSqr(42);
// NOTE: 1764
//=> -1764
```

While tenable, the amount of boilerplate involved in getting this to work for larger capabilities grows quickly. Likewise, I could just change the `note` function to return whatever it's given, and while that might be a good idea in general, doing so here would solve only a symptom rather than the larger disease of incompatible intermediate shapes. That there are functions that can return incompatible shapes, or even no shape at all (i.e., no `return`) requires a delicate orchestration of control flow to compose code. The requirements of this delicate balance work against us in finding a way to compose functions that flow values from one to the next.

By now you might think that the way to fix this problem is to somehow find a way to stabilize the shapes flowing between the nodes—that thinking is absolutely correct.

Finding a Common Shape

The complication in determining a common shape to flow between nodes of a different sort is not picking a type (a regular object will do), but what to put into it. One choice is the data that flows between each node; in the `negativeSqr` example, the object would look like the following:

```
{values: [42, 1764, undefined, -1764]}
```

But what else is needed? I would say that a useful piece of data to keep around would be the state, or target object used as the common target between nodes. Figure 8-9 shows a way to visualize how actions could be composed, even in the face of disparate input and output shapes.

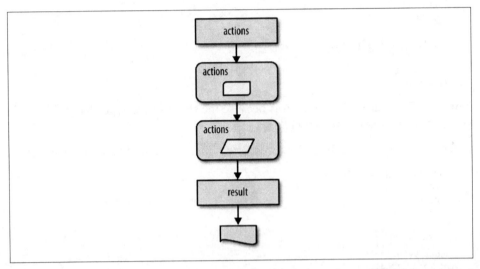

Figure 8-9. The shape flowing between actions is made to be stable using a context object

The last node (i.e., results) operates much in the same way as `force` in that it pulls the answer out of the action object into the real world. In the case of the `negativeSqr` function, the way to get the final answer is to retrieve the last element of the `values` element or just return the state:

```
{values: [42, 1764, undefined, -1764],
 state:  -1764}
```

Now, the implementation of the `actions` function to manage these intermediate states is a hybrid of the `pipeline` and `lazyChain` implementations, as shown here:

```
function actions(acts, done) {
  return function (seed) {
    var init = { values: [], state: seed };

    var intermediate = _.reduce(acts, function (stateObj, action) {
      var result = action(stateObj.state);
      var values = cat(stateObj.values, [result.answer]);

      return { values: values, state: result.state };
    }, init);

    var keep = _.filter(intermediate.values, existy);

    return done(keep, intermediate.state);
```

```
    };
  };
```

The `actions` function expects an array of functions, each taking a value and returning a function that augments the intermediate state object. The `actions` function then reduces over all of the functions in the array and builds up an intermediate state object, as shown here:

```
...
    var intermediate = _.reduce(acts, function (stateObj, action) {
      var result = action(stateObj.state);
      var values = cat(stateObj.values, [result.answer]);

      return { values: values, state: result.state };
    }, init);
...
```

During this process, `actions` expects the result from each function to be an object of two keys: `answer` and `state`. The `answer` value corresponds to the result of calling the function and the `state` value represents what the new state looks like after the "action" is performed. For a function like `note`, the state does not change. The `intermediate` state object might have some bogus answers in it (e.g., the `answer` of `note` is unde fined), so `actions` filters those out:

```
...
    var keep = _.filter(intermediate.values, existy);

    return done(keep, intermediate.state);
...
```

Finally, `actions` passes the filtered `values` (called keep) and `state` into the done function to garner a final result. I could have only passed the `state` or `values` into the done function, but I like to pass both for maximum flexibility, and because it helps for illustration.

To demonstrate how `actions` works, I'll need to break apart `negativeSqr` and recompose it as a series of actions. First, the `sqr` function obviously doesn't know anything about a state object, so I'll need to create an adapter function, called `mSqr`:[10]

```
function mSqr() {
  return function(state) {
    var ans = sqr(state);
    return {answer: ans, state: ans};
  }
}
```

---

10. Monad is the proper term for `action`, but I hesitate to use it in this section because I think that monads are vastly weakened in the absence of a strong-type system and return-type polymorphism. However, that's not to say that monads cannot teach us valuable lessons in deconstruction for use in JavaScript.

I can now use `actions` just to perform a double-squaring operation:

```
var doubleSquareAction = actions(
  [mSqr(),
   mSqr()],
  function(values) {
    return values;
});
```

```
doubleSquareAction(10);
//=> [100, 10000]
```

Since I returned the `values` array directly, the result of `doubleSquareAction` is all of the intermediate states (specifically the square of 10 and the square of the square of 10). However, this is almost the same as `pipeline`. The real magic comes when mixing functions of differing shapes:

```
function mNote() {
  return function(state) {
    note(state);
    return {answer: undefined, state: state};
  }
}
```

The `answer` of the `mNote` function is, of course, `undefined`, since it is a function used for printing; however, the `state` is just passed along. The `mNeg` function should by now seem apparent:

```
function mNeg() {
  return function(state) {
    return {answer: -state, state: -state};
  }
}
```

And now composing these new functions into `actions` is shown here:

```
var negativeSqrAction = actions([mSqr(), mNote(), mNeg()],
  function(_, state) {
    return state;
  });
```

Its usage is shown here:

```
negativeSqrAction(9);
// NOTE: 81
//=> -81
```

Using the `actions` paradigm for composition is a general way to compose functions of different shapes. Sadly, the preceding code seems like a lot of ceremony to achieve the effects needed. Fortunately, there is a better way to define an action, without needing to know the details of how a state object is built and avoiding the pile of boilerplate that goes along with that knowledge.

A Function to Simplify Action Creation

In this section, I'll define a function, `lift`, that takes two functions: a function to provide the result of some action given a value, and another function to provide what the new state looks like. The `lift` function will be used to abstract away the management of the state object used as the intermediate representation of `actions`. The implementation of `lift` is quite small:

```
function lift(answerFun, stateFun) {
  return function(/* args */) {
    var args = _.toArray(arguments);

    return function(state) {
      var ans = answerFun.apply(null, construct(state, args));
      var s = stateFun ? stateFun(state) : ans;

      return {answer: ans, state: s};
    };
  };
};
```

`lift` looks like it's curried (i.e., it returns a function), and indeed it is. There is no reason to curry `lift` except to provide a nicer interface, as I'll show in a moment. In fact, using `lift`, I can more nicely redefine `mSqr`, `mNote`, and `mNeg`:

```
var mSqr2  = lift(sqr);
var mNote2 = lift(note, _.identity);
var mNeg2  = lift(function(n) { return -n });
```

In the case of `sqr` and the negation function, both the answer and the state are the same value, so I only needed to supply the answer function. In the case of `note`, however, the answer (`undefined`) is clearly not the state value, so using `_.identity` allows me to specify that it's a pass-through action.

The new actions compose via `actions`:

```
var negativeSqrAction2 = actions([mSqr2(), mNote2(), mNeg2()],
  function(_, state) {
    return state;
  });
```

And their usage is the same as before:

```
negativeSqrAction(100);
// NOTE: 10000
//=> -10000
```

If I want to use `lift` and actions to implement a `stackAction`, then I could do so as follows:

```
var push = lift(function(stack, e) { return construct(e, stack) });
```

The push function returns a new array, masquerading as a stack, with the new element at the front. Since the intermediate state is also the answer, there is no need to supply a state function. The implementation of pop needs both:

```
var pop = lift(_.first, _.rest);
```

Since I'm simulating a stack via an array, the pop answer is the first element. Conversely, the state function _.rest return the new stack with the top element removed. I can now use these two functions to compose two pushes and one pop, as follows:

```
var stackAction = actions([
  push(1),
  push(2),
  pop()
  ],
  function(values, state) {
    return values;
  });
```

Amazingly, by using the actions function, I've captured the sequence of stack events as a value that has not yet been realized. To realize the result is as simple as this:

```
stackAction([]);

//=> [[1], [2, 1], 2]
```

As shown, the stackAction is just a function and can now be composed with other functions to build higher-level behaviors. Since I've decided to return all of the intermediate answers, the resulting return value can participate in a vast array of composition scenarios:

```
pipeline(
  []
  , stackAction
  , _.chain)
.each(function(elem) {
  console.log(polyToString(elem))
});

// (console) [[1],    // the stack after push(1)
// (console)  [2, 1], // the stack after push(2)
// (console)  2]      // the result of pop([2, 1])
```

This is almost like magic, but by deconstructing it, I've tried to show that it really isn't magical at all. Instead, composing functions of different shapes is possible using a common intermediate type and a couple of functions—lift and actions—to manage them along the way. This management allows me to convert a problem that would typically be a problem of control flow in keeping the types straight, into a problem of data flow—the whole point of this chapter (Piponi 2010).

Summary

This chapter focused on exploring the possibilities in viewing behavior as a sequence of discrete steps. In the first part of the chapter, I discussed chaining. Method chaining is a common technique in JavaScript libraries, reaching the widest audience in jQuery. In summary, method chaining is the act of writing object methods to all return a common `this` reference so common methods can be called in sequence. Using jQuery promises and Underscore's `_.chain` function, I explored chaining. However, I also explored the idea of "lazy chaining," or sequencing some number of method calls on a common target for later execution.

Following on the idea of a chain was that of the "pipeline," or a sequence of function calls that take in a piece of data and return a transformed piece of data at the other end. Pipelines, unlike chains, work against data such as arrays and objects rather than a common reference. Also, the type of data flowing through a pipeline can change as long as the next step in the pipeline expects that particular type. As discussed, pipelines are meant to be pure—no data was harmed by running it through.

While both chains and pipelines work against either a known reference or data types, the idea of a sequence of actions is not limited to doing so. Instead, the implementation of the `actions` type hides the details of managing an internal data structure used to mix functions of varying return and argument types.

In the next and final chapter, I will talk about how functional programming facilitates and indeed motivates a "classless" style of programming.

CHAPTER 9

Programming Without Class

When people are first exposed to JavaScript and its minimal set of tools (functions, objects, prototypes, and arrays), many are underwhelmed. Therefore, in order to "modify" JavaScript to conform to their idea of what it takes to model software solutions, they very often seek out or re-create class-based systems using the primordial ooze. This desire is completely understandable given that in general people will often seek the familiar. However, since you've come this far in exploring functional programming in JavaScript, it's worth tying all of the threads from the previous chapters into a coherent exploration of how to reify functional and object-oriented thinking.

This chapter starts by walking the path of data and function thinking that I've talked about throughout the book. However, while thinking in functions and simple data is important, there will come a time when you may need to build custom abstractions. Therefore, I will cover a way to "mix" discrete behaviors together to compose more complex behaviors. I will also discuss how a functional API can be used to hide such customizations.

Data Orientation

Throughout the course of this book, I've intentionally defined my data modeling needs in terms of JavaScript primitives, arrays, and objects. That is, I've avoided creating a hierarchy of types in favor of composing simple data together to form higher-level concepts like tables (Chapter 8) and commands (Chapter 4). Adhering to a focus on functions over methods allowed me to provide APIs that do not rely on the presence of object thinking and methodologies. Instead, by adhering to the functional interfaces, the *actual* concrete types implementing the data abstractions mattered less. This provided flexibility to change the implementation details of the data while maintaining a consistent functional interface.

Figure 9-1 illustrates that when using a functional API, you don't really need to worry about what types are flowing between the nodes in a call chain.

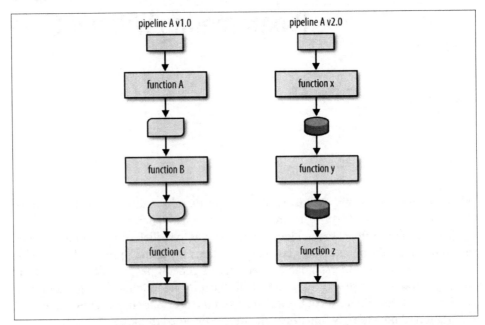

Figure 9-1. When adhering to a functional interface, the type of intermediate data matters little and can evolve (or devolve) as needed especially if you're concerned primarily with the beginning and end of a computation

Of course, the functions themselves should be able to handle the types flowing between, but well-designed APIs are meant to compose and should abstract the details of intermediate types. However, there are times when object-centric thinking is crucial. For example, the LazyChain implementation from Chapter 8 specifically deals with the lazy execution of methods on a target object. Clearly, the very nature of the problem leads to a solution where methods are called on some object. However, the implementation requires that the user of LazyChain deal directly with the creation of instances of that type. Thanks to JavaScript's extreme flexibility, there is no need to create a specialized LazyChain type. Instead, a lazy chain is whatever is returned from a function lazy Chain responding to .invoke and .force.

```
function lazyChain(obj) {
  var calls = [];

  return {
    invoke: function(methodName /* args */) {
      var args = _.rest(arguments);
```

```
      calls.push(function(target) {
        var meth = target[methodName];

        return meth.apply(target, args);
      });

      return this;
    },
    force: function() {
      return _.reduce(calls, function(ret, thunk) {
        return thunk(ret);
      }, obj);
    }
  };
}
```

This is almost the exact code as in the implementation of LazyChain except for the following:

- The lazy chain is initiated via a function call.
- The call chain (in calls) is private data.[1]
- There is no explicit LazyChain type.

The implementation of lazyChain is shown here:

```
var lazyOp = lazyChain([2,1,3])
  .invoke('concat', [7,7,8,9,0])
  .invoke('sort');

lazyOp.force();
//=> [0, 1, 2, 3, 7, 7, 8, 9]
```

There are certainly times to create explicit data types, as I'll show in the next section, but it's good to defer their definition until absolutely necessary. Instead, a premium is placed on programming to abstractions. The idea of how to interact with a lazy chain is more important than a specific LazyChain type.

JavaScript provides numerous and powerful ways to defer or eliminate the need to create named types and type hierarchies, including:

- Usable primitive data types
- Usable aggregate data types (i.e., arrays and objects)
- Functions working on built-in data types

---

1. That the chain array is private slightly complicates the ability to chain lazy chains with other lazy chains. However, to handle this condition requires a change to force to identify and feed the result of one lazy chain to the next.

- Anonymous objects containing methods
- Typed objects
- Classes

Graphically, the points above can be used as a checklist for implementing JavaScript APIs, as shown in Figure 9-2.

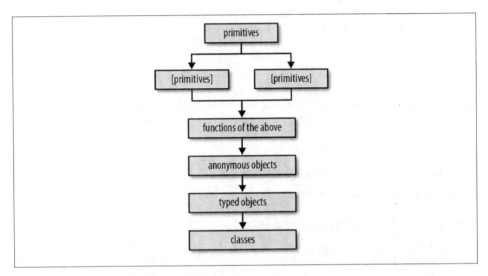

Figure 9-2. A "hierarchy" of data thinking

Very often, JavaScript developers will invert the hierarchy shown in Figure 9-2 and start immediately with constructing classes, thus blowing their abstraction budget from the start. If you instead choose to start with built-in types coupled with a fluent, functional API, then you allow yourself a lot of flexibility for expansion.

Building Toward Functions

For most programming tasks, the activities happening in the middle of some computation are of primary importance (Elliott 2010). Take, for example, the idea of reading in a form value, validating it, performing operations on the new type, and finally sending the new value somewhere else as a string. The acts of getting to and from a string are small compared to the validation and processing steps.

At the moment, the tools that I've created to fulfill this kind of task are a mix of functional and object-based thinking. However, if I factor toward functions only, then a fluent solution can evolve.

First of all, the lazy chains are clearly object-centric and in fact require the stringing of methods to operate. However, lazy chaining can be deconstructed into three stages:

1. Acquire some object.
2. Define a chain in relation to the object.
3. Execute the chain.

The act of acquiring an object is trivial; it simply occurs as part of running JavaScript code. Defining a chain, however, is where it gets interesting. Whereas a lazy chain is defined in terms of the actions to perform on a specific instance, by lifting its creation into a function, I can make lazy operations generic across types of objects instead:

```
function deferredSort(ary) {
  return lazyChain(ary).invoke('sort');
}
```

This allows me to create lazy sorts on any array via a regular function call:

```
var deferredSorts = _.map([[2,1,3], [7,7,1], [0,9,5]], deferredSort);

//=> [<thunk>, <thunk>, <thunk>]
```

Naturally, I'd like to execute each thunk, but since I'm factoring to functions, I'd prefer to encapsulate the method call:

```
function force(thunk) {
  return thunk.force();
}
```

Now I can execute arbitrary lazy chains:

```
_.map(deferredSorts, force);

//=> [[1,2,3], [1, 7, 7], [0, 5, 9]]
```

And now that I've "lifted" the method calls into the realm of functional application, I can define discrete chunks of functionality corresponding to the atoms of data processing:

```
var validateTriples  = validator(
  "Each array should have three elements",
  function (arrays) {
    return _.every(arrays, function(a) {
      return a.length === 3;
    });
  });

var validateTripleStore = partial1(condition1(validateTriples), _.identity);
```

Aggregating the validation into its own function (or many functions, perhaps) allows me to change validation independent of any of the other steps in the activity. Likewise, it allows me to reuse validations later for similar activities.

Double checking that the validation works as expected:

```
validateTripleStore([[2,1,3], [7,7,1], [0,9,5]]);
//=> [[2,1,3], [7,7,1], [0,9,5]])

validateTripleStore([[2,1,3], [7,7,1], [0,9,5,7,7,7,7,7,7]]);
// Error: Each array should have three elements
```

Now I can also define other processing steps that are (not necessarily) lazy:

```
function postProcess(arrays) {
  return _.map(arrays, second);
}
```

Now I can define a higher-level activity that aggregates the pieces into a domain-specific activity:

```
function processTriples(data) {
  return pipeline(data
                 , JSON.parse
                 , validateTripleStore
                 , deferredSort
                 , force
                 , postProcess
                 , invoker('sort', Array.prototype.sort)
                 , str);
}
```

The use of `processTriples` is as follows:

```
processTriples("[[2,1,3], [7,7,1], [0,9,5]]");

//=> "1,7,9"
```

The nice part about adding validations to your pipelines is that they will terminate early when given bad data:

```
processTriples("[[2,1,3], [7,7,1], [0,9,5,7,7,7,7,7,7]]");

// Error: Each array should have three elements
```

This allows me to now use this function anywhere that such a pipeline of transformations might be appropriate:

```
$.get("http://djhkjhkdj.com", function(data) {
  $('#result').text(processTriples(data));
});
```

You could make this process more generic by abstracting out the reporting logic:

```
var reportDataPackets = _.compose(
  function(s) { $('#result').text(s) },
  processTriples);
```

Exploring the use of `reportDataPackets` is as follows:

```
reportDataPackets("[[2,1,3], [7,7,1], [0,9,5]]");
// a page element changes
```

Now you can attach this discrete behavior to your application to achieve a desired effect:

```
$.get("http://djhkjhkdj.com", reportDataPackets);
```

Creating functions in general allows you to think about problems as the gradual transformation of data from one end of a pipeline to another. As you'll recall from Figure 9-1, each transformation pipeline can itself be viewed as a discrete activity, processing known data types in expected ways. As shown in Figure 9-3, compatible pipelines can be strung end to end in a feed-forward manner, while incompatible pipelines can be linked via adapters.

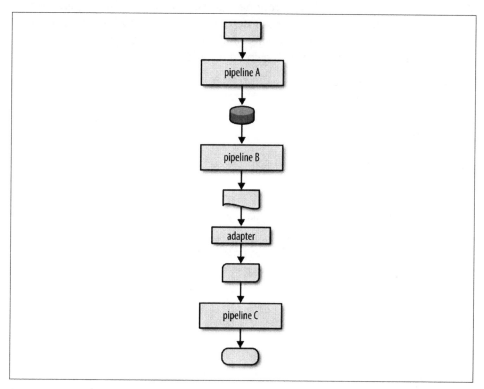

Figure 9-3. Linking pipelines directly or via adapters

From a program-wide perspective, pipelines with adapters can be attached to input and output sources. This type of thinking allows you to compose a system from smaller, known parts, while allowing the flexibility to interchange pieces and intermediate data representations as needed in the future. The idea of data flowing through transformers is a scalable notion, from the level of a single function up to the level of whole systems.

However, there are times when object-level thinking is appropriate, especially when concrete types adhering to generic mixins are the right abstraction. In the next section, I'll talk about the idea of a mixin and how it can be used to build up toward functional abstractions.

Mixins

While I've spent a lot of time and pages outlining a functional style of programming, there are times when objects and methods are just the right solution. In this section, I will outline an approach called mixin-based extension, which is similar to the way that class-based systems are built but intentionally constrained. Before diving into mixins directly, let me take a moment to motivate the need for object-thinking. Imagine a function polyToString that takes an object and returns a string representation of it. A naive implementation of polyToString could be written as follows:

```
function polyToString(obj) {
  if (obj instanceof String)
    return obj;
  else if (obj instanceof Array)
    return stringifyArray(obj);

  return obj.toString();
}

function stringifyArray(ary) {
  return ["[", _.map(ary, polyToString).join(","), "]"].join('');
}
```

As shown, the initial implementation of polyToString can be written as nested if statements where each branch checks the type. The addition of stringifyArray is added to create nicer looking string representations for strings. Running through a few tests shows polyToString in action:

```
polyToString([1,2,3]);
//=> "[1,2,3]"

polyToString([1,2,[3,4]]);
//=> "[1,2,[3,4]]"
```

Seems reasonable, no? However, attempting to create the representation requires that I add a new if branch into the body of polyToString, which is kind of silly. A better approach might be to use something like dispatch from Chapter 5, which takes some number of functions and attempts to execute each, returning the first non-undefined value:

```
var polyToString = dispatch(
  function(s) { return _.isString(s) ? s : undefined },
  function(s) { return _.isArray(s) ? stringifyArray(s) : undefined },
  function(s) { return s.toString() });
```

Again, the types are checked, but by using dispatch, I've at least abstracted each check into a separate function and have opened the door to further composition for extension purposes. Of course, that the use of dispatch works as expected is a nice bonus also:

```
polyToString(42);
//=> "42"

polyToString([1,2,[3,4]]);
//=> "[1, 2, [3, 4]]"

polyToString('a');
//=> "a"
```

As you might imagine, new types still present a problem if they do not already have a nice #toString implementation:

```
polyToString({a: 1, b: 2});
//=> "[object Object]"
```

However, rather than causing the pain of needing to modify a nested if, dispatch allows me to simply compose another function:

```
var polyToString = dispatch(
  function(s) { return _.isString(s) ? s : undefined },
  function(s) { return _.isArray(s) ? stringifyArray(s) : undefined },
  function(s) { return _.isObject(s) ? JSON.stringify(s) : undefined },
  function(s) { return s.toString() });
```

And again, the new implementation of polyToString works as expected:

```
polyToString([1,2,{a: 42, b: [4,5,6]}, 77]);

//=> '[1,2,{"a":42,"b":[4,5,6]},77]'
```

The use of dispatch in this way is quite elegant,[2] but I can't help but feel a little weird about it. Adding support for yet another type, perhaps Container from Chapter 7 can illustrate my discomfort:

```
polyToString(new Container(_.range(5)));

//=> {"_value":[0,1,2,3,4]}"
```

---

2. For the sake of expediency, I've delegated out to JSON.stringify since this section is not about converting objects to strings; nor, for that matter, is it about stringifying in general.

Certainly I could make this more pleasing to the eye by adding yet another link in the chain of calls composing `dispatch`, consisting of something like the following:

```
...
return ["@", polyToString(s._value)].join('');
...
```

But the problem is that `dispatch` works in a very straightforward way. That is, it starts from the first function and tries every one until one of them returns a value. Encoding type information beyond a single hierarchical level would eventually become more complicated than it needs to be. Instead, an example like customized `toString` operations is a good case for method methodologies. However, accomplishing this goal is typically done with JavaScript in ways that go against the policies that I outlined in the Preface:

- Core prototypes are modified.
- Class hierarchies are built.

I'll talk about both of these options before moving on to mixin-based extension.

Core Prototype Munging

Very often, when creating new types in JavaScript, you'll need specialized behaviors beyond those composed or extended. My `Container` type is a good example:

```
(new Container(42)).toString();
//=> "[object Object]"
```

This is unacceptable. The obvious choice is that I can attach a `Container`-specific `to String` method onto the `prototype`:

```
Container.prototype.toString = function() {
    return ["@<", polyToString(this._value), ">"].join('');
}
```

And now all instances of `Container` will have the same `toString` behavior:

```
(new Container(42)).toString();
//=> "@<42>"

(new Container({a: 42, b: [1,2,3]})).toString();
//=> "@<{"a":42,"b":[1,2,3]}>"
```

Of course, `Container` is a type that I control, so it's perfectly acceptable to modify its `prototype`—the burden falls on me to document the expected interfaces and use cases. However, what if I want to add the ability to some core object? The only choice is to step on the core prototype:

```
Array.prototype.toString = function() {
    return "DON'T DO THIS";
```

```
}
[1,2,3].toString();
//=> "DON'T DO THIS"
```

The problem is that if anyone ever uses your library, then any array that she creates is tainted by this new `Array#toString` method. Therefore, for core types like `Array` and `Object`, it's much better to keep custom behaviors isolated to functions that are delegated to custom types. I did this very thing in `Container#toString` by delegating down to `polyToString`. I'll take this approach later when I discuss mixins.

Class Hierarchies

> In Smalltalk, everything happens somewhere else.
>
> —Adele Goldberg

When approaching the task of defining a system using a class-based object-oriented methodology, you typically attempt to enumerate the types of "things" that comprise your system and how they relate to one another. When viewing a problem through an object-oriented lens, more often than not the way that one class relates to another is in a hierarchical way. Say employees are kinds of people who happen to be either accountants, custodians, or CEOs. These relationships form an hierarchy of types used to describe the residents of any given system.

Imagine that I want to implement my `Container` type as a hierarchy of types (see Figure 9-4).

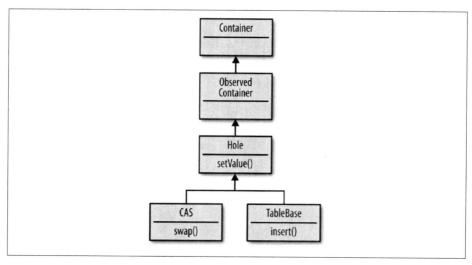

Figure 9-4. Representing Container types in a hierarchy

The diagram in Figure 9-4 states that at the root of the hierarchy is the `Container` type and from that derives `ObservableContainer`, which is used to attach functions that receive state change information. From `ObservableContainer`, I derive a `Hole` type that is "set-able." Finally, I define two different `Hole` types that have differing semantics for just how to assign values.

Using a stripped-down JavaScript class library based on a tiny library created by John Resig, I can sketch how this hierarchy might be constructed (Resig 2008):

```
function ContainerClass() {}
function ObservedContainerClass() {}
function HoleClass() {}
function CASClass() {}
function TableBaseClass() {}

ObservedContainerClass.prototype = new ContainerClass();
HoleClass.prototype = new ObservedContainerClass();
CASClass.prototype = new HoleClass();
TableBaseClass.prototype = new HoleClass();
```

Now that all of the hierarchical relationships are stitched together, I can test if they resolve as I expect:

```
(new CASClass()) instanceof HoleClass;
//=> true

(new TableBaseClass()) instanceof HoleClass;
//=> true

(new HoleClass()) instanceof CASClass;
//=> false
```

This is what I would expect—inheritance travels up the hierarchy, but not down. Now, putting some stubs in for implementation:

```
var ContainerClass = Class.extend({
  init: function(val) {
    this._value = val;
  },
});

var c = new ContainerClass(42);

c;
//=> {_value: 42 ...}

c instanceof Class;
//=> true
```

The `ContainerClass` just holds a value. However, the `ObservedContainerClass` provides some extra functionality:

```
var ObservedContainerClass = ContainerClass.extend({
  observe: function(f) { note("set observer") },
  notify: function() { note("notifying observers") }
});
```

Of course, the ObservedContainerClass doesn't do much on its own. Instead, I'll need a way to set a value and notify:

```
var HoleClass = ObservedContainerClass.extend({
  init: function(val) { this.setValue(val) },
  setValue: function(val) {
    this._value = val;
    this.notify();
    return val;
  }
});
```

As you might expect, the hierarchy is available to new HoleClass instances:

```
var h = new HoleClass(42);
// NOTE: notifying observers

h.observe(null);
// NOTE: set observer

h.setValue(108);
// NOTE: notifying observers
//=> 108
```

And now, at the bottom of the hierarchy, I start adding new behavior:

```
var CASClass = HoleClass.extend({
  swap: function(oldVal, newVal) {
    if (!_.isEqual(oldVal, this._value)) fail("No match");

    return this.setValue(newVal);
  }
});
```

A CASClass instance adds additional compare-and-swap semantics that say, "provide what you think is the old value and a new value, and I'll set the new value only if the expected old and actual old match." This change semantic is especially nice for asynchronous programming because it provides a way to check that the old value is what you expect, and did not change. Coupling compare-and-swap with JavaScript's run-to-completion guarantees is a powerful way to ensure coherence in asynchronous change.[3]

---

3. In a nutshell, run-to-completion refers to a property of JavaScript's event loop. That is, any call paths running during a particular "tick" of the event loop are guaranteed to complete before the next "tick." This book is not about the event-loop. I recommend David Flanagan's *JavaScript: The Definitive Guide*, 6th Edition, for a comprehensive dive into the JavaScript event system (and into JavaScript in general).

You can see it in action here:

```
var c = new CASClass(42);
// NOTE: notifying observers

c.swap(42, 43);
// NOTE: notifying observers
//=> 43

c.swap('not the value', 44);
// Error: No match
```

So with a class-based hierarchy, I can implement small bits of behavior and build up to larger abstractions via inheritance.

Changing Hierarchies

However, there is a potential problem. What if I want to add a new type in the middle of the hierarchy, called `ValidatedContainer`, that allows you to attach validation functions used to check that good values are used. Where does it go?

As shown in Figure 9-5, the logical place seems to be to put `ValidatedContainer` at the same level as `ObservedContainer`.

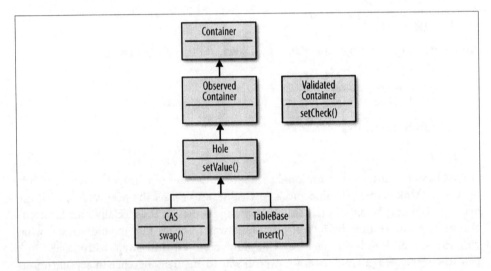

Figure 9-5. Extending the hierarchy

It's conceivable that I'd want all `Hole` instances to allow validation, but I don't really know that for certain (never mind the problem of multiple inheritance). I certainly do not want to assume that my users will want that behavior. What would be nice is if I could just extend it where needed. For example, if the `CAS` class needed validators, then

I could put ValidatedContainer above it in the hierarchy and just extend from it, as shown in Figure 9-6.

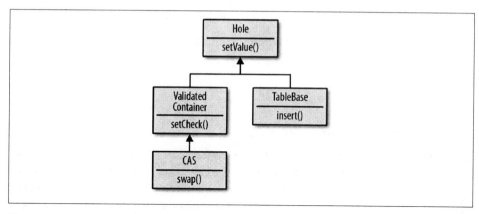

Figure 9-6. Moving a special-case class lower in the hierarchy is tricky

However, if a new type comes along that needs compare-and-swap semantics, but doesn't need validation, then the hierarchy in Figure 9-6 is problematic. I definitely shouldn't force that implementation to inherit from CAS.

The big problem with class hierarchies is that they are created under the assumption that we know the set of needed behaviors from the start. That is, object-oriented techniques prescribe that we start with a hierarchy of behaviors and fit our classes into that determination. However, as ValidatedContainer shows, some behaviors are difficult to classify ontologically. Sometimes behaviors are just behaviors.

Flattening the Hierarchy with Mixins

Let me try to simplify matters here. Imagine if I could take the base functionalities contained in Container, ObservedContainer, ValidatedContainer, and Hole and just put them all at the same level (see Figure 9-7).

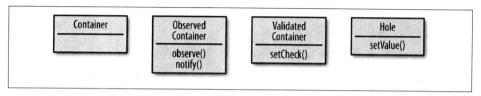

Figure 9-7. Flattening the hierarchy

If you blur your eyes a little, then Figure 9-7 shows that when flattening the hierarchy, what's left is not an implicit relationship between one type and another. In fact, the boxes do not really define types at all. Instead, what they define are sets of discrete behaviors, or *mixins*. If all we have are behaviors, then the way to make new behaviors is to either define them anew or "mix" in existing behaviors.[4] This again hearkens back to the idea of composing existing functionality to create new functions.

So let me start anew with an implementation of Container:

```
function Container(val) {
    this._value = val;
    this.init(val);
}

Container.prototype.init = _.identity;
```

The implementation of this new Container constructor looks much like the implementation from Chapter 7, except this one has a call to an init method. The presence of the init call defines a mixin—or the means by which extension of the Container occurs in addition to the way that clients interact with it. Specifically, the mixin protocol for Container is as follows:

Extension protocol
    Must provide an init method

Interface protocol
    Constructor only

When designing APIs via mixin extension, you'll often need to delegate to unknown functions. This not only provides a standard for interacting with the types, but also allows extension points. In the case of Container, the init call delegates to Underscore's _.identity. Later on I will override init, but for now, see how Container is used:

```
var c = new Container(42);

c;
//=> {_value: 42}
```

So the new Container acts like the old. However, what I'd like to do is create a new type with similar, yet different behavior. The type that I have in mind, called a Hole, has the following semantics:

- Holds a value
- Delegates to a validation function to check the value set
- Delegates to a notification function to notify interested parties of value changes

I can map these semantics directly to code, as shown in the following:

---

4. Mixins in this chapter are a cross between what's commonly known as a "protocol" and the Template method design pattern, minus the hierarchy.

```
var HoleMixin = {
  setValue: function(newValue) {
    var oldVal = this._value;

    this.validate(newValue);
    this._value = newValue;
    this.notify(oldVal, newValue);
    return this._value;
  }
};
```

The HoleMixin#setValue method defines a set of circumstances that must be met in order for a type to qualify as a Hole. Any type extending Hole should offer notify and validate methods. However, there is no real Hole type yet, only a mixin that describes "holiness." The implementation of a Hole constructor is fairly simple:

```
var Hole = function(val) {
  Container.call(this, val);
}
```

The signature for the Hole constructor is the same as for Container; in fact, the use of the Container.call method taking the Hole instance's this pointer ensures that whatever Container does on construction will occur in the context of the Hole instance.

The mixin protocol specification for HoleMixin is as follows:

Extension protocol
  Must provide notify, validate and init methods

Interface protocol
  Constructor and setValue

The need for the init method is derived from the direct use of Container in the constructor. Failing to meet any given mixin, particularly the Container mixin, has potentially dire consequences:

```
var h = new Hole(42);
//TypeError: Object [object Object] has no method 'init'
```

That the Container extension interface was not met means that any attempt to use Hole at the moment will fail. But despair not; the interesting thing about mixin extension is that any given type is composed of existing mixins, either outright or through extension.

Based on the illustration shown in Figure 9-8, the fulfillment of the Hole type requires either implementing or mixing in both ObserverMixin and ValidateMixin.

Figure 9-8. Using mixins to "mix" behaviors

Since neither of these mixins exist, I'll need to create them, starting with the Observer Mixin:

```
var ObserverMixin = (function() {
  var _watchers = [];

  return {
    watch: function(fun) {
      _watchers.push(fun);
      return _.size(_watchers);
    },
    notify: function(oldVal, newVal) {
```

```
      _.each(_watchers, function(watcher) {
        watcher.call(this, oldVal, newVal);
      });

      return _.size(_watchers);
    }
  };
}());
```

The use of the JavaScript closure mojo (function() {...}()); to encapsulate the _watchers object is the common way to hide data, and it is therefore the preferred way to hide a bit of mixin state as well. The watch function takes a function of two values, the old value and the new, and adds it to the _watchers array. The watch method also returns the number of watchers stored. The notify method then loops over the _watch ers and calls each function, finally returning the number of watchers notified. The implementation of ObserverMixin could be enhanced to be more robust in the face of watch function failure, and also to allow the removal of watchers, but I leave that as an exercise to the reader.[5]

The second missing mixin is the ValidateMixin, implemented as follows:

```
var ValidateMixin = {
  addValidator: function(fun) {
    this._validator = fun;
  },
  init: function(val) {
    this.validate(val);
  },
  validate: function(val) {
    if (existy(this._validator) &&
        !this._validator(val))
      fail("Attempted to set invalid value " + polyToString(val));
  }
};
```

As shown, it's the ValidateMixin that finally fulfills the init extension requirement. This makes sense since a valid initialization step is to validate the starting value of the container. The other two functions, addValidator and validate, set the validation function and call it (if set) respectively.

Now that the mixins are in place, it's time to mix them together to fulfill the requirements of the Hole type:

```
_.extend(Hole.prototype
         , HoleMixin
```

5. The ECMAScript.next effort has described an Object.observe method that works similarly to the features described herein. The specification should become a reality in JavaScript core sometime before the heat death of the sun. More information is found at *http://wiki.ecmascript.org/doku.php?id=harmony:observe*.

```
                , ValidateMixin
                , ObserverMixin);
```

I mentioned in Chapter 7 that Underscore's `_.extend` function is tricky because it modifies the target object. However, in the case of mixin extension, this behavior is exactly what I want. That is, by using `_.extend`, I copy all of the methods into `Hole.mix in`. So how does the fully mixed implementation work? Observe:

```
var h = new Hole(42);
```

That the constructor works at all is a good sign to start. What if I add a validator that is guaranteed to fail?

```
h.addValidator(always(false));

h.setValue(9);
// Error: Attempted to set invalid value 9
```

Since I attached a validator returning `false` in all cases, I'll never be able to set another value again unless I remove the validation function directly. However, let me create a new `Hole` instance with a less restrictive validator:

```
var h = new Hole(42);

h.addValidator(isEven);
```

The new instance should allow only even numbers as values:

```
h.setValue(9);
// Error: Attempted to set invalid value 9

h.setValue(108);
//=> 108

h;
//=> {_validator: function isEven(n) {...},
//      _value: 108}
```

That the `Hole` instance h allows only even numbers is of limited value, but for illustration purposes it serves well. Below I'll add a watcher using the `watch` method:

```
h.watch(function(old, nu) {
  note(["Changing", old, "to", nu].join(' '));
});
//=> 1

h.setValue(42);
// NOTE: Changing 108 to 42
//=> 42
```

Passing in the even number 42 shows that the watcher is called, so adding another should also work:

```
h.watch(function(old, nu) {
  note(["Veranderende", old, "tot", nu].join(' '));
});
//=> 2

h.setValue(36);
// NOTE: Changing 42 to 36
// NOTE: Veranderende 42 tot 36
//=> 36
```

So I've managed to create a new JavaScript type by both using constructor calls, and by mixing discrete packets of functionality into a coherent hole…I mean whole. In the next section, I'll talk about how to use mixin extension to add new capabilities to existing types.

New Semantics via Mixin Extension

Adding new capabilities to existing JavaScript types couldn't be simpler; you just muck with the prototype and, *kaboom* you've attached new behavior. Well, *kaboom* is the operative term here because it's rarely that simple. It's not always straightforward to extend existing types because you never know whether you might break some delicate internal balance. Keeping that in mind, I will explore how to extend the capabilities of the Hole type to include new change semantics. First, I like the idea of providing the setValue method as a low-level way to tap into the change machinery. However, I would like to provide another method, swap, that takes a function and some number of arguments and sets the new value based on the result of a call to said function with the current value and the arguments. The best way to present this idea is to show the implementation and some examples:

```
var SwapMixin = {
  swap: function(fun /* , args... */) {
    var args = _.rest(arguments)
    var newValue = fun.apply(this, construct(this._value, args));

    return this.setValue(newValue);
  }
};
```

The swap method on the SwapMixin indeed takes a function and some arguments. The new value is then calculated using the function given the _value and the additional arguments. The mixin protocol specification for SwapMixin is as follows:

Extension protocol
    Must provide a setValue method and a _value property

Interface protocol
    The swap method

I can actually test the SwapMixin in isolation:

```
var o = {_value: 0, setValue: _.identity};

_.extend(o, SwapMixin);

o.swap(construct, [1,2,3]);
//=> [0, 1, 2, 3]
```

So, as shown, the logic behind the swap mixin seems sound. Before I use it to enhance Hole, let me implement another mixin, SnapshotMixin, used to offer a way to safely grab the value in the Hole instance:

```
var SnapshotMixin = {
  snapshot: function() {
    return deepClone(this._value);
  }
};
```

The SnapshotMixin provides a new method named snapshot that clones any object contained therein. Now, the new specification of Hole stands as:

```
_.extend(Hole.prototype
        , HoleMixin
        , ValidateMixin
        , ObserverMixin
        , SwapMixin
        , SnapshotMixin);
```

And now, any new Hole instances will have the enhanced behavior:

```
var h = new Hole(42);

h.snapshot();
//=> 42

h.swap(always(99));
//=> 99

h.snapshot();
//=> 99
```

Mixin extension is not only a powerful way to define new types, but also useful for enhancing existing types. Bear in mind that there are caveats in that it's not always straightforward to extend existing types, and additionally any extension will take place globally.

New Types via Mixin Mixing

Now that I've shown how to define two base types (Container and Hole), let me implement one more called CAS, which offers compare-and-swap semantics. That is, any change to the type occurs based on an assumption that you know what the existing value happens to be. The definition starts by using the construction behavior of Hole:

```
var CAS = function(val) {
  Hole.call(this, val);
}
```

The interesting part of the definition of the CASMixin is that it overrides the swap method on the SwapMixin as shown here:

```
var CASMixin = {
  swap: function(oldVal, f) {
    if (this._value === oldVal) {
      this.setValue(f(this._value));
      return this._value;
    }
    else {
      return undefined;
    }
  }
};
```

The CASMixin#swap method takes two arguments instead of the one taken by SwapMix in. Additionally, the CASMixin#swap method returns undefined if the expected value does not match the actual _value. There are two ways to mix the implementation of the CAS types. First, I could simply leave out the SwapMixin on the extension and use the CASMixin instead, since I know that the swap method is the only replacement. However, I will instead use ordering to _.extend to take care of the override:

```
_.extend(CAS.prototype
         , HoleMixin
         , ValidateMixin
         , ObserverMixin
         , SwapMixin
         , CASMixin
         , SnapshotMixin);
```

While I knew that the SwapMixin was fully subsumed by the CASMixin, leaving it in is not entirely bad. The reason is that if I do not control the SwapMixin, then it's conceivable that it may gain enhancements at a future date beyond simply the swap method. By leaving in the extension chain, I get any enhancements for free in the future. If I do not like the future "enhancements," then I can choose to remove SwapMixin later. To wrap this section up, the CAS type is used as follows:

```
var c = new CAS(42);

c.swap(42, always(-1));
//=> -1

c.snapshot();
//=> -1

c.swap('not the value', always(100000));
//=> undefined
```

```
c.snapshot();
//=> -1
```

And that concludes the discussion of mixin extension. However, there is one more point to make about it: mixin extension, if done correctly, is an implementation detail. In fact, I would still reach for simple data like primitives, arrays, and objects (as maps) over mixin-based programming. Specifically, I've found that when you're dealing with a large number of data elements, then simple data is best because you can use common tools and functions to proccess it—the more generic data processing tools available, the better. On the other hand, you will definitely find a need to create highly specialized types with well-defined interfaces driving per-type semantics.[6] It's in the case of these specialized types that I've found mixin-based development a real advantage.

Simple data is best. Specialized data types should be, well, special.

Methods Are Low-Level Operations

That the types created in the previous sections are object/method-centric is a technical detail that need not leak into a functional API. As I've stressed throughout this book, functional APIs are composable and if created well, do not require explicit knowledge of the intermediate types between composition points. Therefore, by simply creating a function-based API for accessing and manipulating the container types, I can hide most of the detail of their implementation.

First, let me start with the container:

```
function contain(value) {
    return new Container(value);
}
```

Simple, right? If I were providing a container library, then I would offer the contain function as the user-facing API:

```
contain(42);
//=> {_value: 42} (of type Container, but who cares?)
```

For developers, I might additionally provide the mixin definitions for extension purposes.

The Hole functional API is similar, but beefier:

```
function hole(val /*, validator */) {
    var h = new Hole();
    var v = _.toArray(arguments)[1];
```

---

6. If you come from a Scala background, then the mixin-based development outlined here is far from realizing the well-known Cake pattern (Wampler 2009). However, with some work and runtime mixin inspection, you can achieve a rough approximation, providing an additional capability for large-scale module definition.

```
    if (v) h.addValidator(v);

    h.setValue(val);

    return h;
}
```

I've managed to encapsulate a lot of the logic of validation within the confines of the `hole` function. This is ideal because I can compose the underlying methods in any way that I want. The usage contract of the `hole` function is much simpler than the combined use of the `Hole` constructor and the `addValidator` method:

```
var x = hole(42, always(false));
// Error: Attempted to set invalid value 42
```

Likewise, although `setValue` is a method on the type, there is no reason to expose it functionally. Instead, I can expose just the `swap` and `snapshot` functions instead:

```
var swap = invoker('swap', Hole.prototype.swap);
```

And the `swap` function works as any `invoker`-bound method, with the target object as the first argument:

```
var x = hole(42);

swap(x, sqr);
//=> 1764
```

Exposing the functionality of the CAS type is very similar to `Hole`:

```
function cas(val /*, args */) {
  var h = hole.apply(this, arguments);
  var c = new CAS(val);
  c._validator = h._validator;

  return c;
}

var compareAndSwap = invoker('swap', CAS.prototype.swap);
```

I'm using (abusing) private details of the `Hole` type to implement most of the capability of the `cas` function, but since I control the code to both types, I can justify the coupling. In general, I would avoid that, especially if the abused type is not under my immediate control.

Finally, I can now implement the remaining container functions as generic delegates:

```
function snapshot(o) { return o.snapshot() }
function addWatcher(o, fun) { o.watch(fun) }
```

And these functions work exactly how you might guess:

```
var x = hole(42);

addWatcher(x, note);

swap(x, sqr);
// NOTE: 42 chapter01.js:38
//=> 1764

var y = cas(9, isOdd);

compareAndSwap(y, 9, always(1));
//=> 1

snapshot(y);
//=> 1
```

I believe that by putting a functional face on the container types, I've achieved a level of flexibility not obtainable via an object/method focus.

}).call("Finis");

This chapter concludes my coverage of functional programming in JavaScript by showing how it lends to building software. Even though some problems seemingly call for object or class-based thinking, very often there are functional ways to achieve the same goals. Not only will there be functional ways to build parts of your system, but building your system functionally often leads to more flexibility in the long term by not tying your users to an object-centric API.

Likewise, even when a problem calls for object-thinking, approaching the problem with a functional eye can lead to vastly different solutions than object-oriented programming dictates. If functional composition has proven useful, how might object composition fare? In this chapter, I discussed mixin-based design and how it is indeed a functionally flavored style of object composition.

Writing this book has been a joy for me and I hope has been an enlightening adventure for you. Learning functional programming shouldn't be seen as a goal in itself, but instead a technique for achieving your goals. There may be times when it is just not a good fit, but even then, thinking functionally can and will help change the way you build software in general.

Functional JavaScript in the Wild

In no way does this book represent even a modicum of original thinking regarding functional programming in JavaScript. For many years—indeed, for as long as JavaScript has existed—people have pushed the boundaries of its support for a functional style. In this appendix, I'll attempt to briefly summarize what I perceive as a fair sampling of the offerings in languages and libraries on the topic of functional JavaScript. No ranking is implied.

Functional Libraries for JavaScript

There are numerous noteworthy JavaScript libraries available in the wild. I'll run through the high-level features of a few herein and provide a few examples along the way.

Functional JavaScript

Oliver Steele's Functional JavaScript library (*http://osteele.com/sources/javascript/func tional/*) is the first functional library that I discovered. It provides all of the normal higher-order functions like `map`, but it provides a very interesting string-based short-form function format. That is, to square the numbers in an array, one would normally write the following:

```
map(function(n) { return n * n }, [1, 2, 3, 4]);
//=> [2, 4, 9, 16]
```

However, with the Functional JavaScript function literal string, the same code be written as:

```
map('n*n', [1, 2, 3, 4]);
//=> [2, 4, 9, 16]
```

Functional JavaScript also provides currying of the function literal strings:

```
var lessThan5 = rcurry('<', 5);

lessThan5(4);
//=> true

lessThan5(44);
//=> false
```

Functional JavaScript is a masterful piece of JavaScript metaprogramming and well worth exploring for its technical insights.

Underscore-contrib

A long time ago (in Internet years) I wrote a functional JavaScript library named Doris heavily inspired by Steele's Functional JavaScript and the Clojure programming language. I used Doris for some internal libraries but eventually deprecated it in favor of Underscore and (when possible) ClojureScript. When writing this book, I resurrected the Doris source code, ported it to Underscore, cleaned up the code, and renamed it Lemonad (pronounced lemonade), then moved most of the capabilities into the official Underscore-contrib library.

Underscore-contrib (*http://fogus.github.io/lemonad/*) is built on Underscore and provides dozens of useful applicative, higher-order and monadic functions. When importing Underscore-contrib, the functions are mixed into the Underscore _ object, allowing you to turn Underscore up to 11. In addition to the core functionality, I've implemented a number of "extras" for Underscore-contrib, including the following:

Codd
    A relational algebra library

Friebyrd
    A library providing an embedded logic system

Minker
    A library providing an embedded datalog

```
var a = ['a','a','b','a'];
var m = _.explode("mississippi");

_.frequencies(a)
//=> {a: 3, b: 1}

_.frequencies(m)
//=> {p: 2, s: 4, i: 4, m: 1}
```

There are many more functions available. Fortunately, most of the functions defined in this book are available in Lemonad or Underscore-contrib, so consider this the unofficial manual.

RxJS

Microsoft's Reactive Extensions for JavaScript (RxJS) (*http://reactive-extensions.github.com/RxJS/*) is a set of libraries that facilitate asynchronous, event-driven programming models. RxJS works against an `Observable` abstraction that allows you to process asynchronous data streams via a rich, LINQ-like functional query model.

When I was a younger man (this of course dates me) I spent a seemingly limitless amount of time playing my old Nintendo NES system. The Japanese company Konami created many interesting games, but prime among them was my favorite, *Contra*. The goal of *Contra* was...well, no one cares anymore, but one interesting point was that there was a cheat code that you could enter to get 30 extra lives. The cheat code is described as follows:

```
var codes = [
    38, // up
    38, // up
    40, // down
    40, // down
    37, // left
    39, // right
    37, // left
    39, // right
    66, // b
    65  // a
];
```

The cheat code was entered via the game controller before the game started, and it was the only reason that I ever completed the game. If you want to add the Konami Code (as it's commonly called) to a web page, then you can do so with RxJS. A useful method to compare a sequence of values with RxJS is called `sequenceEqual`, and can be used to check that a stream of integers matches the Konami Code:

```
function isKonamiCode(seq) {
  return seq.sequenceEqual(codes);
}
```

RxJS allows you to tap into many sources of asynchronous events, including a page document's key presses, as shown:

```
var keyPressStream = $(document).keyupAsObservable()
  .select(function (e) { return e.keyCode })
  .windowWithCount(10, 10);
```

The `keyPressStream` represents a stream of keycodes built from keypress events. Rather than observing on every keypress, RxJS allows you to chunk the stream into aggregate segments using the `windowWithCount` method. One additional point is that RxJS adorns jQuery itself with relevant `Observable` creating methods, and will do the same for various other JavaScript frameworks. This seamless integration with existing libraries is a pleasure to work with.

Now that I have a stream of keycodes, I can declaratively tell RxJS what I would like to do with them:

```
keyPressStream
  .selectMany(isKonamiCode)
  .where(_.identity)
  .subscribe(function () {
    alert("You now have thirty lives!");
  });
```

Of note is that the `where` method could transform the data values along the way, but I chose to pass them through using Underscore's `_.identity` function. The function given to the `select` method is what will run whenever the function assigned via the `selectMany` returns a truthy value. If I were to load the preceding code into a web page and push the correct sequence of arrow keys followed by the characters "a" and "b," then an alert box would launch.

RxJS is an amazing library that provides a way to capture asynchronous flow as a value—a truly mind-bending paradigm.

Bilby

If Lemonad turns Underscore up to 11, then Bilby turns Lemonad up to 12 or beyond. A self-contained functional library, Brian McKenna's Bilby (*http://bilby.brianmcken na.org/*) stretches the possibilities of functional style in JavaScript. It's worth exploring Bilby to learn its entire feature set, but one that is particularly nice is its implementation of multimethods.

Bilby's multimethods are similar to the `dispatch` function defined in Chapter 5 but more robust and flexible. Using Bilby, you can define functions that dispatch on any number of interesting conditions. Bilby provides a module system called environments that aggregate related methods and properties:

```
var animals = bilby.environment();
```

Before adding a multimethod I can define a few helper functions:

```
function voice(type, sound) {
  return ["The", type, "says", sound].join(' ');
}

function isA(thing) {
  return function(obj) {
    return obj.type == thing;
  }
}

function say(sound) {
  return function(obj) {
    console.log(voice(obj.type, sound));
```

```
        }
    }
```

Using these helpers I can tell Bilby:

- The name of the method
- A predicate that checks the arguments
- An action function that performs the method behaviors

The `Environment#method` takes the three arguments just listed:

```
var animals = animals.method('speak', isA('cat'), say("mew"));
```

As shown, adorning an environment with a new multimethod returns a new environment. I can now call `speak`:

```
animals.speak({type: 'cat'});
// The cat says mew
```

Adding a new polymorphic behavior is simple:

```
var animals = animals.method('speak', isA('dog'), say("woof"));
```

And calling `speak` with a dog object works as expected:

```
animals.speak({type: 'cat'});
// The cat says mew

animals.speak({type: 'dog'});
// The dog says woof
```

Of course, I can match an arbitrary condition within the dispatch predicate:

```
var animals = animals.method('speak',
  function(obj) {
    return (isA('frog')(obj) && (obj.status == 'dead'))
  },
  say('Hello ma, baby!'));
```

So passing in a dead frog works the same:

```
animals.speak({type: 'frog', status: 'dead'});
// The frog says Hello ma, baby!
```

Bilby provides much more than multimethods, including a trampoline that allows you to return functions, monadic structures, validation helpers, and much more.

allong.es

Reginald Braithwaite's allong.es library (*http://allong.es/*) has a bevy of useful function combinators in its arsenal. However, an interesting aspect from my perspective (and something that I didn't cover in depth) is its support for stateful iterators:

```
var iterators = require('./allong.es').iterators
var take = iterators.take,
    map = iterators.map,
    drop = iterators.drop;

var ints = iterators.numbers();
```

Aside from the necessary import seance required to get the correct allong.es iteration functions, I also defined an iterator, ints, over all numbers. I can then "perform" some operations over the ints iterator:

```
var squares = take(drop(map(ints, function(n) {
  return n * n;
}), 100000), 100);
```

Just for fun, I squared all of the integers, dropped the first 100,000 results, then grabbed the next 100. The magic of the allong.es iterator is that I've not actually performed any calculation yet. Only when I query the iterator using an external iterator (in my case, for) will any of the calculations occur:

```
var coll = [];
for (var i = 0; i < 100; i++ ) {
  coll.push(squares())
}

coll;
//=> [10000200001,
//      10000400004,
//      10000600009,
//      10000800016,
//      10001000025,
//      10001200036,
//      ...
//      10020010000]
```

I can check the math by manually squaring the number 100,001 (because I dropped 100,000, recall):

```
100001 * 100001
//=> 10000200001
```

And, as shown, the manual calculation matches with the first element in the coll array. There is too much in allong.es (and about iterators in general) to do justice here. I highly recommend you explore.

Other Functional Libraries

There are a growing number of JavaScript libraries supporting varying degrees of functional programming. The grandmaster of them all—jQuery—has always been somewhat functional, but with the inclusion of promises has gotten more so. A nice project that I've followed since its inception is Reducers (*https://github.com/Gozala/reducers*), which implements a generalized reducible collections API inspired by Clojure's reducer functionality. The Lo-Dash project (*http://lodash.com/*) is a major fork of Underscore that attempts a cleaner core and more performance. The Mori project (*https://github.com/swannodette/mori*) by David Nolen is a facade over the ClojureScript core library, including its persistent data structures. The Udon library (*https://github.com/beastaugh/udon*) is a very straightforward functional library akin to Lemonad. Finally, the prelude.ls project (*http://gkz.github.com/prelude-ls/*) is also a straightforward functional affair. However, where prelude.ls differs is that it's originally written in the statically typed language TypeScript and compiled to JavaScript.

Functional Programming Languages Targeting JavaScript

When a functional library simple doesn't cut it, more and more programmers are turning to new languages using JavaScript as their compilation target. I'll outline just a few of the languages that I'm familiar with (to varying degrees herein). Don't take a language's inclusion as an endorsement and don't take a language's exclusion as a rejection. Included are only the handful that I've either used on real projects, contributed to in some way, or studied in my spare time.

ClojureScript

The ClojureScript programming language (*http://www.clojurescript.net*) is a variant of Clojure that compiles down to JavaScript. It has many of the same features as Clojure, including but not limited to the following:

- Persistent data structures
- Reference types
- Namespaces
- Strong JavaScript interop
- Laziness
- Destructuring assignment
- Protocols, types, and records

A taste of ClojureScript is as follows:

```
(defn hi [name]
  (.log js/console (str "Hello " name "!")))

(hi "ClojureScript")

;; (console) Hello ClojureScript
```

ClojureScript is an exciting language targeting the large-scale JavaScript application space. Indeed, I've used it to great effect in building robust single-page applications with the Pedestal web framework.[1] You can find out more about ClojureScript in the second edition of my other book, *The Joy of Clojure*.

CoffeeScript

CoffeeScript (*http://coffeescript.org/*) is a popular programming language that is the very embodiment of "JavaScript: The Good Parts" with a very clean syntax. The "hello world" example is simply trivial:

```
hi = (name) ->
  console.log ['Hello ', name, '!'].join ''

hi 'CoffeeScript'

# (console) Hello CoffeeScript
```

Some of the additional features above JavaScript include:

- Literate programming support (something I love a lot)
- Varargs
- List comprehensions
- Destructuring assignment

Its level of support for functional programming is effectively that of JavaScript, but its balance of features and syntax can act to make a functional style much cleaner.

Roy

Roy (*http://roy.brianmckenna.org/*) is a statically typed functional programming language inspired by ML in the early stages of its life. While Roy provides many of the features common to ML-family languages including pattern matching, structural types, and tagged unions, its type system is most interesting to me. If I implement a hi function that attempts to concatenate strings s in JavaScript, then I'm set for a rude surprise:

```
let hi name: String =
  alert "Hello " + name + "!"

// Error: Type error: String is not Number
```

Roy reserves the + operator for mathematical operations, disallowing the concatenation overload. However, Roy provides a ++ operator that will suffice:

---

1. And its predecessor. Pedestal is at *http://pedestal.io/*.

```
let hi name: String =
  console.log "Hello " ++ name ++ "!"
```

And calling the hi function is as simple as this:

```
hi "Roy"

// Hello Roy!
```

I, for one, will follow Roy's progress and hope to see good things come from it.

Elm

Like Roy, Elm (*http://elm-lang.org/*) is a statically typed language that compiles down
to JavaScript. Also like Roy, Elm will not allow willy-nilly string concatenation using +,
as shown here:

```
hi name = plainText ("Hello " + name + "!")

-- Type error (Line 1, Column 11):
-- String is not a {Float,Int}
-- In context: + "Hello "
```

Once again, like Roy, Elm reserves the ++ function for such use:

```
hi name = plainText ("Hello " ++ name ++ "!")

main = hi "Elm"

-- (page text) Hello Elm!
```

However, where Elm really departs from Roy is that instead of merely being a programming language, it truly is a system for development. That is, Elm provides a language centered around the Functional Reactive Programming (FRP) paradigm. In a
nutshell, FRP integrates a time model with an event system for the purposes of sanely
building robust systems centered on system-wide change effects. I could never ade-
quately cover FRP in these pages, as it could in fact, fill its own book. If you're looking
to stretch your mind, then Elm is a nice system for just such an exercise.

Annotated Bibliography

Papers/Books/Blog Posts/Talks

Structure and Interpretation of Computer Programs by Harold Abelson, Gerald Jay Sussman, and Julie Sussman (MIT Press, 1996)

> This book is among the most influential programming books ever written. Every page is a gem and every other sentence worthy of highlight. It moves very quickly through the material and requires focused attention and study—but it's well worth the effort.

Extreme Programming Explained: Embrace Change by Kent Beck (Addison-Wesley, 1999)

> An engaging book that elucidates the tenets of a revolution in programming.

Introduction to Functional Programming by Richard J. Bird and Philip Wadler (Prentice Hall, 1998)

> I prefer the first edition.

Closure: The Definitive Guide by Michael Bolin (O'Reilly, 2010)

> Bolin's ideas on JavaScript pseudo-classical inheritance have been very influential to my own style.

JavaScript Allongé by Reginald Braithwaite (Leanpub, 2013) (https://leanpub.com/javascript-allonge)

> I was fortunate enough to read an early draft of Reg's great book and think it would make a nice follow-up to my book. *Functional JavaScript* turned up to 11.

JavaScript: The Good Parts by Douglas Crockford (O'Reilly, 2008)

> Crockford's book is like a well-written, beautifully shot horror movie. It's the Suspiria of programming books. It'll give you nightmares, but you won't be able to look away.

An Introduction to Database Systems by C.J. Date (Addison-Wesley, 2003)
A must-read.

SQL and Relational Theory: How to Write Accurate SQL Code by C.J. Date (O'Reilly, 2011)
An amazing book for truly understanding the underpinnings of relational algebra and why the queries we write are so slow.

JavaScript: The Definitive Guide, 6th Edition by David Flanagan (O'Reilly, 2011)
The ultimate book on JavaScript in my opinion.

Domain Specific Languages by Martin Fowler (Addison-Wesley, 2010)
A profound writer and thinker on a profound topic.

Design Patterns: Elements of Reusable Object-Oriented Software by Erich Gamma, Richard Helm, Ralph Johnson, and John Vlissides (Addison-Wesley, 1995)
Much loved and derided, the original goal of the Gang of Four's book, to find a common language for describing system building, was a worthy one.

Java Concurrency in Practice by Brian Goetz, et al. (Addison-Wesley, 2005)
Absolutely essential reading if you ever plan to write a pile of Java code.

On Lisp by Paul Graham (Prentice Hall, 1993)
Considered by many to be the definitive book on Lisp.

Effective JavaScript: 68 Specific Ways to Harness the Power of JavaScript by David Herman (Addison-Wesley, 2012)
Like *JavaScript Allongé*, Herman's book would make a nice companion to my book.

The Joy of Clojure, Second edition by Chris Houser and Michael Fogus (Manning, 2013)
One of my goals in writing *Functional JavaScript* was to provide a smooth transition to understanding *Joy* without prior Clojure knowledge.

Hints for Computer System Design by Butler W. Lampson (Xeror Palo Alto Research Center, 1983)
Lampson has influenced much of modern programming even though you might never have heard his name.

ML for the Working Programmer, Second Edition by L.C. Paulson (Cambridge University Press, 1996)
What could you possibly learn about functional JavaScript by reading about ML? A lot, as it turns out.

Applicative High Order Programming: Standard ML in Practice by Stefan Sokolowski (Chapman & Hall Computing, 1991)
A long-forgotten gem.

JavaScript Patterns by Stoyan Stefanov (O'Reilly, 2010)
> Not really patterns in the "design patterns" sense, but rather patterns of structure that you'll see in JavaScript programs. A very nice read.

Common Lisp: A Gentle Introduction to Symbolic Computation by David S. Touretzky (Addison-Wesley/Benjamin Cummings, 1990)
> What could you possibly learn about functional JavaScript by reading about Lisp? A lot it turns out.

Programming Scala by Dean Wampler and Alex Payne (O'Reilly, 2009)
> A well-written book on Scala, available free online.

High Performance JavaScript by Nicolas Zakas (O'Reilly, 2010)
> An essential read when it's time to speed up your functional abstractions.

Presentations

"Pushing The Limits of Web Browsers...or Why Speed Matters" by Lars Bak (http://bit.ly/144rBkj)
> An invited keynote presentation at the 2012 Strange Loop conference. Bak is an engaging speaker who has been a driving force behind language-speed optimizations for decades.

"Programming with Values in Clojure" by Alan Dipert (http://bit.ly/Z1zrwS)
> A presentation given at the 2012 Clojure/West conference.

"The Next Mainstream Programming Language: A Game Developer's Perspective" by Tim Sweeney
> A presentation given at the Symposium on Principles of Programming Languages in 2006.

Blog Posts

Can functional programming be liberated from the von Neumann paradigm? by Conal Elliott (http://bit.ly/Z1zrwS)
> An exploration into how and why I/O corrupts the functional ideal that strives for declarativness.

Markdown by John Gruber (http://daringfireball.net/projects/markdown/)
> Markdown's ubiquity is nigh.

Rich Hickey Q&A by Rich Hickey and Michael Fogus. Code Quarterly 2011. (http://codequarterly.com/2011/rich-hickey/)
> Chock full of gems about programming, design, and languages and systems.

Monads are Tress with Grafting by Dan Piponi (http://bit.ly/12Hhe56)
> The paper that helped me tremendously in understanding monads. YMMV.

Simple JavaScript Inheritance by John Resig (http://bit.ly/ZN2nr2)
> While I tend to dislike hierarchy building, Resig's implementation is very clean and instructive.

Understanding Monads With JavaScript by Ionut G. Stan (http://bit.ly/109vWDm)
> Stan's monad implementation was highly important for my own understanding of monads. Additionally, the `actions` implementation is derived from his code.

Execution in the Kingdom of Nouns by Steve Yegge (http://bit.ly/19FFUgz)
> Yegge popularized the verbs vs nouns argument in OO vs functional programming. While his points are debatable, his imagery is stellar.

Maintainable JavaScript: Don't modify objects you don't own by Nicholas Zakas (http://bit.ly/10yBkQ0)
> Zakas has been thinking about good JavaScript style for a very long time.

Journal Articles

"Why functional programming matters" by John Hughes. The Computer Journal (1984)
> The definitive treatise on the matter. While the examples given are sometimes unfortunate, the prose is well worth a read.

Index

Symbols

We'd like to hear your suggestions for improving our indexes. Send email to index@oreilly.com.

L

lazy data, definition of, 131
LazyChain object, 168, 192
Lemonad library (Fogus), xiv, 218
lexical scope, 51
lookup schemes, 52

M

makeUniqueString function, 78
map function, 34, 140
Math#max, 70, 72
_.max function, 70, 72
McKenna, Brian, 220
metaprogramming, 33
method chaining
    benefits of, 165
    _.chain function, 166
    downsides to, 176
    lazy chains, 168
    overview of, 189
    promises, 173
    _.tap function, 167
    _.value function, 167
methods
    definition of, 33
    as low-level operations, 214
Microsoft's RxJS library, 219
Minker library (Fogus), 218
mixin-based extensions, 198–216
mixins, 198–216
    and class hierarchies, 201–211
    definition of, 206
    flattening hierarchies with, 205
    need for, 198
    new semantics with, 211
    new types with, 212
    vs. core prototype munging, 200
monads, 185
mutations
    as low-level operation, 92
    avoid by freezing, 151–153
    hiding, 83, 149–151, 153–154
    in JavaScript, 146, 148
    policies for control of, 160
        (see also immutability)
mutually recursive functions, 124
myLength operation, 114

N

nexts function, 118
_.noConflict function, 50
number, generating random, 139

O

_.object function, 42
object oriented programming (OOP), 4, 10, 32, 191, 216
object validators, 82
Object#freeze operation, 151
object-centric thinking, 192, 198
objects
    comparing arbitrary, 70
    deep cloning of, 125
    defensive freezing of, 151
    as low-level operations, 159
    mutability of, 148
    pervasive freezing of, 155
_.omit function, 43
OOP (see object oriented programming)
optimizations, 22

P

_.pairs function, 42
parseAge function, 9
partial application, 100–108
    of arbitrary number of arguments, 103
    vs. currying, 101
    of one and two known arguments, 102
    overview of, 111
    and pipelines, 180
    preconditions, 104
_.pick function, 44
pipelining, 176–180, 189, 197
_.pluck function, 41, 44
plucker function, 67
polymorphic functions, 87
predicates, 14
program optimizers, 23
promises, 173
property testing, 143–144
prototype chains, 32
prototype-based object-oriented programming, 32, 200
purity, 139–147
    determination of, 139

About the Author

Michael Fogus is a software developer with experience in distributed simulation, machine vision, and expert systems construction. He's actively involved in the Clojure and Underscore.js communities.

Colophon

The animal on the cover of *Functional JavaScript* is an eider duck (*Somateria mollissima*), a sea-duck that ranges between 50–70 cm in length. Eider ducks can be found along the coast of Europe, North America, and the east coast of Siberia. They spend their winters in temperate zones after breeding in the Arctic and other northern temperate regions. In flight, eider ducks have been clocked at speeds of 113 km/h (70 mph).

Eider nests are often built close to the ocean and are lined with eiderdown—plucked from the breast of a female eider. The lining has been harvested for use as pillow and quilt fillers, a sustainable practice that happens after the ducklings have left the nest without harm to the birds. Eiderdown has been replaced in more recent years by synthetic alternatives and down from domestic farm geese.

Male eider ducks are characterized by their black and white plumage and green nape; the female is brown. In general, eiders are bulky and large with a wedge-shaped bill. They feed on crustaceans and mollusks. Their favored food, mussels, are swallowed whole, the shells crushed in the gizzard and excreted.

This species has populations of between 1.5 and 2 million in North America and Europe; the numbers in eastern Siberia are large but unknown. One colony of eiders—about 1,000 pairs of ducks—on the Farne Islands in Northumberland, England, enjoys a bit of fame for being the subject of one of the first bird protection laws in the year 676. The law was established by Saint Cuthbert, patron saint of Northumberland, giving the ducks a local nickname of "Cuddy's ducks" ("Cuddy" being short for "Cutherbert").

In the 1990s, there were eider die-offs in Canada's Hudson Bay that were attributed to changing ice flow patterns. According to data gathered by the Canadian Wildlife Services, the population has shown recovery in the years since.

The cover image is from *Wood's Animate Creation*. The cover font is Adobe ITC Garamond. The text font is Adobe Minion Pro; the heading font is Adobe Myriad Condensed; and the code font is Dalton Maag's Ubuntu Mono.

Get even more for your money.

Join the O'Reilly Community, and register the O'Reilly books you own. It's free, and you'll get:

- $4.99 ebook upgrade offer
- 40% upgrade offer on O'Reilly print books
- Membership discounts on books and events
- Free lifetime updates to ebooks and videos
- Multiple ebook formats, DRM FREE
- Participation in the O'Reilly community
- Newsletters
- Account management
- 100% Satisfaction Guarantee

Signing up is easy:

1. **Go to: oreilly.com/go/register**
2. **Create an O'Reilly login.**
3. **Provide your address.**
4. **Register your books.**

Note: English-language books only

To order books online:
oreilly.com/store

For questions about products or an order:
orders@oreilly.com

To sign up to get topic-specific email announcements and/or news about upcoming books, conferences, special offers, and new technologies:
elists@oreilly.com

For technical questions about book content:
booktech@oreilly.com

To submit new book proposals to our editors:
proposals@oreilly.com

O'Reilly books are available in multiple DRM-free ebook formats. For more information:
oreilly.com/ebooks

O'REILLY®

Spreading the knowledge of innovators   oreilly.com

Lightning Source UK Ltd.
Milton Keynes UK
UKOW02f0840160414

230009UK00005B/23/P